In Strangers'

In Strangers' Arms

The Magic of the Tango

BEATRIZ DUJOVNE

Foreword by Alejandro Martino

McFarland & Company, Inc., Publishers
Jefferson, North Carolina, and London

Endorsement:
In March 2010, the governing body of the Buenos Aires National Academy of Tango endorsed this book as a vehicle for the enhancement and the dissemination of the national genre, the tango.
Resolución CD No. 0006/2010

LIBRARY OF CONGRESS CATALOGUING-IN-PUBLICATION DATA

Dujovne, Beatriz E. (Beatriz Elena)
    In strangers' arms : the magic of the tango / Beatriz Dujovne ; foreword by Alejandro Martino.
      p.   cm.
    Includes bibliographical references and index.

    ISBN 978-0-7864-6389-3
    softcover : 50# alkaline paper ∞

    1. Tango (Dance) — History.   2. Tango (Dance) — Social aspects. I. Title.
GV1796.T3D85   2011
793.33 — dc23   2011023799

BRITISH LIBRARY CATALOGUING DATA ARE AVAILABLE

Front cover image: Guillermo Merlo and Fernanda Ghi, internationally acclaimed professional dancers and instructors from Argentina, dance the social tango at a milonga in Sweden (photograph courtesy Jerzy Dzieciaszek, Stockholm, Sweden).

Manufactured in the United States of America

McFarland & Company, Inc., Publishers
  Box 611, Jefferson, North Carolina 28640
  www.mcfarlandpub.com

To Carlos
for his infinite patience and unfailing support

Acknowledgments

This book could not have come to fruition without the generous spirit of dancers from the international tango community. Countless exchanges with them illuminated the intriguing world of the tango, as a phenomenon existing both inside their hearts and as a pulsating alternative community. Many dancers from the United States and from Buenos Aires trusted me with their innermost feelings. Some agreed to long, taped interviews. Some wrote candid narratives. Some responded to surveys. Hundreds of anonymous tangueros of Buenos Aires showed me, through their desire to connect, their curious gaze, their romanticism and their playfulness, that tango is who they are.

I was fortunate to find in Jake Spatz an editor knowledgeable of tango in its various aspects. In addition to helping me shape and revise every aspect of the manuscript, he captured the spirit of the original "letras" in his English translations quoted in the text, despite the difficulties inherent to the task of translating poetry.

Talented photographers from various countries caught the visual dimension of the tango with their camera lenses, and Steve Anderson contributed his expert assistance by helping prepare the archival and personal illustrations for publication.

For the time invested, I am especially indebted to Korey Ireland, Jim Roberts, David Gibbin, Guillermo Ibarra, Sabine Zubarik, Mikas Kalinauskas, Mila Vigdorova, Murat Erdemsel, Ozlem Elgun, Damian Lobato, Judith Chinea, and Keith Elshaw. Peers and colleagues joined me during various phases of this project, which began in 2005: Vera Anderson, Ravi Bhaskar, Jack Brannon, Marilyn Dawson McCarthy, Michael Figart,

Acknowledgments

Richard Keith, Susan Lawrence, Horacio López, Taisuke Nakata, Jason Pollen, Julia Pugliese, Mary Spalding, Peter Theoharis, Patricia Touagliaro, and Daniel Zárate.

Mary Posses, Laura Allen, and Dotti Pope were my dear supporters and sounding boards throughout this project.

At the Buenos Aires National Academy of Tango, the mentorship of Alejandro Martino opened a new path in my research. I thank Alberto Romeo of the same institution for his availability.

The personnel of the Archivos de la Nación Argentina, of the Instituto Nacional de Estadística y Censos de la República Argentina, and of the Archivos de la Academia Nacional de Tango graciously assisted me in data collection. So did Libertad Marilef of the "Blas Parera" library of the Sociedad Argentina de Autores y Compositores de Música.

The final critical evaluation of the manuscript by Enrique Binda of the Buenos Aires National Academy of Tango, and by Sergio Pujol of the Consejo Nacional de Investigaciones Científicas y Técnicas, motivated me to seek publication of this book.

Dancing with all of you throughout the creation of this work has enriched my life.

Table of Contents

Table of Contents

Foreword

BY ALEJANDRO MARTINO

The art of bodies moving through space, an original art with world recognition and a global foothold — the dance of the tango is for me not just those two generalizations, but also my profession. As flutist and director, I have accompanied the most distinguished stage dancers in performances all around the world, as well as a countless number of anonymous *milongueros* (social dancers) in the dance halls of my native city, Buenos Aires.

I used to think I knew quite well what dancing is because I carry it engraved on my retina and because I have taken part in it, in communion, by contributing the sounds essential to the dance's existence. However, as a popular adage in my country has it, "he that plays never dances," and with the passing of time, I have witnessed the inexorable accuracy of this. I do not dance the tango.

Today, I can change the verb tense and say that I *did not* dance the tango until I fell into the cosmic embrace of Beatriz Dujovne.

Her book, *In Strangers' Arms*, let me grasp the transcendent value, the profound value of this art form, the one I used to watch from the outside. Today I know that there is much more, and I invite you to experience it as a reader.

Having said that, a question keeps going around in my mind: How could an impact of such magnitude be made by a citizen of the United States? Beatriz Dujovne has with her book produced a phenomenon — fusion — that is only arrived at by whole peoples in conjunction or by great artists in their deepest selves. Tango, jazz, and bossanova are products of

1

the fusion that would not exist were it not for the social phenomenon of our continent. Tango, jazz, and bossanova, like so many other marvels, would not exist without America.

In Strangers' Arms is the offspring of a singular fusion because its author was born in Buenos Aires, completed her graduate studies in Argentina and the United States, and lived and practiced her profession in the United States, before beginning her research on the tango, which she later brought to conclusion in Buenos Aires, breathing the same air that nourished the tango's mentors; but above all, since Beatriz dances the tango, what she talks about in her work is not solely a research topic but a life experience profoundly her own.

In conclusion, I would say that it's not often you encounter such knowledge expressed in so transparent a form; Beatriz Dujovne has written a document that turns no reader away.

Alejandro Martino is founder of the School of Popular Music of Avellaneda, and a Senior Member of the National Academy of Tango of Buenos Aires.

Introduction:
More Than Fishnets and Fedoras

We might say that ... in heaven there awaits us...
the Platonic idea of the tango, its universal form.
— Jorge Luis Borges

The tango ... the most iconic dance of the twentieth century — and now of the twenty-first ... the one that kick-started the modern age, that cut down old boundaries, that gave a new world its first credible picture of elegance and intimacy ... the dance of illusions and dangers, its origins shrouded in myth ... the one that hands you your heart, when the world has stolen your hat.... These images of the tango are as familiar as an old friend, but are they the whole story?

Today's popular culture is fascinated by manly men and womanly women with slicked-back hair, wearing provocative costumes, fishnets and fedoras who dance the tango on stages around the world. It is held spellbound by the severe-looking choreographies of couples swirling around and performing skillful leg movements with utmost precision at the "speed of light." Dramatic lifts and drops add drama to the high energy of dancing couples enlaced in an open embrace.

To the passion of music and song, they dance stories of sex and violence in the midst of shady characters who live in the dangerous part of town. "Elegant," "seductive," "passionate," "alluring," "exciting," and "lustful" are adjectives typically used to describe magnificent performances. As art and entertainment, stage tango consistently brings thundering audiences to their feet.

This photograph, from a 1905 article in the magazine *Caras y Caretas*, shows that tango was embraced by a cultural mainstream in Argentina well before "Tango-mania" hit Paris, London, and New York in the 1910s. Teatro Victoria (formerly Teatro Onrubia), in which the photo for this article was taken, had been since 1895 the dancing venue predominantly attended by the working class. The accompanying article remarks: "Come Carnival, the tango becomes the owner and señor of all dance events, and the reason is that, being the most libertine of dances, it can only be tolerated in these days of craziness.... All theaters announce new tangos, which is a great motivator for a dancing clientele aspiring to show off.... As a spectacle it is something original.... The Victoria hall is filled with happy people, everywhere one could hear expressions that would make a policeman's helmet turn red. Male youngsters of good family, and young ladies of even better, sit in the boxes. Suddenly a tango plays and couples form. And the couples move swinging with cadence to the rhythm, voluptuously, as if this dance contained all their desires." Signed by one "Goyo Cuello," the commentary reflects the discomfort that the tango elicited in the conservative media at the beginning of the 20th century. *Photograph and article courtesy of the Photographic Department, General Archives of the Nation, Argentina.*

These same audiences are often perplexed upon learning that there is another tango, one where real people in dance halls pair up to dance a pure form of gentleness and physical closeness that involves neither sexual passion nor any relationship beyond the moment of dancing. Social dancers express what their hearts feel to the music, to their partners, and to particular moments on the dance floor. They improvise. They dance for themselves, introspectively. Shunning the external world, their eyes turn inward. This circumspect dance comes from a different heart and culture than the stage tango.

The Marginal Root of the Sexual Stage Tango

Shows rarely fail to feature the colorful bordello protagonists — the prostitute, and the so-called "compadrito" who acts as the lover or the pimp. These rough characters are assumed to be the originators of tango. Shows enact tango's relatively small marginal root, which writers on the subject (and the general public) assume to be the whole history of tango's beginnings. This early "history" is an elaborate mythology: the tango was the creation of criminal or quasi-criminal characters who lived outside the law, around the always-dangerous port areas; it was first danced in brothels while men waited for sexual commerce, and while women were not available for dancing; the upper classes, and the majority of decent people with them, rejected the tango born around the 1880s until after its acceptance in Paris around 1913. The myth would have it that because of this illicit origin, the dance and the music underwent a specific period of prohibition in Argentina. And the myth has proven to be so appealing that people resist letting it go.

This myth of the tango's origins still passes for history today, both at home in Argentina and abroad. Yet it remains a widely *unknown* fact that this lurid mythology began to find circulation only some three decades after the tango was born. How did these beliefs develop in the first place?

Two Argentine brothers, Hector and Luis Bates (notorious for their radio program interviews), in their 1936 book *La Historia del Tango*, introduced many attractive errors. Their book remains the unfortunate source of most "historical" references (including academic ones) in English-language publications about the tango's beginning. The myth excludes the majority of the actual originators of the dance who were decent, hard-working, law-abiding people.

Since the 1980s, when shows took off and exposed stage tango to millions of people, the *tangueros* of Buenos Aires (people who dance the tango in dance halls, at social events called *milongas*) have insisted that *el tango* is not in the legs. Pejoratively they call stage tango "of the legs" and "for export" to differentiate it from the social tango (*tango salón*) they dance. The mythology, which re-enacts the tango that they disdain, has been a great source of alluring material for the stage, but it mismatches in emotions and form the sweetness and circumspection of the social tango.

There is more than the myth to the history of tango.

The Popular Root of Social Tango

At social dances we see neither sexual passion nor violence. The dance's form is different as well. Legwork is minimal; feet are kept on the floor; the size of the steps is small. People dance closely embraced to one another, bodies connecting, chests close together, heaving and retreating with every breath, heads resting delicately together, moving as one, immersed in total improvisation that forbids them to hide behind choreographed steps. Beauty radiates from the emotions inside the dancers, not from external displays of skill.

What is the root of this social tango? Carefully documented studies did not exist prior to the 1990s. The *Antología del Tango Rioplatense* (1991), published by the Instituto Nacional Musicología, cites "chronicles, news, and newspaper advertisements" as early as 1900 that establish "the presence of tango as a popular fact." Marisa Donato came to the same conclusion in her 1993 article published in *Institute of Tango*. The watershed finally came in 1998, with the publication of the book-length study *El Tango en la Sociedad Porteña (1880–1920)* by the researchers Hugo Lamas and Enrique Binda — a book entirely devoted to facts about the early days of the tango, gathered from more extensive public sources than any previous study had looked to for evidence: the General National Archives, the Police Archives, the Police Historical Center, and the National Library in Buenos Aires. These two independent scholars documented in minute detail and with extensive quotations the role of a wide popular mass in Argentina during the early days of the tango. They showed definitively that the widespread myths about the tango's origins — that it was declassé or scorned until it became the toast of Europe — are flat-out contradicted by the evidence of its early commercial boom in Argentina. The numbers speak for themselves. Tangos had been recorded professionally since 1902, and between 1903 and 1910 no fewer than 350 recordings had been pressed; between 1902 and 1909, more than 3 million scores of sheet music were sold nationally (this figure includes only the documented sales: as with Tin Pan Alley years later, there was also a substantial trade in pirated copies of sheet music). Do these statistics support the theory that tango music was forbidden, or even unpopular? Who bought all these modern articles — the indigent people of the margins?

Rather, these statistics suggest that people with means were not only interested in the tango but also backing up that interest with their disposable income. The cost of a gramophone then (at a time when a policeman's monthly salary was 60 pesos) ranged between 150 and 300 pesos. Tango music was never forbidden and was, in fact, played throughout the city of Buenos Aires in restaurants and cafés, by trained musicians, early in the 20th century. In 1910, tangos were played at the city's official 100th anniversary festivities — an event organized by the government to honor foreign dignitaries and royalty. A formerly well-kept secret of early tango history even demonstrates that the upper classes were not merely fond of the tango but also instrumental in creating it. As music historian Vicente Gesualdo reports in his 1961 book *Historia de la música en la Argentina* (and in a 1991 article included in *Todo es historia*), seven of the earliest tangos, thought to be composed between 1872 and 1885, are not by an "anonymous composer," but were in fact written by Eloisa D'Herbil de Silva, the Spanish baronness and concert pianist who lived 75 of her 100 years in Buenos Aires. Gesualdo asserts of this noblewoman: "She is the author of our first tangos."

Neither was the dance forbidden. Police reports indicate that dancing did not happen in brothels, of which there were many in the city, and that these locales operated strictly for business. Lamas and Binda argue that with an immigrant population that was 70 percent male, the demand for this business was indeed considerable; the city brothels had neither space enough for dancing nor any incentive to waste time and money on it. The *Antología del Tango Rioplatense* had reached the same conclusion: "The presence of tango in the brothels of Buenos Aires was virtually zero, due to the prohibition of dancing [in brothels], the consumption of alcoholic beverages, etc." Furthermore, they cite a 1919 ordinance that only one prostitute was permitted to work in a brothel. The "brothel mythology" neglects to account for the wide appeal tango had and the popular market it was enjoying at the turn of the century. It also overlooks the fact that men did not have to go to brothels for dancing; they could and did dance with women at "academies" (public dance halls where men could pay per song to practice tango with professional women dancers), which were abundant in the city and unrelated to prostitution activities. Some of the academies were called "clandestine" because they disregarded dress codes and hours of operation — not because they were brothels. That the police kept a close watch on all of this, and knew what was what, is documented in their archives and arrest records.

Dancing did take place in the larger prostitution houses in the interior of the country, because there the venues were also used for other kinds of social activity: men gathered in them to drink, play music, and dance — sometimes without sexual commerce being included at all. (The action of *Amarillo*, a 2006 Argentine independent film, takes place in a social gathering/bordello venue in the interior of the country). Early tango bands played in this type of venue, but they traveled there for the gigs: tango may have been played in the country, but it was born and raised in the city. The tango is a Buenos Aires native — a *porteño*, born in the port city.

What about Argentines rejecting the dance before its acceptance in Paris? The wide appeal of the tango among the popular masses is documented as early as 1900 in *El Tiempo* and 1901 in *El Diario*. A 1902 newspaper article reports that at the gigantic popular theater Victoria, with its capacity for 2,600 spectators, the best tangos were danced. A 1903 article in *La Prensa* states: "The tango is triumphing!" Newspaper articles of 1904, 1906, and 1910 continued to report events at elegant theaters in the center of the city. There were dances at Teatro Ópera, an aristocratic venue; tickets for the evening were the most expensive in the city. A 1910 article in *La Nación* firmly places the dance among the upper class as it describes the attire of women "of beautiful silhouettes" and "elegant poise."

In light of the documentation presented, the assertion that tango was forbidden as music and dance due to its marginal roots is unsustainable. Ironically, the most famous examples of the tango being prohibited occurred not in Argentina but rather in the very countries that the mythology credits with making it "acceptable." Articles published in the *New York Times* between 1913 and 1916 report tango prohibitions in Paris, Rome, and New York.

So was there any prejudice against tango in Buenos Aires? Indeed there was. The lower and middle classes had accepted and practiced the dance, but the conservative media looked down on it, and so did the

The interior of the Teatro Ópera. From its opening in 1872 until 1908, this was the most aristocratic venue in the city, where touring European artists of the caliber of Caruso, Puccini and Toscanini performed. As early as 1902, newspapers report that dances were held at the Ópera (the seats were removed for these dancing events), and that tangos were featured prominently among other popular genres. *Photograph courtesy of the Photographic Department, General Archives of the Nation, Argentina.*

nationalistic literary elite. For the writer Leopoldo Lugones the tango was the "reptile of the brothel"; for writer Enrique Larreta, cultural representative in Paris during the "tangomania" (circa 1913), "tango was unjustly identified as Argentine during the times of its shameless triumph." For Carlos Ibarguren, academic, historian, politician, and writer, tango was "an illegitimate product ... hybrid or mestizo." The nationalists of the 1910s wanted country music, not tango, to represent the national identity: tango was unsuitable in their view because they considered it the music of immigrants. The prejudice of the literary elite was indeed more against the people of tango than against the music and dance per se. The tango phenomenon conflicted with their expectations of what should be considered culturally Argentine at a time when the issue of national identity was of foremost importance. Historians and politicians were asking themselves: How might this society, which is a tapestry of cultures, feel united? How might the state facilitate a sense of national identity? These preoccupations, however, did not stop tango from becoming an icon of national identity — especially for the urban masses.

Who made up the wide popular mass that supported tango? Let's go back to the second part of the 19th century, when tango was brewing and Argentina was becoming one of the ten richest nations in the world. Let's also explore the first part of the 20th century, when the burgeoning middle class sealed its consolidation.

The city of Buenos Aires had two faces: the north and the south. The elite of the north had a tradition of looking up to England for economic models and to France for education, fashion, art, and lifestyle. Oral tradition says that when they traveled to Europe they brought their own cows on board, to have the best milk for their young. The south comprised the poorer districts where tango evolved; they were semi-urban areas, also called *orillas* or outskirts. There, people lived closer to the earth. *Arrabaleros* (working-class people of the suburbs around the outskirts) breathed not the French scents El Centro enjoyed in the north, but the stench of nearby leather tanneries, meat processing plants, and polluted rivers (some of which were later covered by asphalt). Blood was a common part of life in the outskirts, whether from the inhabitants' past association with cattle slaughtering, from their current occupations in the meat industry, or from occasional fights in the marginal areas located around the port.

In 1867 Buenos Aires had a mere 161,000 habitants. By the middle of the 19th century, when exportation of agricultural products from the Pampas unleashed an economic boom, the nation began attracting a continuous stream of immigrants that reached massive proportions between 1880 and 1920. This "deluge" transformed the "big village" ruled by the elite into a dynamic and cosmopolitan metropolis of 1,240,000 habitants by 1909. The rapid growth and assimilation was an unprecedented sociodemographic world phenomenon. (Buenos Aires was the only metropolis that entered the 20th century with more immigrants than natives.) The vast majority of poor rural immigrants had came from practically all over the world, but the predominant lands of origin were Italy and Spain. The poor immigrants settled in the indigent and remote outskirts, which formerly had been occupied by urban and rural natives. (The ones with money settled in nearby districts.) According to sociologist Gino Germani of Buenos Aires and Harvard universities, immigrants became rapidly assim-

Coachmen on strike, 1906. These are the *compadritos*, the city-born men of the outskirts, who made up a large percentage of the population of Buenos Aires from the 1880s through the early 1900s. The one on the far left is sipping *mate* through a *bombilla* (metal straw), a typical Argentine drink. These natives were born from the union of immigrants with immigrants, or immigrants with natives, and implanted their sometimes-exaggerated movements and personality on the tango, in both its dance and its lyrics. *Photograph courtesy of the Photographic Department, General Archives of the Nation, Argentina.*

ilated, partly because they outnumbered natives, partly because they did not look up to the existing culture, and partly because they did not feel compelled to fit in. The laws of the land facilitated integration, so ghettos did not develop in Buenos Aires as they did in New York and other cities. During the second half of the 19th century, those who came from European countries had directly or indirectly experienced the process of industrialization and the conflicts between capital and labor. They transplanted to Buenos Aires the anarchist and anticlerical ideologies quite popular in Europe at the time.

Julio Mafud, in his book *Sociología del Tango* (1966), noted the coincidence of the anarchist movement in Argentina and the tango's gestation.

An undated photograph showing gauchos outside a *pulpería* (general store) in "Old Buenos Aires," the outer fringes of the city. Gauchos became immigrants in their own land when the Pampas were fenced during the latter part of the 19th century. They passed on a tradition of improvisational poetry and song, usually to the accompaniment of a guitar, called *la payada*. Rebellion and nostalgia, quintessential traits of the tango, were part of this gaucho tradition before tango was born. *Photograph courtesy of the Photographic Department, General Archives of the Nation, Argentina.*

The movement represented the urban proletarian voice as it wove together with the long-standing attitude of protest in the Argentine gaucho literature. Old and new ideas, attitudes, and aspirations underwent a rapid metamorphosis. The colonial structure, with power in the hands of the elite, also became transformed. Within a short time, the strata of mostly rural origin that had settled in the outskirts became an urban proletarian mass that began migrating to other districts of the city. Immigrants shook up the traditional colonial social stratification. They began transforming the social order even while the wealth and power remained in the hands of a small, entrenched elite. Their rapid social mobility transformed them into a substantial middle class "in five minutes."

Typically when we picture the melting pot that created the tango, we think of Argentine natives alongside Italian and Spanish immigrants. As this turn-of-the-century photo documents, other ethnicities were present as well: the writing on the storefront behind these Polish immigrants is displayed in several Slavic languages. *Photograph courtesy of the Photographic Department, General Archives of the Nation, Argentina.*

This unprecedented human mix of local and foreign people of disparate geographic origins, races, colors, religions, customs, and languages rapidly mixed with one another. Before tango came into being, native Afro-Argentines danced the *candombe*—a dance that did not involve an enlaced couple. According to George Andrews of the University of Wisconsin, between the 1860s and 1870s they favored imports such as the waltz, schottische, and mazurka. Once a large percentage of the Buenos Aires population, with a large working class and a small middle class, the Afro-Argentines had suffered an "irreversible decline" by the time tango was born. The Afro-Argentine influence in tango dancing is considered important by some historians and insignificant by others.

A mix of the black and the creole; the homegrown and the sophisticated European; nationalities, races, and cultures; pluralistic religious tolerance; various musical traditions; poor and working-class people; secular

13

education; anarchist ideas — all of these were part of the tango's birth context during a process of rapid demographic, economic, social, and ideological transformation that began around 1880 and was more or less completed by 1910. The 120 newspapers in various languages registered in Buenos Aires in 1914 are a testament to the long-prevailing diversity of the city. Each different culture entered the pot during a process of fusion that *porteños* call "the stew." This unprecedented, non-segregated mix — with its unique international and multiethnic DNA — was the blood that went into the veins of the tango. And it was a nostalgic blood that came from shared losses. As other artistic expressions have been regarded as products of individual nostalgia, we can think of tango as the product of the collective nostalgia of a large majority of voluntarily displaced people.

With this enormous, diverse mix in its blood, the tango emerged as a genuine local art, with a soul from Buenos Aires and the world, fused in the unique liberal ethos that prevailed at the end of the 19th century. It catalyzed "the stew" into an identity — the new porteño who created a new art: the tango. The new porteño was a fusion, and so was the tango.

How to characterize the tango? It is a complete genre: it has its own music, dance, and poetry. Its early music conveys a sense of popular expression with a quality of nice old days, and yet a complexity that mirrors the ethos in which it was born; it is as earthy as its stomping grounds in the outskirts, and as sophisticated as the European culture of the nearby north. It represents the culture of Buenos Aires, where it has its strongest presence. (Other Argentine music is more representative of the social realities of the interior of the country: the folkloric music of the provinces.) At first, the tango's phrasing, or way of saying things, tends to elicit surprise in many foreign cultures. After the exotic first impression is overcome, tango music is felt in the heart, brings tears to the eyes, and melts us in a true emotional experience. Multi-layered, it fuses melodic romanticism with rhythmic vigor, life energy with tragedy, happiness with despair, roughness with refinement. It connects us with something rich, deep, as real as life is.

A Century Later: Gripped by Social Tango

Popular misconceptions based on the highly visual stage tango do not really capture the internal depth of what happens to dancers. When the spirit of tango grips us, we don't so much want to dance — we need to dance. And our need to dance can be every bit as strong as the need to eat, to rest, to be loved. Dancers know of this power; and throughout these pages, dancers themselves will tell us about it in detail. It possesses us. Surreptitiously it entwines with our flesh and soul. It may even place itself at the epicenter of our existence. Most dancers do not question their healthy addiction to high doses of tango any more than you would question your instincts if you woke up in bed suddenly craving a glass of water. We, social dancers in tango halls across the world, cannot get enough of it.

Tango is the only popular dance I know of where the partners move tightly embraced. In other dances, bodies either do not touch or, if they do, remain loosely enlaced — not literally embraced, with chests in contact and held closely together. Unlike in ballroom dances, Latin or smooth, where dancers follow a set choreography, the social tango is improvised in the moment: thus the expression, "You cannot dance the same tango twice."

Tango defies us to surrender to the rhythms and melodies of the music. We do not choose the tango: it chooses us — it holds us captive, and it leaves us mystified. The dance is our artistic expression, therapy, tribal rite — an integral part of our lives and even our very integrity.

With feelings of trepidation and a sense of adventure, in the tango two strangers embrace each other closely, find a common ground, and move as one. Not through our eyes but through our physical contact and intuition, we dancers immediately know something deep and private about one another. We dance who we are. If we feel sad, we dance sadness. If we feel confident, we dance confidence. If we feel empty ... yes, we dance emptiness. We dance emotions so primal that often they cannot be expressed with words.

In a close embrace, established in a few moments and lasting until the end of the song, we are totally vulnerable, with our inner beings exposed to an unknown other. The tango plunges to the core, revealing every strength and insecurity, every bit of us that is true and real. With every breath, with the scents and the textures of our skin, all that we are comes together in a séance of circular motion.

We wallow in the pleasure of making art with a stranger. Without thinking or talking, two collaborators experience the hurts and joys within, and may at times rise above all this and reach something above and beyond the self. I can only define as "transcendent" the moment when the dance becomes a connection of two strangers in a feeling of oneness.

On the Fringe Between the Sensual and the Sexual

Throughout its evolution, the revolutionary tango has challenged the tolerance of public sensual expression. It still does. In primitive dances sexuality was explicit, but as humans became more refined we also became more censored. Eventually the explicit became transformed, sublimated: the choreographed European dances that enjoyed great social popularity prior to the 1900s are a testament to this sublimation.

The tango, on the other hand, has lived on the fringe between the sensual and the sexual since its inception. Despite the physicality of the dance, porteño tangueros — the dancers of Buenos Aires — have always claimed the dance is sensuous, not sexual. And they are adamant about this despite the many ongoing discussions held on the subject. The discussions will probably continue because a strand of the marginal root of tango is forever likely to be woven into the social tango.

The masses that gave it an initial impetus felt free to transgress white European norms, and to defy religious notions that considered any gratification of the senses sinful — including listening to music. (This freedom, in a predominantly Catholic country, can only be understood in light of the secular and integrationist ethos of the late 19th century in Buenos Aires.) Comfortable with their bodies and their sensuality, urban native creoles took the lead, and everybody else followed: rural native mestizos, rural and urban Europeans, Afro-Argentines, adults and youngsters.... These people, some indigent, some working-class, and some upper-class, followed no social prescriptions about who was to mix with whom. They transformed the anonymous embrace from a cultural way of being into a world-encompassing art form.

It is no wonder that this tango that pushed the limits was considered scandalous (by some) both inside and outside Argentina. It was the natural reaction of conservatives to a dance that broke the physical barriers between men and women, and that thereby threw the dancing world with its established societal norms upside-down.

With the Fullness of an Imagined Memory

History points to the fact that the creators of the tango were people like you and me, not just marginal ruffians, not prostitutes, not criminals. But setting the record straight makes me wonder.... These myths endure for a reason — why so? Is there pleasure in imagining that we dance to the sexually and legally forbidden, or in watching this during a performance? Do we like to think of it as marginal and as countercultural, so that a certain dark side of our heart can live on the edge?

As Borges put it: "Tango creates a turbid unreal past that somehow is true, the impossible memory of having died fighting, in a corner of the suburb." The mythical tango is, in other words, a fiction we indulge in — and one that we can now indulge in with the certitude that it is unreal. Now we can accept these myths for what they are, and enjoy what they give us, with the fullness of an imagined memory.

Symptoms of a Powerful Heart

Now that we have cleared the air, we can say that the most popular dance of the 20th century is not about fishnets and fedoras. In fact, it seems to be much more than just a dance if we consider its birth circumstances and its world trajectory. The tango was born in a relatively minute area of the Río de La Plata; it began its world rise in the 1910s, over two decades after its gestation in the cities of Buenos Aires and Montevideo. In the beginning it dazzled France, England, Germany, Italy, Finland, Spain, the United States, and Japan. Gradually it dazzled the entire world. The same world that supposedly was not ready for the tango's new carnality in dancing proved itself more than eager to embrace it with passion.

From that point on, the tango enjoyed immense popularity at home in Buenos Aires, reaching a high point at the end of the 1920s before inaugurating a three-decade Golden Age with its utmost peak in the 1940s. By this time, the tango had become a staple of popular music around the world. Much like other forms of pre-war popular culture, however, it gradually fell into decline when Rock hit the scene in the late 1950s. Even before that time, the new immigrants who descended from the provinces to Buenos Aires, and who played a significant role in the 1946 election of Juan Perón, gave new impetus to the folkloric dances that were part of their identity. The frequent curfews during the Perón era precluded attendance at many evening *milongas*, or tango-based social dances. Due to a combination of factors, tango dancing skipped an entire generation. During those quiet years of tango, a vanguard in music and poetry emerged with Astor Piazzolla's revolutionary music and Horacio Ferrer's revolutionary poetry. Piazzolla died in 1992; Ferrer, who broke the traditional canons

of poetry both in form and in content, remains the beloved poet of today's Buenos Aires. The Piazzolla-Ferrer collaboration went beyond tango; "María de Buenos Aires," a chamber opera, continues to be staged not only in Buenos Aires but also around the world. In the 1980s, a resurgence of the dance was set in motion by touring stage shows, and this soon prompted people all over the world to embrace the social tango of the milongas with a renewed voracity and unrelenting passion, which has not abated but in fact has continued to redouble up to the present.

A poster placed on the streets of Buenos Aires when UNESCO added tango's deep-rooted tradition of dance, poetry, and song to its "List of the Intangible Cultural Heritage of Humanity" on September 30, 2009. The poster features bandoneón virtuoso and composer Astor Piazzolla (1921–1992). *Photograph by Beatriz Dujovne.*

If the dance has reached your community, and it probably has, it has most likely been changed by your culture. Each culture feels and expresses this art through its unique sensibilities. Today tango belongs to the world. On September 30, 2009, UNESCO added tango's deep-rooted tradition of dance, poetry, and song to its "List of the Intangible Cultural Heritage of Humanity" for safe-

18

guarding and preservation. And no wonder: the dance has established "nests" throughout the world, with ongoing weekly dances and instruction. There are nightly milongas in almost every big city in the world, with the biggest cities sometimes offering three or four events on the same evening. But it is not just the metropolis that features milongas: a small town like Totnes, in Devonshire, England, offers two milongas a week and hosts a festival every two months. It is no news that on any given evening, a milonga in Buenos Aires may gather 500 people or more; it is the tango's motherland; but it *is* impressive that a monthly milonga in Tel-Aviv gathers 120 to 220 dancers on a regular basis.

Today hundreds of thousands of dancers cross national and international skies regularly to be with others at weekend tango festivals, or camps that might last anywhere from one to several weeks. Large camps have been featured for years in Germany, Italy, Sweden, and Greece. The Berlin-based website Tango.info lists tango events in 75 countries and 918 cities — probably conservative estimates. From 1996 through 2009, 999 festivals made this list. During 2009, world festivals were held in cities as diverse as these: Alghero (Sardinia), Ankara, Athens, Baltimore, Basel, Barcelona, Berlin, Brussels, Bonn, Budapest, Buenos Aires, Capri, Casablanca, Denver, Dubai, Houston, Istanbul, Krakow, Lisbon, Leipzig, Ljubljana, Lugarno, Montevideo, Montreal, Nijmegen, Paris, Perugia, Pesara, Portland (Oregon), Rome, St. Petersburg, Salerno, Salt Lake City, San Diego, Seoul, Singapore, Sudan, Sydney, Taipei, Valencia, Washington, Zurich, and 130 others. More than 120,000 dancers attend the annual Seinäjoki Tango Festival in Finland once a year. On special occasions large numbers of dancers meet anywhere in the world; in September 2008, more than 25,000 dancers gathered for an outdoor milonga in Piazza Navona, Italy. Unknown thousands of people from all nationalities fly to the Mecca of tango, the city of Buenos Aires, where the dance is part of the culture and where the sheer number of milongas makes it feasible to dance from noon into the night and until dawn.

The world's omnipresence of the dance is a symptom of its powerful heart, which is capable of shaking people from all points of the compass regardless of social strata, age, religion, race or sexual orientation. In these times of personal isolation, unconcern for others, and the cult of the mighty ego, the tango as a dance offers people a refreshingly sensitive human rapport where strangers need each other, where we communicate directly and delicately with our bodies in silence, where we together create an art of unique and arresting beauty.

Dance with Me

The might of the tango calls to porteños from a collective unconscious; it is who we are. But how is it that people with such diverse nationalities and religious affiliations, with such disparate educational and racial backgrounds, and belonging to almost every age group, can identify with this porteña-born dance? What enabled it to rise above cultures and resonate around the globe as loudly as it does? For years, I did not raise these questions. Then my life shifted in ways that propelled me to ask: What is inside the heart of this dance that makes it possible to embrace a stranger, and become instantly familiar? What is the power within its heart that enables it to speak to all, and to connect all? How can I demonstrate that this art of the heart embodies a culture, a cosmology, a way of life? And how can I accomplish this task in a way that's consistent with the personal nature of the dance?

To grapple with these questions I set out to discover the *inner* social tango, the one that observers' eyes cannot see. In the pages that follow, we will meet the people of tango today, look for ghosts of its past people in the places and the culture of tango, and navigate the heart of its poets. Each chapter will take us through one or more strands of the emotions and the cultural way of being infused into tango. In the end, all the strands of the tapestry we call "tango" will shed light on its powerful heart. A first-person narrative style seemed more fitting than an impersonal, "objective" approach: my commentaries are backed up by the most current research, but there's no aesthetically satisfying way to unveil the heart and culture of this art form without subjectivity. My personal memories and evocations, along with those of many others whom I interviewed while writing this book, offer a subjective vehicle that I believe delivers the "real thing" more convincingly, and more accurately, than a more distanced perspective could. The tango, as a dance, is not about distance in the first place!

But let me back up: I mentioned a shift in my life. To understand what I mean by tango as a "way of being," you need to understand this. Call it the first motive that made me look at things sideways, and that put me on the path that has led to me writing this book and you reading it.

In the weeks following September 11, the day that changed all of our lives forever, my view of the world got shaken. I had been embracing strangers on the dance floor, of all ethnicities, for several years, without really reflecting on it as a social phenomenon. Then a different social phenomenon forced me to. It was October 2001. Six policemen broke into the home of a friend, a petite Mexican woman, a law-abiding, sweet, and hard-working person of the same caliber as the immigrants who made this country strong. She was alone at home. The men turned her house upside down. They found nothing incriminating. She was driven away to a secret location. No note was left of her future destination for her husband or child. She was the mother of a 10-year-old American-born boy. She had a permit to work, paid her social security, and filed her taxes. *It did not matter.* We searched jails and police stations to no avail. When we found her at the immigration detention center, she was brought out of the cell handcuffed and with her ankles chained. No one would explain to us why she had been detained. We were told she would be deported the following day. We weren't given any reason. *It did not matter.* She was a suspect. She was handled like a convicted felon. Seeing this family broken apart, I engaged an attorney who was able to figure out that she had not been notified — by her own attorney — of the impending expiration of her work permit. As is done with dangerous criminals, my friend kept being moved from prison to prison. It was an ordeal to find out where she was. But I kept finding her and visiting her through the glass barricade, choking and unable to talk through the phone for the few allotted minutes. All we could do was to look at each other in horror, cry, and place the palms of our hands on the glass barrier so we could symbolically "touch." At one point I obtained permission for her to see her child in a regular room. The visit took place under police surveillance. This mother could not touch her boy because she was handcuffed, and she was hiding her arms to keep her child from getting scared. *It did not matter.* A community of over one hundred people sent pleas to the attorney general, the senators and the representatives. The case reached a judge's desk, but he refused to give her a hearing. In his notes, he acknowledged she had overextended her stay because of her attorney's negligence to notify her that she needed to apply for an extension. That attorney was later disbarred. *It did not matter.* It was October 2001. Handcuffed and chained at the ankles, she was put on a plane to the Mexican border. Her child's last memory of his mother is seeing her in jail. He has probably been wondering, as children do, what he had done wrong, what action of his made his mother disappear from his life. How to explain what happened, to a kid? *It did not matter.* A mother-son bond was severed, a woman's heart was broken, a child lost his mother, a family was torn apart. *It did not matter.* Under the Patriot Act, everything was legal.

In the days, months, and years following the 2001 world tragedy and the wreckage in my own backyard, I became painfully aware of the values that destroy our humanity. Of our impotence to change them. The attacks of September 11 fell 15 years after Chernobyl, 4 years before New Orleans was flooded, and 9 years before the Gulf oil spill — three more events that reflect how human lives are becoming increasingly dispensable and how we are becoming increasingly complacent about it. And right in the middle of this same world is the tango, a dance so dignified and emblematic of the human condition, of our need for each other, that it might be danced, ceremoniously and not offensively, at a funeral.

Tango dancing, in the wake of these events, took on a different dimension of meaning for me. It became an activity where I celebrate our common humanity. It became my act of dissent against the facelessness and heartlessness in this world that has to yet figure out how to stop terrorizing itself.

I am a porteña with a second culture: I have lived most of my adult life in the United States. I move in and out of my two cultures and speak their two languages. I dance in various U.S. tango communities and in Buenos Aires' tango halls. A citizen of two nations, I have deep roots in both. The essence of the traditional tango that has been danced in Buenos Aires milongas is the one that runs in my veins.

The tango is, for me, a cocoon of sweetness, an instinctive innocence with a touch of mischief, a beauty, a might. If it were a person, I would draw it with rough hands, a face marked by pain, a throbbing vitality, and a rich, oversized heart. But this is my view. Tango people of my two cultures and other parts of the world, who are deeply entrenched in the tango way of life, will share with us their own perspectives. We will learn from many messengers, from inside the embrace and inside the culture. They know the intoxicating secrets of the dance that outside observers do not even imagine to exist.

This dance begins as our lives begin: by embracing and trusting a stranger. I invite you, whether you dance or not, as strange as it may seem, to join me in taking this first step and to "tango" with me while you read. Self-discoveries await us, for the tango is a mirror wherein we see ourselves in unexpected new ways.

Follow me, and discover the powerful heart and the culture of this dance. I am convinced that our tango will touch or change something inside of you. I believe it knows nothing else.

1

In Strangers' Arms

On the outside, the Refinery is a total anomaly. It's one of the only things you can see from a distance here in the flatlands. Its ultra-contemporary exterior stands out from the nondescript surroundings: the split-face stone façade, the high brick siding leading up to a green roof, the modern-looking columns that frame large panels of darkly tinted glass.... The building doesn't seem like it was built here; it seems more like it landed amid the white fences of this small Midwestern town's pastel two-story homes. In contrast with this looming stranger, the residential neighborhoods around it seem even quieter. It made me imagine that even the dogs and cats here lead normal Christian lives.

On the outside, there's a red sign over the entrance. In the basement, there's a brightly lit gym buzzing with technology and polished chrome, along with a steam room and a juice bar. Above that, on ground level, are the sprung maple floors of a peach-themed ballroom, where the table settings, down to the patterns woven on the napkins, match the ornate decor of the walls. Behind the tables and the dancing area, a futuristic bar spreads itself in a corner. With its shower of halogen lights, the bar itself, shaped with the undulating curves of an amoeba, seems both to receive the energy of the room and to pulse with it.

I shifted for a moment and looked at how my hand sat on the bar, lit by one of the spots like something underwater. I was enjoying the setting from within the timeless zone that evolves during three consecutive days of tango dancing at a festival. By Sunday night, it's half wonder and half fatigue. This place, with its magnificently polished wood floors and ceiling-high windows, which had been our home away from home since Friday,

Milonga in Italy. *Photograph courtesy of Leone Perugino (Catania, Italy).*

was a refreshing opposite to the usual, stark festival venues set up to meet our basic dancing needs. I stared at the smooth motion of the couples navigating the floor. This, our last *milonga* (social dance), was more sparsely attended; many had returned home already. I would be gone the next day. And in that twilight mood, the thought of leaving drifted away from me.

I was. I was, simply, being; lingering at a curve of the bar. Time had condensed itself into a place, and the place was so far inside time that it had come loose from it. With my hand growing hazy in the halogen light, I listened to the lyrics of the tango "Nada" ("Nothing"):

> *¡Cuánta nieve hay en mi alma!*
> *¡Qué silencio hay en tu puerta!*
>
> How deep a snow my soul is under!
> What a silence fills your doorway!

The voice of Alberto Podestá singing these images in the 1940s seemed to flow like the present. The scene before me, the place I was in, the dancing couples, the ultra-contemporary everything, seemed like the memory.

In the tango it is not uncommon to embrace an unfamiliar person regardless of age differences. The dance offers the freedom to bypass external differences that often separate people in daily life. ***Photograph courtesy of AlexTangoFuego (Driftwood, Texas).***

The Encounter

The predictable unknown of going to a tango festival, which adds intrigue to the mystery of the dance itself, was a known by then. I had done my dancing. I had met my strangers in an embrace on the dance floor, had taken my classes, and had done some interviews for the book I thought I was writing. On the outside, it had been a good enough time, and now it was a wrap. And then I was talking to a dancer I didn't know, about how two of the Argentine instructors epitomized the tango I was learning: open, warm, a bit naughty, funny ... about how they updated my *lunfardo* (the slang of Buenos Aires) every time I saw them, and how when they danced, even when they performed, they seemed to be hypnotizing each other. And by then we had transitioned to the stranger's recent visit to Buenos Aires. And he said, "In five minutes, porteños tell you who they are."

My eyes searched his face; and then I looked away, to the close-grained wood in the circle of light on the bar. He had sharpened me: his perceptiveness had captured, in startlingly few words, one of our salient traits. I was impressed, and my North American self was remembering my Argentine self. I asked him to elaborate, to tell me what else about us caught his attention, and after a moment of recollection he related a snapshot of Buenos Aires:

"There was a couple standing on a downtown corner. They were arguing, they kept going away and coming back together. They were talking out loud, gesticulating. Not shouting, but intensely involved in disagreement. They were such a potent image for me. I didn't even hear their words; but their emotional lives were in their bodies, everything about them was so readable. They seemed unperturbed by people passing by. Argentines do not conceal — it is all out there. With them, if you feel you make a connection, you do."

My fellow dancer was not only an astute observer of cultural idiosyncrasies, but also appreciative of them. In his observations, he had inadvertently described intrinsic traits not only of Argentines but also of the tango: its being inescapably personal, and the public nature of its emotionality.

We talked a bit about ourselves and our home communities in the United States. He was an avid student of our dance's history, a thinker. He had a good command of Spanish. I guessed, to my pleasure, that he understood the poetry in our music, and that we could talk about its beauty and realness at some future time. Then he told me about his first impression, as a North American, of our dance:

"When my wife and I took our first tango lesson, I could see right away that tango was deep like the ocean, and I knew I would never know it fully even if I immersed myself in it until the day I died. That's what grabbed me."

I told him about my writing, from the inside of the dance, from the invisible ocean that our eyes cannot see. I was curious about how and why it gets so intertwined with our bodies and souls, no matter who we are, no matter where we live or which culture we come from. He seemed genuinely interested in my project; and I was interested in gaining his perspective. As we heard the first chords of the tango "La cumparsita," the one that closes milongas all over the world, we arranged to stay in touch.

Tomorrow I would be gone, and maybe he would be gone to his hometown too; but we had made a connection.

"La cumparsita" is the most well-known tango in the world. Gerardo Hernán Matos Rodríguez first composed the tune in Uruguay to sing with his fellow students at "a carnival comparsa." According to Oscar Del Priore, the pianist, composer and bandleader Roberto Firpo, who was in Uruguay at the time, arranged a new version of it, since Matos Rodríguez's musical knowledge was rather limited. There are two versions of the lyrics: one by Matos Rodríguez, and the other by Pascual Contursi with Enrique Maroni. ***Photograph courtesy of Alexander Zabara (Moscow).***

Correspondents

Soon thereafter I traveled to Buenos Aires and emailed him my daily observations of the tango, sending him my notes about the dance and its culture. My office in this city was an outdoor table at *confitería La Biela*. In no other office does *chamuyeo* (conversation) with waiters get as good as it gets here. I am usually greeted by Luis, the waiter, with a kiss on the cheek. When he is not serving my area, he usually brings me chocolates, one in each hand: he knows I do not eat them, but he also knows I like them, so he brings (he says) one for each one of my eyes. My notes to my new friend in the United States were about milongas or tango shows; sometimes about my mental adventures differentiating tourists from locals at a place like La Biela (which attracts both). It is not the clothes. It is not the food they order. Only two hypotheses had been consistently correct: non-locals put ketchup on their French fries, and they sit up straighter. Porteños have a way of sitting leaning forward, often with their hands on the table close to the other person's hand, and they *chamuyean* (talk) as if they were sharing the most intimate of secrets of their lives. And probably they do.

It was a pleasure to correspond with him because he responded enthusiastically. We developed a rich exchange during those weeks. A few months after my return to the United States, we reconnected personally at a tango festival in another city. The first evening, buses arrived at the downtown hotel where the rest of the events took place, and transported the dancers to a rather desolate industrial area. The only light there came from an inconspicuous open door. Upstairs, more than one hundred people were packed in a room, dancing under the warmth projected onto the naked brick interior by some light bulbs dangling from the ceiling. The dancers weren't fazed by the poor ventilation: in the tango embrace, mundane inconveniences go away — we get used to improvising. We get to be experts in surprise management.

I spotted my friend at the other end of the moving mass. After about an hour we found each other and danced together. Inwardly, I was celebrating my new friendship with him.

Each of us danced with many partners as the night went on. I decided to leave before the very end, and he accompanied me down the narrow stairs. As we descended, the DJ began to play the next song of the night, "Niebla del Riachuelo" ("Fog on the Riachuelo River"), and the opening phrases struck a feeling of nostalgia into my heart. Indulging the mood, I mentioned something to my friend about the inherent nostalgia of the tango. His unexpected response — "I know some happy tango music" — had the tone of a direct challenge.

I let the comment go because we had already planned to meet the following day, and I could respond then.

A Day Later and a Life Ago

I was caught off-guard by his serious demeanor when we exchanged greetings the following evening: it didn't match the softness that I had sensed in our first encounter, or during our correspondence, or in our dances last night in that stuffy brick room so different from the elegant, air-conditioned hotel lobby where we were meeting now. To settle myself a bit, I went to take a peek inside the ballroom where that night's milonga was about to begin. The setting was definitely European-looking and luxurious; the lights dimly illuminated the floor, which was more than ready for the first dancers, who were already beginning to show up wearing handsome evening attire.

After I heard the first sounds of a tango, I turned back and saw my changed friend. He had gone looking for seating in some semi-private corner, and waved me over. Little did I know when I sat down next to him that this hotel lobby was about to become a psychoanalytic couch where the remnants of my life would wash over me.

"You know," I said without preamble, "'Desde el alma,' the happy music you mentioned yesterday, has very sad lyrics. Tango can be both happy and sad. The music feels one way, the poetry another. It is like us. It is our mirror. It is our contradictions and paradoxes. Sometimes I visualize the tango as a person with a form my eyes can see, with inner layers waiting to be discovered, and with an unconscious that totally eludes me."

He looked pensive. Then he asked, "Did you grow up with tango at home?"

"Oh, yes. Tango," I defended myself, "has been entrenched in my life from day one. Like the Spanish language. Like Argentine culture. My home was filled with it; we did not miss any of Hector Gagliardi's tango poetry recitals on Radio Belgrano. Yes, it has been part of me since I was born, even when I did not know it, even when I walked away from it during my teens. The immigrant soul of the tango has always been in my life, one way or another."

He seemed curious, so I went on.

"From my earliest days I was an immigrant by osmosis, by virtue of growing up with Spanish grandparents, Spanish father, Spanish uncle; and distant relatives came from the old country to live with us until they found work. Later on, I became a full-fledged immigrant in my own right. That happened when I came to live in the United States. I feel my own heartbeat in that longing to go back home, in that *missing* that throbs in the veins of the tango."

He asked, "Do you think you feel tango more deeply because you left your country and relocated in another?"

"We do not actually have to change countries to be an immigrant, do we? We all go through cycles of leaving and arriving, through the yin and the yang of losing and finding. Just by being alive. We are immigrants for the first time when we get kicked out of the womb. We are born and — bang! New territory! Breathing! Feeding! Can we cope? Tango speaks to the disorientation, to the hope, to the panic of those transitions."

He was quiet again, and I had more to say.

"When we approach a partner to dance, aren't we just like anxious immigrants arriving in the world of an unknown other? *Immigrant* is the tango's condition."

"I like seeing the tango through your heart, Beatriz. I hear so much talk about tango that represents it as something that it is not."

It moved me to be understood again after our uncertain exchange the night before. That he knew that the tango is more than a dance, something beyond the fishnet-and-fedora show posters. It even moistened my eyes. Despite our correspondence, we were still barely acquainted; but we were both highly emotional about something, even if the "something" might be different in the details for each of us.

"How do you feel, Beatriz, when the tango is bought and sold as a bunch of acrobatic figures?"

We exchanged a wince. Then, with a bit of anger that I was delighted to see, he added, "It disturbs me that the rhetoric of religion or romance is brought in to explain an aesthetic experience. Tango is not a trance state. Tango is not Zen. Tango is not transcendental meditation. Tango is not a dark night of the soul. Tango is not love and kindness. Tango is not seeing into the true nature of things. These are ill-chosen metaphors...."

We had a good rant going, but it seemed to frustrate itself into a different topic:

"Did you learn to dance in Argentina?"

"No. I learned here, in the mid–1990s. When I started, it helped me recognize the initial fabric of my life. Tango brought back parts of my flesh, blood, heart. I recovered a lost 'mi.' Somehow tango shocked — in a good way — the 'me' that I had become in my second culture, the one that did not fit me well. Tango challenged what was not real in me. It did its work while I was in the arms of strangers, where I was vulnerable."

We shared a moment of silent reflection.

"Is that when you started writing?"

"No, I started several years ago, when my 'kitchen' memory came to me. This was on a winter evening in Kansas, maybe around 2002. We had freezing temperatures. I was looking outdoors through a picture window, watching icy tree branches, amazed at nature's crystal chandeliers. A few defiant autumn leaves were hanging on, resisting the winds. I kept watching a twelve-inch snowdrift accumulating outside the window, and on the inside, streaks of condensation were draining down into a small puddle on the windowsill. As soon as I touched it, I flashed back to a memory of my six-year-old index finger drawing figures in the glass of another window fogged with steam. To the radio playing tangos.... That's the 'kitchen' memory."

I held back mixed feelings tied to the kitchen memory. A torrent of emotions burst through the double door of my heart: being six years old in that kitchen, but also being 20-something at the Buenos Aires airport. The airport. The kitchen. Two lost "homes." Two times of mourning.

Uncompromised Concentration

I looked at him, hesitantly. These memories made me uneasy.

"You said the radio was playing tangos. Do you remember what it sounded like?"

"In the kitchen memory," I answered, "my father was listening to the tango. His favorite program was the Glostora Tango Club, which broadcasted live performances by the orchestra of Alfredo De Angelis at 7:55 in the evening, on Radio El Mundo. It came on between my two favorite soap operas, 'Blanquita y Héctor' and the one about the family of 'Los Pérez-García.' Would you like me to tell you how the announcers introduced my program?"

"Yes, what did they say?"

[In a low voice] "*Esta es la casa de Los Pérez-García. Todas las noches un nuevo programa. Todas las noches una nueva emoción....*" ("This is the home of the Pérez-García family. Every night a new program. Every night a new emotion....")

"I feel like a new emotion is what I'm hearing about now!"

"Can you hear the fun-loving kid? And then at 8:25, everything stopped, and a strange male voice came on to say: '*Son las veinte y veinticinco, hora que Eva Perón paso a la inmortalidad.*'"

"What does that mean?"

"It is 8:25, the hour that Eva Perón passed into immortality."

I rolled my eyes, as my parents did back then, whenever they heard those words. We laughed. And I continued: "That wooden radio, with those sounds and music coming out of it ... the voice of the MC in his poetic prose, and the invisible audience applauding with such fervor ... it was so mysterious. But the biggest mystery was my father's expression listening to the tango, with uncompromised concentration."

I supposed that he thought this was a happy memory, but it was mixed with loneliness. It marked the beginning of my second life in a new house, living with just my parents — a time when I was missing my extended family, when I was longing for the play and noise of my first life. I could feel the bereavement I knew, and it made me anxious. The other memory of the airport made me anxious, too.... How could I explain all this to him? Did I even want to go there? These two memories marked big personal losses for me. The kitchen was the end of feeling that I was held secure within a nest of loving arms. The airport was the end of feeling held by lifelong connections and things familiar. Could he relate to this?

"To get back to your question, I started writing about tango on that freezing evening I was telling you about, in that different time zone in Kansas, in that place so far away from my second kitchen in Buenos Aires. I wrote a brief poem then. All about how life had lost color in my second childhood home, how lonely I felt with just my mother and father. How the three of us lived in a grayish, introverted silence. Except when music played: the tango was our bridge. Perhaps the music expressed what we could not say. Could my parents have been as sad as I was? Were they missing the same connected life I was missing? That's what I wondered with those circles I drew on the steamy glass."

He turned out to be a good catalyst. He kept close track of my feelings:

"Where does the scene of the airport come from?"

"The airport memory is too ... it's too intense."

I wanted to push ahead and name the pain. But I had to swallow first. My throat had gone dry.

"I was wearing high heels and the Chanel-style burgundy suit my mother, the family tailor, had made. I was clutching a fur-lined leather coat to fend off the Chicago winters. Going up the metal stairs at Buenos

Aires International airport — I can still feel their coldness. I was afraid my parents would die of grief. I was their only child. I kept turning back, sobbing. Looking at how sad they were. To board the plane was to part from life as I knew it. Everything changed at that precise instant; I lost something that had to do with my essence, with my identity, with who I was. Parts of *mi* are still there at the terminal."

I left the matter there.

His expression invited me to keep going.

I gambled on a segue, to get away from the topic:

"This violent feeling of yanking myself from my roots is my bridge to the heart of those who invented the tango. I have not thought about these memories since that winter evening at the window, in Kansas, when I started writing. Until now, with you, here — and in Chicago of all places."

This had not even occurred to me. Boomerang segue.

"I lived here for three years when I first came to the States. In Chicago people were cordial: they welcomed me to their homes, and they were helpful — but they kept their opinions and feelings private. They did not show me who they were 'in five minutes.' And I stopped showing who I was in five minutes. My Argentine self had been interrupted; I had to figure out who I was and how to be in this new city, in this new country. Life was different here: orderly, predictable, safe. But without the old salt and pepper. I missed that a lot."

At that moment, in the hotel lobby, I felt grateful for what my second country had given me. To my surprise, an immense love for my father welled up in me for no apparent reason; and with it came an inconsolable sadness for being far away when he died, 11 years after I first left Argentina. These feelings stormed inside me, quiet container that I was on the outside. On the inside they stormed, and on the outside he matched my silence.

Dancers had been entering the ballroom for a while now, and at this instant we both seemed spent from emotional labor. He looked like he had been traveling through his own internal losses as I was reliving mine.

Having already collected ourselves for a moment, we had nothing to do but stand and hug each other. I thanked him for having been such a good listener and catalyst. With teary eyes and the softest of expressions, he gestured "vice versa" with his hands.

Part I. The People

After we parted, I had no idea whether I would ever see him again. Maybe it would be like at tango dances, where even the most meaningful encounters quite simply end.

That is the code.

2

Buenos Aires:
Connection Metropolis

Smitten.

That's how we natives feel about our city.

Poets are in love with "her," too; some of their lyrics are declarations ~~her city~~ of love to her. In "Mi ciudad y mi gente" ("My City and My People"), poet-composer Eladia Blázquez confesses that it is hard to make a living in Buenos Aires, where a tango hurts; yet she wants to stay, she would not feel proud living "under any other skies."

Abandoned.

That's how we natives feel about our city.

Our romantic hearts easily turn angry at "her." We have felt forgotten ~~emotion of her city~~ by our own motherland. Many of us sought voluntary exile; others had no choice but to live under other skies. To leave is to miss the creative energy and the connectivity that very few other cities have. It dooms us to dream about returning, and to question our wisdom. The 1935 tango "Volver" ("To Return") by Carlos Gardel and Alfredo Le Pera sums up the predicament of the porteño in exile:

> *Yo adivino el parpadeo*
> *de las luces que a lo lejos,*
> *van marcando mi retorno.*
> *Son las mismas que alumbraron*
> *con sus pálidos reflejos*
> *hondas horas de dolor.*
> *Y aunque no quise el regreso,*
> *siempre se vuelve al primer amor.*

I can already see the twinkle

Part I. The People

Musician, composer, and director Leopoldo Federico (b. 1927) playing the bandoneón, the instrument that represents the voice of tango and the voice of Buenos Aires. Federico began his career at age 17, playing with the orchestras of Juan Carlos Cobián, Alfredo Gobbi, Alberto Marino and Emilio Balcarce, Osvaldo Manzi, Héctor Stamponi, Miguel Caló, Lucio Demare, Mariano Mores, Carlos Di Sarli, and Astor Piazzolla. He was a soloist in Piazzolla's "Octeto Buenos Aires." In 1953 he formed his own orchestra with Atilio Stampone. In 2009 he won a Latin Grammy for "Best tango album." *Photograph by Carlos Furman photography (Buenos Aires).*

of the lights that from afar
are marking my way home.
They're the same that used to cast
their pale, reflected rays
on deep hours of sorrow.
And I didn't want to come back,
but you always return to your first love.

Charm, aesthetics, imagination, intimacy, pride, and elegance are in the air, all spiced up with French romanticism and Italian spiritedness, filtered through the warmth and sensibility of Buenos Aires. This urban landscape has a pinch of dark as well: the last economic debacle (in 2002) left ugly casualties in its wake, with the sight of *cartoneros* — cardboard collectors — sorting through the trash in downtown neighborhoods. They place their findings in contraptions that allow a single person to push a heavy load. The official story of these bins changed over time: at first people said the city assigned a train to carry the cartoneros' recyclables; since the first train was white, it became called the "white train" (*tren blanco*) or the "ghost train" (*tren fantasma*). The story porteños tell me more recently is that the cartoneros were employed by marginal organizations, which sent out vehicles to load up the materials and take them to the train; "ghost train," they say, means it has an unofficial status. During my last visit I noticed that the cartoneros, who were once the indigent "unemployed," now wear impeccable uniforms with neon stripe bands for protection, and have become formal city employees, at least in some districts of the city.

Protest demonstrations are part of everyday life as well. A handful of demonstrators can block the 19 traffic lanes of Avenida 9 de Julio and paralyze the core of the downtown area. Radio and television announce the daily traffic interruptions regularly, giving the places and times. The police who march alongside protesters to prevent violence obey instructions from above not to disband protesters no matter how much inconvenience they may cause.

But downtown, particularly on Corrientes Avenue, life never quite stops. Stores that sell new and out-of-print books keep their doors wide open until the wee hours of the night. It is not uncommon to watch someone browsing Nietzsche or Dostoyevsky past midnight. During the "night of the bookstores" that takes place in December, a human sea moves up and down Corrientes, enjoying the events prepared for the occasion; couches are placed in the middle of the avenue for more comfortable enjoyment of audiovisuals featuring the text and the readings of classic poets. Cafés, sometimes more than two or three per block, are everywhere in the city center and surrounding districts; there is always one in sight when it is time to sit down for a *cafecito*.

Most of the architectural landmarks were completed before the city's 100th anniversary in 1910. Many are stunning. Residential buildings with carved wooden doors and massive bronze hardware contribute to the solid feel of the city. These doors can be fully appreciated when they are not blocked by human traffic; but this only happens on Christmas day. And tucked amid the period architecture, there's the red and yellow of a McDonald's here and there.

Experiencing the city's way of life is the best way to understand why

Avenida Corrientes, in downtown Buenos Aires. The obelisk marks its intersection with Avenida 9 de Julio. Many tangos were written about this avenue, including "Corrientes y Esmeralda," "Corrientes bajo cero," and "Tristezas de la calle Corrientes" among others. As early as 1921, Paquita Bernardo (1900–1925) played with her Orquesta Paquita at Bar Domínguez on Corrientes, with Osvaldo Pugliese on piano and Emilio Vardaro on violin. At the peak of tango's splendor, this avenue was lined with dance and music venues. The "Palacio de la papa frita," whose sign is visible on the right, was a favorite of Astor Piazzolla. *Photograph courtesy of Gregorio Donikian (Buenos Aires, Argentina).*

tango is more than a dance: this is the one place in the world where tango is a way of being, a part of a larger culture. Anywhere else, tango is an art form without a culture to nourish and sustain it. Every time I return here, little shocks sink into my bones before I have time to realize what has happened. When I come from the United States, I have to forget about life being orderly, predictable, "safe," efficient…. "The warm invisible something" of Buenos Aires drips from every one of its pores, connecting me with others, with the air, the jacaranda trees, the birds, the aged brick walls, the intimacy of neighborhoods, the bohemia of the night, the sweetness of couples kissing outdoors. Within an hour, I have become part of a passionate pulse that never abates: the energy is contagious.

This is the city of hugs and kisses. Locals like to connect through impromptu repartees. Gazes are always turned on; they come in all shapes and colors: the imaginative, the subjective, the introspective, the dancing ones, the ones that cross each other, the ones filled with questions and answers.

This city is warm. It is hot. It is searing. I am not an island here.

Two Hours during Any Afternoon

"Taxi! Taxi!"

After letting the driver know the destination point, I look at the person sitting in the car on my right. The driver of the other car looks at me. This looking that happens from car to car is quite lively. There is curiosity and desire. A certain mystery. Who are you? A certain intrigue. What can I tell from your expression?

As I do "this looking thing" the taxi driver engages me; he lays some of his life out there in front of me. He asks me something about my life, too, but only if he senses I am in the mood. Typically, I am in the mood. We talk about real "stuff"; how I feel about this, how he feels about that. He turns his head to meet my eyes on red lights. We get to the destination. I have a general sense of who he is. Maybe he has a sense of who I am. We exchange warm goodbyes.

I step out carefully; always looking down: the sidewalks are a calamity! I seem to step in every single hole. My ankle — ouch!

Litter here, litter there. Not a trash can in sight. I walk amid a stream of people getting attracted by something or other. Like the vendor who sells parrots outside his pet shop on Rivadavia Avenue. Or the proud shoeshiner with his tools artistically placed on a black velvet mat. Most windows demand my attention for one reason or another. My taste buds get tantalized by showcases full of freshly baked sweets. What a loud cacophony of horns and traffic noise. My ears — ouch!

The signs: I read some of them twice in disbelief: *We sell pizza by the meter*. What? Well, why not? Why do pizzas always have to be round and sold by the slice? Why can't they be rectangular and sold by the meter? Signs like this tell me there is thinking outside the box in this busy neighborhood of barrio Once.

A poster announces an art workshop for children: *Forbidden not to touch*. Did I read that correctly?

Traffic keeps moving fast in this wide avenue. I breathe pollution; I am very conscious of the hot weather. Looking for air conditioning, I enter a café and sit down. No glass of water gets placed on my table immediately. No waiter comes for 10 minutes. My North American side gets impatient. The waiter finally arrives! He and I do "the looking thing."

After eating I read the newspaper for as long as I want. I am not rushed out of my table. I can linger here forever. What would my friend Celina be doing right now? I miss her. I call, and we arrange to get together later in the day, for a *cafecito*, of course.

I do not have to make an appointment with her three weeks in advance.

I am in Buenos Aires.

Hugs and Kisses

Remember how teachers, physicians, bosses, colleagues and just about most people keep a physical distance in the States? Maybe we get small doses of vitamin touch, or else *nada, niente, rien*. Physical distance is a comfortable, safe, self-inflicted deprivation we get used to.

In Buenos Aires I undergo more kissing and touching in a single month than in my entire lifetime thus far in the States. Kissing and hugging friends and family is commonplace. So is stroking the arm, the hand or the body of the person we are conversing with. This is not surprising either. Because most of us talk and listen with our bodies as little children do. We like this fleshly nature of ours. That's how we are. That's what went into the dance's physical nature. It surprises visitors whose cultures squelch this natural need to touch and be touched. "Natural" because we are born with this need. Don't little ones want to touch everything and everybody no matter where they are born?

What surprises me here is to kiss the cheek that the cleaning lady offers me when I greet her at the door. It surprises me in a good way. Or kissing hello and goodbye the manicurist, the hairdresser, or just about everybody with whom I have even a passing business connection.

Sometimes I persevere in my North American mode during the first few days of my stay and say *hola* without kissing. "Give me a kiss," the other person usually says. So I do. And I like it. Hugs, kisses, and touches are not rituals: through them we give some of who we are, and receive some of who the other is.

The kissing culture of the medical profession amazes me the most. I kiss the receptionist and the nurse, whether I have seen them before or not. The physician greets me with a kiss, whether he has seen me before or not. Recently a physician gently played with my hair as he was talking to me. He gave me his and his nurses' cell numbers in case I needed access to them during the weekend. He called me the day after the visit to find out how I was doing. I cannot imagine getting the doctor's cell phone number in the United States. Or kissing the receptionist and the nurse.

Impromptu Repartees

Consider this way of starting a Saturday.

It is breakfast time. I go with Carlos to my favorite *confitería* (eating establishment). Voila! A table next to the window is available. Good: I like the light and the people-watching. We sit, craving a *cafecito* and the obligatory *media luna* (croissant). I watch how people are with one another. Such animation! No two people at a table are having breakfast in silence. At the tables for six, they are gesturing and talking vivaciously. I watch two of them, a woman and a man — presumably friends — stand up, give each other a hug that lingers, lingers, lingers ... lingers ... and after this eternal embrace, they sit down and keep on conversing.

A waiter passes by our table. Craving the morning caffeine, I get impatient:

"Who waits on this table?"

"Joaquín: he will be with you soon."

Five minutes later Joaquín appears (he knows us — we are frequent customers), looks at Carlos' cute and oversized leather hat and says, "Señor, what fell on your head? A UFO? Let's be careful, we do not want NASA to interrogate us, or the FBI to put us in jail."

Joaquín is not being rude to his customers. It is his respectful way of being creative and playful. He "hooks us" (*nos engancha*) into an interesting brief conversation. We share a good laugh. In one of tango's figures called *gancho* (a direct reflection of what Joaquín just did) the men and women hook each other's legs in movement.

It is raining outside. It is Carlos' turn to "hook" Joaquín: "Can you do anything to get sun inside this place?"

(Joaquín responds to the "hook.") "You are going to have to pray a lot. While I get your breakfast, why don't you go across the street and pray... see that church there?"

Another waiter comes by to take our order. Still coveting breakfast, Carlos "hooks" him: "Joaquín has already taken our order, but if you want to bring another one gratis we have no objection."

(Smiling, the waiter "hooks" back.) "I am going to have to study the subject. I will come back in a few minutes and give you an answer." (The three of us smile at his comeback, knowing this is not true.)

Breakfast arrives. We enjoy it. Then we read three newspapers, looking for artistic events to go to tonight. Carlos leaves the table. I am alone when Joaquín passes by. He tries to "hook" me: "Where did the extra terrestrial go?"

"He went next door to change money."

"I was hoping you would say he went next door to buy another hat. But let's keep this between us. Don't say anything to the UFO man."

I laugh with gusto: he keeps a straight face. To someone from my second culture who could have watched and heard the "hooking" with Joaquín, it would have seemed disrespectful to the customer. But it's creative play, healthy play. Repartees between strangers add salt and pepper to daily life in this city.

This repartee would not have occurred if Joaquín had not looked and noticed Carlos' hat. Which leads me to the gazes — always alive in this city, whether at the cafés or at the milongas.

The Imaginative Gaze

Imagine you are with me in busy Corrientes and Larrea Streets. The usual traffic congestion: cars, buses, taxis, bumper to bumper. Five available taxis to choose from. This one is in bad shape: dismissed. That one is independent: dismissed. This belongs to a fleet; it looks well-taken-care-of: acceptable. The driver's face? He's in his 30s and reminds me of someone I know and like: acceptable.

"Are you available?"

"Sí, Señora."

"Please drive me to Uriburu 2600."

As usual, stuck in traffic. The activity in this predominantly Jewish business district is frantic.

"Chauffeur, I am changing my mind; maybe I want to go to 2600 Austria instead. Let me make a phone call, so I can tell you for sure."

At least five minutes go by. I am unable to get a ring at the other end. I hear the soft voice of the driver engaging me: "Señora, if you would allow me, I could make a proposal to you. I could suggest going to the corner of Avenida de Mayo and Bartolomé Mitre."

(I don't get it.)

"You would then say to me, 'That is an irresolvable matter, driver.' Or I could propose to drive you to the corner of Gascón and Medrano, and you would say to me, 'That is an impossibility, chauffeur.'"

I smile as I begin to realize that he is proposing corners that do not exist; he is naming parallel streets. I tell him I like his humor. My attention floats from him to the business in the narrow Larrea Street. I do not have enough eyes to take in the frenzy of activity going on.

The driver's soft voice comes back: "We could create a Kafkaesque scenario, looking for places that do not exist."

I am taken aback by his mentioning Kafka, but I tell him, "Yes, I suppose we could drive in circles all day long."

Another red light. Along this street all lights turn red when we approach them. Infallibly so. It takes 15 minutes to drive 15 blocks at any time during business hours, which is all day. The driver's voice brings me back to him: "I was digressing like this with a friend the other day. She said, 'You are spongy.' When she used the word 'spongy,' I said to myself, either she has been reading Borges, or she's high on marijuana. I wanted to kill her, but she was my friend's girlfriend. So I did not."

Wow, I say to myself, this man is an intellectual; he mentioned Kafka before and now Borges. Time was flying by listening to his witty imagination. I was so entertained now I could not care less if it took one hour to get to the destination. Red lights again! A sign jolts me: *Open 25 hours a day*. I like to read signs in this city. They tell me, "Come on, improvisation is on." People unloading rolls of fabric from trucks to stores catch my attention. Lots of colors: solids, prints. Lots of textures: silks, wools, embroideries, laces, sparkles—what a multicolored tapestry this neighborhood is! Another sign makes me laugh: *Hours: We open when we arrive. We close when we leave.* The calm and serene voice of the driver looks for me again. My attention floats between the interesting street scene and the fascinating imagination of the driver.

"Evolution has taken away our animalism. If we had lived in the times of Charlemagne, I would have used the dagger on my friend's girlfriend. If we had lived in the times of Henry VIII, I would have had her beheaded." I admire his knowledge; now he's into history. I get curious about a building that seems familiar and unfamiliar: "Chauffer, I do not recognize that building."

"It is the medical school. Señora, maybe you are getting disoriented because I have scared you. You are probably thinking, 'This guy is undergoing a schizophrenic break.'"

Actually, I am not afraid but amused and wondering if he was a former professor of psychology, history, or literature, an intellectual who had to drive a taxi because he could not get a professional job. He continues engaging me: "Here in Buenos Aires, psychologists surround themselves with books of Lacan, Melanie Klein, Freud. They like to think about how crazy others are. Never about how crazy they are. We have arrived, Señora: Austria 2600."

"Gracias. If I had lots of money, I would really like to hire you as my private chauffer. I could sure learn a lot from you. I regret not having your words on tape. I did take a few notes as you were talking. A souvenir?"

"Oh, no, not a tape recorder! If you had me on tape, it could eventually incriminate me."

I smile. "Because of your homicidal thoughts?"

I am out of the vehicle, about to close the door when his calm voice reaches me again: "Señora, don't ever feel guilty about doubting. Doubt is the basis of all knowledge." After such a Cartesian comment, I shake my head in disbelief, go across the street, and ring the bell.

This ride brought to mind an article written by a U.S. psychiatrist, published in a North American psychoanalytic journal. He described how a taxi driver, on the way from the airport, upon learning that his passenger was attending a conference in Buenos Aires, asked what his theoretical orientation was. An interesting discussion of the subject ensued between driver and passenger. The visitor was so bewildered that he wrote this story in a scientific journal. We find this natural.

Like Joaquín, this driver is a natural at noticing the other, at connecting, playing, and improvising. This is our day-to-day dance, one and the same as the improvisation of the tango.

The Lounging Gaze

La Biela. This is a *confitería* in the heart of the upscale Recoleta district. Few spots in Buenos Aires enjoy the combination of urban life and bucolic mood one finds here. This is what draws me here day after day. Imagine a city center with traffic noise and possibly more pollution than New York. But this place feels green and tranquil. A surrounding park keeps noise away; and behind this park lies the ultimate silence: the Recoleta cemetery. This landscape is an oasis away from the city's cement.

Elegant outdoor cafés and restaurants surround the green. No hot dogs here; no self-service either. No cleaning your own table. What a perfect place to indulge in idleness! What a balm for the soul!

Selecting the right outdoor table under the colossal *ombu* tree branches is as important as selecting a good theater seat. The branches of the enormous two-hundred-year-old ombu tree (rubber tree) make a natural roof about 30 feet wide and 20 feet long. It is like sitting on a stage with ombu branches and luminous blue skies above, with majestic French architecture to the south (Palais de Glace) and a backdrop of neoclassicism (Recoleta cemetery entrance) and colonial architecture (Iglesia del Pilar). We, the customers, are the actors in this privileged setting.

Once I sit down, I do what porteños do. To scan the people scene is a must. What do we see? Hair textures and colors under the midday sun are lusciously shiny. Some people look up, trying to tan their faces. Most talk with friends. Those who are alone read or simply look at people. Eyes meet. Eyes talk. Eyes dance. When only a little eye contact goes on at La Biela, it is because the patrons are mostly foreign visitors.

On weekends, this oasis-park pulsates with artists of all persuasions. During my last Sunday here, I ate breakfast and lunch in one sitting. Six hours! The melancholy voice of a bandoneón playing tangos was the ultimate hook. I could not think of any place in the world I would rather be.

Fortunately, waiters let the customers be, even if they are not consuming, even if they only had a *cafecito* three hours ago.

In a PBS interview, Robert Duvall said that this was his favorite corner in the world. Can you tell this corner had been mine before it became Duvall's? Every waiter here knows when the actor is in town. He is passionate about the tango and about Buenos Aires. One waiter told me Duvall usually comes here directly from the airport, with his luggage. Well, since he likes this place so much, maybe this corner could be both his and mine.... La Biela easily can be as addictive as the tango.

People-watching is a favorite pastime everywhere in this city. I relish this quiet inquisitiveness and desire to connect: how nice it is, to be warmed by people's gazes. How validating it is, having one's presence so firmly acknowledged.

The Gaze Turned Inward

I send a hand signal to an oncoming taxi, but he keeps going. Hmm: unusual. A few yards ahead, a red light stops him. I run. Here is where the internal ride begins, and it becomes as subjective as the psychoanalytic couch ever gets.

"Señor, are you available?" He motions yes. "I tried to stop you but —"

"I apologize. I was in my internal world. You took me out of my inside-myself-ness [*ensimismamiento*]. I was thinking about my two girls. I had just seen that airline sign all over the city that shows two 10-year-olds. I just drove by one. I would like to buy one. If I just knew where to get it. The girls in the sign look just like my daughters."

He looks too old to have two 10-year-old girls.

"They are women now. I am sorry I missed you. But I don't want to get upset about it. I am learning not to get upset about things. My blood pressure is high. I am a great candidate for a heart attack. Too many crazy ones in the street. I have 61 years on top of me, and I do not understand a lot of what is happening in the world today."

Like most taxi drivers, he thinks about life! That's why I like to talk with them. I like to hear their strong opinions. I know their opinions come from self-reflection and critical thinking. How refreshing!

"A few hours ago, I was driving three 13-year-old passengers; one of them was using foul language — *boluda* here, *boluda* there. All the persons she talked about were *boludos*."

Boludo is an empty word without consensual meaning, an adjective people may use either with a pejorative tone or with affection.

"Luckily she got out of the cab before the other two girls did. One of them said to me, 'Papá, I could tell you did not like the language this girl [*piba*] was using. You were listening to her and became uncomfortable. We find her unbearable, too. And we have to put up with her in school every day.'"

"Señor, what a nice story. These two girls were watching you, and noticing you were uncomfortable — how sweet! And they called you papá. Very tender!"

"I am already a grandfather. And you, what do you do?"

"I write."

"About what?"

"Mostly about psychology."

"Ah … I cannot lie to the guy that looks at me in the mirror when I shave every morning. This is my psychology. Homemade psychology. I strive for simplicity, good manners, humility. Humility is my definition. I mean being humble. Many *villeros* [those who live in the slums] are not humble; they are arrogant [*soberbios*]. Do you only write about psychology?"

"I write about the tango, too."

"Ah … *El tango*. I admire Cátulo's poetry. Look at everything he says in just a few words: '*Paredón, tinta roja en el gris del ayer, sobre el callejón, con un borrón, pintó la esquina.…*"

He is reciting the lyrics of the tango "Tinta roja" ("Red Ink").

"'Bounding wall, your emotion of brick, happy over my alley, with a sketch painted the corner.…' And how about Discépolo? His poetry is so pertinent today. '*Que el mundo fué y será una porquería ya lo sé … En el quinientos seis y en el dos mil también.…*'"

He is reciting the tango "Cambalache" ("Pawnshop").

"'That the world has been and will always be a shame, I always knew.… In the year 506, and 2000 all the same.…' And Piazzolla. I remember the day I gave him a ride. It was after he divorced his second wife. He was living with Laura Escalada in Libertador and Ortega y Gasset. Piazzolla asked me: 'Is your old man still around?' 'Yes,' I told him. 'I hope you keep him for many years. The day he dies, you will become the old man.' When I listen to 'Hora cero,' I hear Buenos Aires. And when I listen to 'Adiós, nonino,' I think Piazzolla composed it after talking with me about his old man. Here we are, Señora, Rivadavia 2500. Shall I drop you at the corner?"

The driver's internal gaze was constantly on. He showed me who he was "in five minutes," in his feelings, in what mattered to him. I know he could have conversed with me about anything. He had the kind of wisdom that comes to a person who makes thinking a priority. Before getting out of the cab, I read his name out loud from the vehicle registration card: Víctor Hugo Bonacoza. "Basque-French," he said. This was enough to guess that his parents had given him a love of poetry.

Like most porteños, this driver lives in a subjective mode. Other cultures look more toward the outside, to what others think, to what is socially or politically correct. Not so much here.

This driver is as introspective as the tango.

The Searching Gaze

"Taxi!"

It stops.

"Please drive me to Callao and Corrientes."

After some personal conversation, the driver asks me what most of them ask me.

"Where are you from?"

How can all these drivers tell I don't live here?

"From Buenos Aires. I was born in Barracas."

He inspects me in his rearview mirror. Our eyes meet there. I wonder if I can maintain my disguise of being half-foreigner. I can see he does not believe me. With typical porteño forwardness, he tells me so.

"You must have lived a long time abroad."

"You are right. I don't know how taxi drivers know. Would you tell me? I am dying to find out."

He keeps examining me in the mirror. After a bit of silence he lets me know: 'There is a different music in the way you talk.'

Porteños naturally seek connections with others. This way of being mirrors the silent asking of questions and listening to answers in the dance.

The Freudian Gaze

Placita Pichón Riviere. Today I read in the newspaper about a commemorative event at this petite plaza. It is the day of the social psychologist, I learn. How unusual! We do not have a day of the psychologist in the United States. I read that a plaque to Enrique Pichón Riviere will be placed there. I am astonished: I remember the man. He was one of the founders of psychoanalysis in Argentina. I never met him, but I studied his textbooks. He was the psychotherapist of our admired tango poet Enrique Santos Discépolo. I think about Café Freud in barrio Palermo, with Sigmund's face engraved on the glass door. A café named after the founder of psychoanalysis is not surprising in this city, where the general population is so interested in psychoanalysis. Could there be a Café Freud in any other city? I believe there is one in London ... but Freud lived there. I have never seen a plaza named after a psychoanalyst, except for the Sigmund Freud Park in Vienna; but he lived and worked there, too. But we have a Plaza Freud in barrio Palermo Hollywood (at the corner of Honduras and Salguero). In Vienna it was not easy to find Berggasse 19, Freud's one-time home and office. But (I keep talking to myself) even though a Café Freud is not surprising in Buenos Aires, a "Placita Pichón Riviere" is! But on second thought: why would this be strange in a city that is in love with psychoanalysis? Does the regular person in the street have a basic knowledge of what psychoanalysis is? Yes. How come? Books and magazines on the subject are easily available in newspaper stands. Just recently, five volumes of *The Complete Works of Sigmund Freud* were abridged and printed in pocket size. Can you imagine common people carrying Freud's books in their pockets in any other city? I cannot.

Porteños are also familiar with psychoanalysis because so many sign up for it. Do we need treatment more than other cultural groups? No. Is this hard to believe? Not if you're familiar with the culture. Porteños thrive on subjectivity and introspection. Remember the taxi drivers? How they didn't talk about externals? How subjective their comments were? In Buenos Aires we believe that being in psychotherapy or psychoanalysis "is the smart thing to do" because it helps us become more self-aware. We do not hide our "patienthood." On the contrary, we flaunt it.

Leti was giving me a facial. I asked her about the steps for a certain skin treatment.

"I have not 'internalized' the steps. Let me find the instructions so I can read them to you."

"'Internalized'? This is shrink jargon. Are you in psychoanalysis?"

"Yes, I am. For 20 years. I wanted to be a psychologist but decided against it, because I did not want to spend a lifetime in psychoanalysis. I went into cosmetology instead, and I have spent my life in psychoanalysis anyway."

Víctor, my hairdresser, mentioned his 32 years in psychoanalysis, as he was opening his personal life to me, while cutting my hair.

Buenos Aires has been the epicenter of psychoanalysis in the Americas. It has the greatest number of psychologists per capita of any city in the world (one in every 649, according to a *New York Times* article). It is also the epicenter of the tango as well. A coincidence? Not at all.

I understood our love of psychoanalysis after I meditated on our love for tango. Subjectivity is the right soil for both. We like to dig into the meanderings of our beings through tango and through psychoanalysis. We take our pain to both. We hurt in both. We heal in both. We ride our internal, wondering gaze in both.

Crossing Gazes

Piropos are flattering comments porteños offer, typically in the streets when a woman approaches a man from the opposite direction. When their gazes cross. We porteñas like piropos. They do not offend us. In fact, if a day goes by and I do not get at least one piropo, I know I must look anywhere from nondescript to bad. These piropos come in many flavors: plain, poetic, or a bit mischievous. They do not ask for anything. They are playful improvisations. Overall, they are well intended.

A North American-Swiss woman living in Buenos Aires had this to say: "I may be going across the street; a man may pass by; he may let me know with words or grunts that he likes me. The other day a young man saw me coming down the sidewalk and began to make swiping motions with his arms. He looked crazy. I could not figure out what was happening to him. When I passed by, he said he liked cleaning the sidewalk for beautiful women. I loved it. I like how men look at women here."

I remember a poetic piropo given to me by another customer as I walked into a store. I did not see the person, but I heard his voice:

"I know spring is here when I see a flower bloomii
I turned toward him, smiled and replied:
"I am sorry to rain on your piropo, Señor. Today h;
21, the first day of winter...."
"No, no, no. What matters is what I feel inside. I f
not matter what season it is. I feel you are spring, and I feel young inside."
He walked a few steps toward me, faces me, and said:
"How old do you think I am?"
I evade the question because I cannot tell people's ages. He insists.
"Just look at my face and just say a number ... please.... But do not look too long. I do not want you to fall in love with me."

"I could never live with pride...."

Yes. We are smitten with the life-energy, paradoxes, aesthetics, creativity, sensuality, interest and desire of this city. Yes. We like to be part of its grand connecting circle of life. Our imaginative and subjective gazes have always been our survival skills. They have kept us sane in political and economic seas of madness. Yes, it is hard to make a living in this land. We suffer if we stay, and we suffer if we leave. But we are in irredeemable love with her ... and angry at her. We surrender to her, as Rubén Garello puts it in "Buenos Aires conoce" ("Buenos Aires Knows"):

> *Buenos Aires me tiene,*
> *apretado a su nombre,*
> *atrapado en sus calles,*
> *ambulando a sus pies.*

> Buenos Aires holds me
> pressed against her name,
> trapped amid her streets,
> walking on her feet.

And she gave us her child, with its mighty, invisible heart, which is all of us: *el tango*. To find the dance we must step behind the scenes of this exuberant and dynamic metropolis, and enter the slower pace of the tangopolis that lies pulsing just behind some of its ornate doors.

3

Shadows in the Temple: Inside the Milongas

The milonga is the tango's art museum.

— Horacio Ferrer

As I raise the bedroom blinds, a tearful Buenos Aires winks at me. It drizzles. I remember the lyrics of Enrique Cadícamo's 1943 tango "Garúa," named after this foggy, misty type of rain. I hum its melody of immense nostalgia:

> Las gotas caen en el charco de mi alma
> Hasta los huesos calados ... y helados

> The drops are falling on the puddle of my soul,
> my very bones are soaked through ... and frozen

The view from my eighth-floor Buenos Aires apartment is seductive on this gray, winter day. I stare out at Recoleta, one of the grand cemeteries of the Western world. Its Doric columns welcome mourners as well as those just out for a stroll. Scattered people with umbrellas and raincoats walk along its manicured paths. The burial sites, all of them architectural setpieces, impress me once again.

The country's history is here, from the fathers of the nation to its governors and presidents, its literary personalities, its eminent scientists. Eva Perón is here, too, resting in a black marble monument amid the aristocracy she hated.

As I look out the window through the dense mist, the wet domes of the monuments form a supernatural stage where the protagonists might

Milonga "El beso" in Buenos Aires. The history of the city's inhabitants — their way of being, connecting, walking — are present in the tango, as the fully embraced dancing couples move slowly to the music. Unlike dances that express the "happy" side of life, the tango is a "serious" dance that connects us with our deepest selves, our need for others, and our experience of life's losses. *Photograph courtesy of Jerzy Dzieciaszek (Stockholm, Sweden).*

rise from their majestic burials. Maybe they will act out the life of 26-year-old Liliana Crociati, who died in Austria during her honeymoon. In the life-sized sculpture that was commissioned by her father, she now stands in her wedding dress, accompanied by her dog, with a replica of her bedroom extending underground beneath the level tiles of the walkway.

Maybe the dead wait in the wings to act out the story of 15-year-old Luz María García Velloso, now in Carrara marble, sleeping on a white bed of roses beside the concrete pad where her mother slept night after night following her death. We would probably not want to see the phantasmagoric story of Rufina Cambaceres, supposedly buried alive in a cataleptic state in 1902 — an incident that changed the funeral customs and started the trend of placing bell chimes besides corpses in case they should "wake up." The 2,400 stained-glass windows built inside the monuments, hidden from the view of visitors, could also tell us inside secrets that only they know.

Part I. The People

All other cemeteries I know, whether manicured or in disrepair, are places where I feel the deceased are unequivocally dead. Recoleta is an exception, and can be disorienting; it stirs up the fantasy that Liliana still lives in her bedroom ... that Luz María merely sleeps ... that corpses could wake up and rattle their bell chimes ... that the stained-glass windows are there for the "enjoyment" of those not quite so deceased. Paradoxically, in this place of death, there is something that inspires creativity and that soothes the spirit. One of our great presidents, Cornelio Saavedra, came here for meditation. The poet Borges strolled here on Thursday afternoons, and left us these lines in his memorable early poem "La Recoleta":

> Beautiful are the sepulchers,
> the bare Latin and the bonded dates of fate,
> ...
> and the many yesterdays of history
> now arrested and unique.

In this cemetery and in tango poetry, I find a similar perplexity. Both are like two rapidly spinning coins with their faces changing: death, life, past, present. As they spin, these faces coexist in dynamic motion. Neither in these lyrics nor in Recoleta is the "before" a clear discrete past. I feel the present in the poets' hearts, even though their eyes are typically looking toward the past. The before is constantly evoked by their memories of bygone childhood, youth, and loves. These tango poets hold on to memories the same way Luz María's mother held on to the presence of her dead child.

The poetry of Alfredo Le Pera's tango "Volver" ("To Return") illustrates this ever-present theme:

> *Vivir,*
> *con el alma aferrada*
> *a un dulce recuerdo*
> *que lloro otra vez.*
>
> To live,
> with the soul clutching
> one sweet memory
> that I cry for once again.

My nostalgic mood wants company, which I know I can find in the numerous temples where the ceremony of the tango dance is performed. The weather does not invite outdoor living today, but it is perfect for milonga-hopping. I look at the milonga schedule in the newspaper. Three

56

of the 25 for today catch my attention. I like *La Ideal*, where a certain 3 P.M. milonga happens. This other one, *El Arranque*, was excellent last year; I could get to the first one by 3 P.M. and to the other one by 6 P.M. A definite "yes" to both; a tentative "yes" to *El Beso*, which lingers on past midnight.

It is time for my dressing ritual. Nothing flashy. Sobriety. I choose a black skirt and fitted top, red earrings. The black is for rituals; the red, for life. Unlike the sexy tango of Madison Avenue advertisements, I follow the traditional codes I have observed since I started attending milongas. It is nothing like the tango postcards. No femme fatale outfit, no fishnet hose, no see-through tops. No rhinestones. Red high-heeled shoes travel in my purse, protected from street damage, so I can better do pivots and turns. I'm on the sidewalk outside my building, and a taxi is approaching; I wave it over, open the door, and sit: "*Buenas tardes.* To Suipacha 384, Confiteria Ideal, please."

Sacred Space for Ceremony and Rituals

The French-inspired Argentine façade of the *Confiteria Ideal* reflects the aristocratic origins of this two-story building, a one-time exclusive teahouse that first opened its doors in 1912. At that time, the wealthy gathered in sumptuous European-style buildings like this one: the tango, born around 1880, was already danced throughout the city. Today one finds no aristocracy among its patrons, only common people mostly from the south districts of the city, dancing their hearts out. Tourists, celebrities, and foreign tango dancers pay obligatory visits to this historic temple.

Inside, a marble staircase curling around a turn-of-the-century elevator points me upstairs. Music reaches my ears, at first faintly. Something inside me swells at the sound of the Golden Age orchestras. The nostalgic strains of this music, recorded during the peak tango era that stretched from the 1930s into the late 1940s, are a balm for my mood today. It speaks for our collective *nostalgia porteña*. So does the music of the 1920s, which we admittedly dance to less often. This dance and these sounds belong together. As I continue upward, I feel the relief of knowing that I will not be exposed to "alternative" music, the jazz, club, chamber, and salsa music that I hear at some tango festivals and milongas in the United States. That music is definitely not a match for the tango's heart I can feel inside me today.

When the Confitería opened its doors in 1912, the city had more than 1,250,000 inhabitants, but only aristocratic patrons from the city center frequented it, in formal attire, for its elegant afternoon teas. Today, Confitería Ideal is both an historical site and a milonga venue, but it is also an institution of tango culture, featuring shows and the major orchestras, along with other cultural events related to the tango genre. *Photograph courtesy of the Archives of Confitería Ideal and general manager Jorge Vieites (Buenos Aires).*

3. Shadows in the Temple

Once in the upstairs foyer, my eyes marvel at the salon's decor. I could be in Paris or Belgium; the high ceilings, wood paneling, French light fixtures — what a visual feast! Yet everything here is touched as well with a moribund splendor: the red tablecloths are worn out, the chairs are in need of repair, the walls are crying for a new coat of paint. I miss the grand chandelier that used to preside over the dancing area. This old familiar place looked so much better in the 1990s. I miss some of the baroque trappings that gave such a sumptuous setting to Carlos Saura's movie *Tango* and Madonna's film *Evita*. Last year I saw Sally Potter here, director and protagonist of the film *The Tango Lesson*. I wondered what it was like for her to be back in the setting of her movie. Like most, she was nursing a *cafecito*. Like most, her gaze was fixed on the couples swirling on the dance floor (*la pista*). That day, she was sitting at one of the small tables that border the dance floor amid its frame of marble columns. Today, men are sitting solo in this area next to the entryway.

When the milonga manager greets me at the foyer, I tell him where I want to sit. "Not there," he explains. "Those tables are reserved for regulars. You have to sit [pointing faraway] in that area. I am sorry."

Swallowing my frustration over this constraint on a freedom that I take for granted in my second culture, I enter the salon following him. Men and women stare at me. What do they see? Tango dancers can tell a good dancer by the poise of his or her walk. I will certainly scrutinize those coming in after me. We do the dance of the gaze ritual in this land; we look at each other with reciprocal curiosity and interest.

"Do you like this table?"

(I do not, but I take it.) I sit where I am told. A seemingly capricious code preserves the old traditions; the temple has to be set up exclusively for dancing, not for socializing. The codes are clear. Men who sit alone dance with women who sit alone. A woman who is accompanied by a man won't get invited by other men. To ask for a dance, one sends a gaze to meet the gaze of the person one wants to dance with. That is a dancing survival skill: those who do not use this "looking" communicate that they are not interested in dancing.

Men and women agree to dance from a distance. That's the code. It is called *cabeceo*, the "nod." From the man, cabeceo may include a friendly slight rising of the eyebrows or tilt of the head. From the woman it is the brief gaze, holding the man's eyes, inviting him to invite her to dance.

59

Cabeceo exists consistently in Buenos Aires, though not in the interior of Argentina. The uninitiated do not even see these visual telegrams crossing the room.

(As an aside: In the United States tango world, I had heard that Argentine men send invites from afar to avoid rejection. I had never questioned this conjecture — until this very moment. On this particular afternoon, I realized that the eye-invite at milongas is just an extension of what we all do in this city around the clock. We look! And look! Incessantly! Whether sitting at cafés, paying bills at restaurants, buying newspapers, entering or leaving establishments, or riding elevators, we look, handling the world and people around us with our gaze. The insight struck me like a minor epiphany on this 60-degree winter afternoon.)

Once seated, I stretch my antennas to feel out this group. I like what I feel and what I see. I decide just to watch here, and dance later at another venue. I am happy just to absorb the deep respect for music, tradition, and dance that I find today. Some men wear suits, others jackets, others turtlenecks or shirts. Clothing is less formal this year among the men. Up to the late 1990s, both jacket and tie were the norm. The majority of Argentine women in this hall, however, still dress as they did some years ago; most of them wear skirts. With one exception: at the far end of the hall, by the bar area behind the tables, I spot a couple dancing with large steps, wearing sneakers and cargo pants with pockets up and down the legs. Their dancing style and their clothes tell me they are foreigners.

The Inner Circles

Déjà vu! I see a dancer at the same table he occupied here last year. His hair is a bit grayer, but he is wearing the same attire he wore when I last saw him: burgundy shirt, burgundy pants, burgundy socks, and burgundy shoes. How can I forget that?

Then I spot — let's call him Alonso. (I don't know his name.) Last year, a dancer acquaintance played go-between, asking me if I would partner his friend who had expressed interest in dancing with me. It was strange, I thought at the time: I felt I had to accept, but this unusual invitation was an omen of bad dancing. So, Alonso and I went out to the floor. Little did I know what a great dancer he was. This man, half my height, had such skill that at the end of the *tanda* (set of dances) I said:

Confitería La Ideal was built during European Belle Époque, the period between the last decade of the 19th century and the beginning of the First World War in 1914. Its façade of granite and marble reflects the aesthetics and opulence of those years. A prominent fleur de lis emblem stands over the balcony. The wife of don Manuel Rosendo Fernández, founder partner of the Confitería, was French. All display cabinets and chandeliers with the inscription "Flor de Lis," which is a royal emblem, were ordered from France. *Photograph courtesy of the Archives of Confitería Ideal and general manager Jorge Vieites (Buenos Aires).*

"With a lead like yours, I bet you can resuscitate the dead and make them dance." I had to ask him what his tango story was. He told me he sometimes performed in the dinner show downstairs. I had been to the show a few weeks earlier, and I clearly remembered him after his mentioning it. Alonso, in his late 50s, is a combination of milonguero and stage dancer. I am happy to see him here. Rarely do stage dancers show up at daytime milongas.

I continue watching the dance floor. Of the roughly 80 couples here, I can see only those around the periphery. They move at a snail's pace. Those in the middle travel slowly as one compact mass. Each dancing couple that passes by reminds me of people holding each other and saying goodbye before going away for a long time. In their inwardness and seriousness I feel the passionate and soulful people that made the tango, embracing each other so as not to die of sorrow. Are these dancers embracing just their partners, or are they holding everyone they ever lost and still want back? When the 15-minute tanda of four dances is over, and the *cortina* (interlude) music plays, I can see individuals emerging from the mass. Dancers exchange a look, a smile, or a "gracias"; he follows her to her seat and then moves apart without looking back. That is the code. The floor empties swiftly. The cortina gives us time to sit, to signal, to receive invitations, and to join new partners. After another four dances the cortina plays again.

Cycles of intimacy and distance. Of closeness and separation. These, the great dilemmas of human relationships, are enacted in the tanda-cortina sequence over and over, again and again.

As couples begin the new tanda, my attention is drawn to the multiple invisible circles I visualize the couples making on the dance floor. Smaller ones revolve within bigger ones in a galaxy of spheres. The embraced couples form the smallest circle. Each of these small circle-couples rotates and pulsates with its own energy. Sometimes the man walks in a bigger circle around his partner. Sometimes she moves in a larger circle around him as well. Couples are like spheres floating around each other in the orbit of the biggest circle of all, the counter-clockwise line of dance.

What balance and harmony! In the bohemia of the urban dance hall, our dance has a celestial quality, even if I do not see the stars from inside the temple. Tango circles; eternal cycles of life.

The invisible circles lead my eyes to focus on the feline movement of the men's feet. I scan the feet on the floor, looking for milongueros. These habitués of the milongas have been going to them since they were teenagers. They are in their 70s or 80s now. They did not learn tango in schools: they grew up watching others, learning to dance from family or neighbors. They embody the essence of the tango and are admired for being naturals at an art that takes us a "life and a half" to learn. Women love to dance with them. They are the "high priests" of the temple. The milonga feels sanctified when one or a few of them are present. They exemplify the traditional rituals and ceremonies: filling themselves with the music before they choose a partner; taking ample time to embrace, fitting body to body with their partner before starting; dancing from the heart, inwardly; maintaining a silence while they dance, talking only between the songs of the tanda.

Ah ... their feet. The forward-moving foot pulls back a bit in calculated vacillation, like the knife-fighter's hand that retreats only to aim at its target with greater precision. I rediscover how naturally men move *al piso* (feet always on the ground), without breaking the embrace, with small unhurried steps, with pauses, with simple or intricate figures — maybe *giros* (turns), *ochos* (figure-eights), and *calesitas* ("carousels"). These men walk the dance with the naturalness of their walk in the street. The women's legs and feet are also a spectacle: they have a unique personality, a quality of assertive womanliness that seems to broadcast: "This is the woman I am."

Some time later, my heart overflowing from watching the beauty and tenderness of this dance, with sweet remembrances of my childhood filled with this music and poetry, delighted with the respect and solemnity I find today, I am ready to leave this temple.

It is pouring now. This heavy rain is not as dreamy as this early afternoon's misty *garúa*. It takes a while to spot an available taxi. I wave, *Taxi! Taxi! Taxi!*

"*Buenas tardes.* To Salón La Argentina in Bartolomé Mitre 1759."

Each Dance Is Its Own Story

This architecturally plain venue, Salón La Argentina, is tucked among the other nondescript buildings on the block. Its inside is as bare as its outside, without the Old World character of Confitería Ideal. It holds the milonga El Arranque today.

My first ritual is to change shoes in the bathroom. It is run by a female attendant, *la señora del baño*, an invaluable character mixture of mother and counselor who is behind the scenes. Her dancer's "emergency room" is equipped with essential paraphernalia for the milonga: combs, makeup, lipsticks, nail polish, nail files, super glue, hand mirrors. I begin to grasp the milonga mood right here. Women talk about the dances they had, and the ones they could have had. La señora del baño listens with empathy. Amid this bathroom camaraderie, my stilettos leave the darkness of my purse and become a part of me.

Now I am a dancer. Completed, I walk into the dance hall.

The usual. The staring. What are those eyes thinking?

Most porteños are so precise in their dance; I can feel intimidated. These men know when a woman is a millimeter off their lead. I know I can dance with as much heart as they do. But will I be able to dance as meticulously as they expect? Will I pass the challenge of figuring out the unique personal styles some of them have? At the beginning of each of my return trips, it takes me a while to feel relaxed amongst them.

Several tandas go by while I look without looking — watching the women and the men, but not gazing at any man's eyes in particular. When I was uninitiated, an experienced woman dancer at another milonga, *Viejo Correo*, shared the secret of how the invitation really happens. "Do not move the head around looking at all men, just look at the one you would like to dance with. It looks as though the man invites," she said, "but the woman chooses which men to look at." She invites the invitation. True, the man may or may not respond, but he cannot invite someone who does not look at him. When I look without looking, I am scanning the environment to figure out who could be the two or three good dancers I would "invite to invite me" when I feel ready to dance.

Tango shoes — the dancer's coveted possessions and endearing companions. *Photograph courtesy of MicMac (Catania, Italy).*

I am ready for the most important ritual. To choose whom to look at, to get invited to dance, maybe....

Seventy-Something with Green Beads

From the third row I watch the back of a man in his 70s seated in a front-row chair at the edge of the dance floor. He seems to be a regular who gets a strategic place reserved for him every week. He has been attentively watching dancers as if judging a competition. He looks back and sends me a friendly invitation with a smile. We go to the floor. A beaded green necklace peeks through the three opened buttons of his black shirt and distracts me a bit. As it happens, once we embrace, reality recedes, necklace and all. Embrace. End of distractions. Period.

From step one, I realize his dancing personality is harder to decipher than most. I trust I will figure it out shortly. Never has anyone wrapped me around his shoulders as this man does. I have become a diva's silk shawl, gently draped around his body before the next aria. With minute torso movements, he moves my left arm exactly where he wants it, more around his shoulder. He also glues my right shoulder to his left shoulder. He has one of the strongest signatures I have ever encountered. After the first song he introduces himself, which is rare among porteños. They usually prefer to keep their anonymity; but he sticks to the code by giving me only a nickname:

"My friends call me *Ché Milonga*."

"Because you go to milongas every night?"

"Noooo!! Not every night. Only Thursdays, Fridays, and Saturdays. I have no other vices; I do not smoke, I do not do drugs, I do not go to the horse races. Are you enjoying yourself?"

"It was hard to follow you at first. I would say it was a challenge. I am enjoying the challenge now."

"I have been dancing since I was 13."

"Really? You must have grown up in a family where everybody danced tango all the time."

"Ahhh ... yes. Bajo Flores."

"Bajo Flores — 'barrio tango.' Were there milongas every Sunday at home?"

"Every Sunday? Noooo!! All the time! Everything was an excuse to organize a milonga. If one of us kids lost a tooth [he points to a tooth] we would get a dance going. My grandfather would yell at my uncles: 'Eh you, get your body straight, what kind of posture is that?' That was my school. My grandfather teaching my uncles. I do want you to enjoy the dances with me."

It took me half a song to decode Ché Milonga's unique style. This happens to me, to some extent, with many dancers in Buenos Aires. Encountering the unique styles of the porteños is encountering each person's history, which has been invariably drenched in tango since birth. It takes me a little longer to find a groove with them, compared to the dancers in my second culture, where we have all undergone the same schooling and where tango dancing and music is not part of the culture.

Like Ché Milonga, many men ask women if they are enjoying the dances. Sometimes directly, other times with expressions such as *"Qué tal?"* which is an open-ended invitation to talk, or *"Todo bien?,"* which asks if everything is all right. These are not rhetorical questions. They really want an answer, and an honest one. I believe men who are very good dancers know they are not going to get complaints. I think that the purpose of the question is to open a personal dialogue in the present.

Twenty-Something with a Touch of Red

Something out of place interrupts my musings. I notice him right away, a 20-something among older men, and one who is wearing a red neckerchief like those worn by the Argentine men who invented the dance. He approaches my table with a verbal invitation; I notice the code change. A generational change? Had he sent me a cabeceo I failed to notice? He looks like a conservative older man in a younger body. In between songs I praise him for being a young carrier of our national dance. He likes to dance *tango salón* at traditional milongas like this, he says; many women his age do not know how to dance this tango. He is preparing to enter a competition. I inquire about the particulars: he says the judges give points for musicality, connection and embrace. Tango *al piso* is expected. As to the figures, only walks, turns, and *ochos* are permitted. The competition disqualifies dancers who lift their legs off the floor to do adornments.

As I slip back to my seat, I am baffled, once again, at the irrelevance of age at milongas. So far I have danced with a 70-something and with a 20-something. I cannot help but reflect on how equalizing the milonga culture is in this aspect. Little matters other than how a person feels the dance. (Up to a point, of course. Looking at the floor I'm reminded that there are always men who only dance with young and sexy women, whether they can dance well or not.)

The Purist in Blue

Three related subgenres of tango music are played and danced at milongas: tango, milonga (the name of a rhythm and dance, as well as the name for the gathering itself), and Argentine vals. Tangos might be vibrant, poignant, or nostalgic; milongas are generally faster and more playful. Tango vals is often happy and sweet, danced like tango but with a waltz rhythm. The tango vals evolved naturally as musicians began to creolize the form and compose their own songs.

Some people only dance when the music moves them, choosing partners likely to enhance their experience. They are the purists. A man in a blue suit and tie, carrying a briefcase, sitting close by, will tell me so. I thought it was strange that he was not dancing for one hour, until he sent an invitation, and we made our way to the floor. "Why now?" is the question I will ask him between songs.

"Before I dance, I want to watch the dancers, listen to the music, and absorb it all," he says.

He could not resist this particular tango vals — that's why he was moved to dance. We dance another vals. After the second song he asks if I want some advice. "Yes, of course I do," I answer, playing dumb.

"You should choose who you dance with. I watched you dance with someone who came to your table."

"But ... he did come to my table."

"You should say no, especially to those who come to the table. They are not worth dancing with."

He advises me to look at those whose dancing I really like. He even chooses specific partners to dance to certain orchestras. He is not being haughty. This implies that each dance is a commitment of the heart, and he wants to live it to the fullest. He is implying that each dance is a ceremony.

I will see him again, by chance, at various milongas, always dressed in a blue suit and tie, always carrying a briefcase, and always choosing carefully.

Grandpa's Bandoneón

I look at a sturdily built man in his 40s who has been sitting nearby without dancing. In my mind, I have already concluded he is not going to dance today: perhaps he is feeling melancholic and wants to get lost in the music and just watch. But surprise, surprise: he invites me after all!

We meet on the floor to dance our first song. While we wait for the second, this man whose body feels so very tango in its earthiness tells me, in response to my question, that he has been dancing for eight years. He has taken lessons at La Viruta and at Gricel, the group lessons offered before milongas.

"But you have given me dances that are older than eight years. Much older."

"I swear I have only danced for eight years."

During the intervals between the following songs, always searching for a window into my partner's life, I ask if he heard tango at home when he was a child. He tells me how much he loved his grandfather's bandoneón music, how it animated family parties where he watched the grownups dancing. "Ah, that's why your dance is older," I tell him. "You are your grandfather's bandoneón."

With this man, as with the others, I had to switch gears to encounter his personality. I had to enter his life. He grew up with tango at home, even if he did not dance as a child or as a young man. In this city, most dancers' lives are like that. When they dance, their every intention passes through individual and ancestral layers of memory and experience on its way to becoming movement. That's what makes a porteño's dancing signature rather cryptic to me when I return to this tangopolis after living for several months in my second culture. I have to decode quickly, interpret the style; from initial moves I have to imagine a whole, and then draw the plan of all the forms their dance may possibly take, the universal form for that particular person. The mind does not do the decoding. The body intelligence does.

If You Look at Me....

Certain codes are followed rather strictly in this city.

I go out to dance with a man who sends me an invitation. Why would he ask me out at the tail end of the set? We dance the last half of a song and head back to our seats. This is odd, I am thinking.

As we walk back he says, "We hardly danced. I invited you late because I could not engage your eyes earlier. I did not want to miss the chance to ask you when our eyes met. I would like to dance a full tanda with you. If you look at me from your seat, I will invite you to dance the next set."

We sit, apart. In less than 30 seconds, the new tanda begins. I do look at him. Why not? He is a good dancer. His strict adherence to ritual is intriguing. We go out again, right after returning to our seats. We dance a full set. He thanks me, and we return to our seats again.

The U.S. part of me is baffled. Could this have happened in my other culture? Never. Why? In the United States, if a man wanted to dance with a woman, he would approach her even if their eyes had not met. In the United States, we do not follow the cortina code strictly; a couple who wanted to dance more would just stay on the floor and disregard the cortina. In Buenos Aires, it's a signal to change partners, and breaking the code can send other signals. At a different milonga once, during a previous visit, my partner walked me to my seat after we had danced three consecutive tandas: although the dancing was over, the story went on. He soon came back to extend multiple invitations to go dancing together the following day — a porteño dancer's way of picking up a woman. When I declined, he argued that it would be just natural to pursue a man-woman relationship because he liked dancing with me and I "obviously" liked dancing with him, otherwise I would not have danced three consecutive dances!

The Provocateur

A new tanda is about to start. I engage the eyes of a tall man in his 50s. Moustache, pink shirt, gray pants, casual look. I stand up and wait, unsure if his invitation is for me, or for one of the five women around me. When he comes close, I step toward him. That's the code; that's how things are done. He tells me he is angry because he had looked at me for two hours the previous day at another milonga, and I did not make eye contact. He was ready to cut his veins if I did not look at him today.

"I do not remember seeing you yesterday. Where were you sitting?"

"Behind your chair."

He is joking but keeps a straight face. I smile. He does not.

We embrace. Before taking the first step he says in his simpático Spanish tone: "This is tango, your body is already moving too much; you have to be calm; I am the leader. You are too independent. Men are the bosses at milongas. This is the only place where we can tell women what to do."

I have heard this cliché before. His seemingly scolding tongue-in-cheek remark is gentle. I figure he just wants to make an impression. Canaro's music is playing, the orchestra that tends to send earthquakes through my body. That may be what prompted his remarks. Between dances he talks more about my unruliness. I smile and play dumb. He keeps a straight face.

"Maybe I will have to hold you still or tie you up to get you to follow the lead."

In the same spirit, when the tanda is over, I thank him for his astute observations.

"I will try to be submissive next time."

"You will never be able to do that."

I smile. He does not. He is not breaking any milonga codes. He wants to be noticed. And he succeeds.

I am aware of and feel undisturbed by his flirtatious banter. The provocateur knows I am not planning to be submissive, and that I am not serious when I thank him for his astute observations.

Later in the evening he invited me for a second set.

Irredeemable Poet

This tall, frail man in his late 70s is impeccably dressed in a light gray suit, white shirt, and gray tie. He seems to have a halo around his angelic grandpa's face; he looks blissful. Between songs he wonders why he has never seen me before. I tell him that he is not unknown to me, that I have seen him at Club Gricel several times. I have admired the way he keeps the old dress code of the milongas; and I have observed how he keeps dancing and never misses a tanda.

"I do not dress to keep up any milonga code. This is the way I dress when I get up in the morning."

"Oh ... what elegance! How about not missing any dances? Am I correct about this?"

"I love the tango."

"What is tango for you?"

He looks upward and smiles. "It is like touching the heavens with my hands."

"You are a poet."

He extends his arms and touches my elbows. Sweetly, looking at me in the eyes he says, "See the heaven I am touching at this moment?"

"You are definitely a poet."

The Lost Moment

My next partner has a self-made style much less traditional than most. He walks with unusual adornments, rises, and descents, and improvises a wide variety of small figures. It takes me a while, about 20 steps, to decipher his dancing signature. Easily and gradually, he leads me into all the figures his heart wants. Our connection is solid and grounded. His embrace is one of those that makes a woman feel treasured and taken care of. After the first song we converse in a mix of Spanish and lunfardo (slang). I tell him he is more playful than most milongueros with whom I have danced today. He knows others are critical of his style; he does not care.

"The tango is not a public dance; it is for me and my partner. It is not for those watching."

When he returns later to invite me for a second tanda, I notice he has changed his black shirt. He is wearing a white one now. He always brings a change of shirts in case one gets wet. We dance a Pugliese tango. During the cortina, he tells me that we were dancing to his favorite orchestra.

"I like Pugliese too, but isn't it too bad that his granddaughter conducts an electronic tango orchestra?"

With hurt feelings in gesture and voice he says, "How can you think about Pugliese's granddaughter at this moment? In tango you have to be fully present in the moment with me. Your mind and heart should be here."

He may have offended someone not familiar with the directness of porteños. He felt a slippage in our connection. He called my attention to it. Gently. Unlike the provocateur who was talking tongue-in-cheek, this man was serious. He expected my full presence between dances. Why act differently just because we were waiting for the next song?

Conversation with him and with most of my partners today starts from a personal core but remains anonymous. Typically no addresses or phone numbers are exchanged. At the milonga we are not in the roles we perform during our regular lives. There is no hiding behind them. We do not even have names; only Che Milonga told me his nickname — not even his real name. I am ready to leave so I can make the third milonga on my list.

Outside the rain has abated, and I am enveloped in garúa again. I see 10 taxis approaching this busy intersection of Callao and Bartolomé Mitre. I pick one and wave.

"*Buenas noches.* To Riobamba 416, at the corner of Corrientes, please."

The Temple of Temples

I am going to El Beso, a short taxi ride away, just to watch excellence. It is a closed circle there: regulars dance with regulars. I don't expect to dance because no one will invite me. From the sidewalk I remember the secretive narrow stairs that stand behind the red entry door. In what hellish place will I be seated? I head toward the small restroom to put my shoes on just in case: there's just a sink, two stalls, and a chair for changing shoes. No *señora del baño* here.

I approach the dance floor, which is tiny compared to the ones I came from. The walls are painted dark green, the columns are red, and light is minimal. I like the smallness and intimacy of this place.

The manager offers to seat me. (Actually, he commands me to follow him.) I knew it: the fourth row of the poorly lit all-women's section, in total darkness, touching elbows with those next to me.

"I made a reservation for a good seat," I protest.

"The best tables around the *pista* are for regulars who come every week, I am sorry," he replies.

I do as he says and begin to blend in with the wall.

Ah, the politics of the milonga! There is a strong macho atmosphere here. Men know they are excellent and fluff their feathers. They may stare an unfamiliar woman in the eye, then never invite her to dance. Habitués, both men and women, play the same power games. The very best dance with the very best, no exceptions. As in life, some people are more equal than others. If you do not belong to the caste, you remain an "untouch-

Milonga Porteño y Bailarin, Buenos Aires. *Photograph courtesy of Jerzy Dzieci-aszek (Stockholm, Sweden).*

able." (Some milongas have broken away from old codes and now adopt free seating policies instead, to make themselves more newcomer-friendly and to tone down the pronounced macho scent. Not this one.)

I watch the *pista*. I try to figure out who belongs to the higher and lower echelons, but I soon get distracted by beauty. I notice many women wearing expensive shoes. The majority of dancers are art. Some move like live sculptures. With perfect posture. With perfect balance. With minute steps. With legs that move slowly and with weight, as if by earth's gravity. With feet that land with precision where they are supposed to. This is tango heaven.

In many of the prouder men I find a diluted version of the arrogant — and admired — Argentine men who invented the dance shortly before the turn of the 19th century, the so-called *compadritos*. One of the dancers, Daniel, a porteño who lives both in the States and in Buenos Aires, happens to pass my chair on his way to the bar. We had met at a milonga in the States (we tend to exchange names in my second culture) and recognize each other.

"What are you doing sitting way back here?"

"I did not have a choice; plus, no one invites me to dance anyway, not even if I sit in the front row under a spotlight. I keep coming because I enjoy watching the dancing here."

"Dance with me. After others see your dancing, you will get invitations. Men will not invite unless they see you dance. They do not want to look ridiculous dancing with a novice."

I appreciate Daniel's offer. He had told me, in the States, that he had studied with master teacher Carlos Gavito, who insisted that the tango was not about steps, but about what happened between steps. Tonight I feel his maestro's philosophy in his pauses and unhurriedness. From the moment of the embrace he feels like a human dancing tree with long roots deep into the earth; he is the trunk, I am a branch connected to the earth through his body. When the tanda is over, we exchange "gracias," and I go back to my dungeon with a different attitude. With confidence, I send my gaze to a man whose dancing and demeanor I have admired. Daniel was right: this man responds with an instant invitation.

A Tanguero Who Doesn't Dance

Back in my prison seat, I glance at the stairway randomly and see a familiar profile entering the place, now that the milonga is almost over. In the dim light, I see he is my friend Florencio. I had asked him many times to come up to this temple just to watch, since he does not dance, but he had consistently refused. He has devoted every aspect of his non-working life to tango, and has amassed a large collection of early tango recordings, all without ever setting foot in a milonga in his very own city. He knew which nights I go to El Beso: he was in the neighborhood, and after so many deferrals, here he comes to surprise me! It delights me that he will finally get to see this skillful dancing in a proper setting.

Florencio sits down next to me and says nothing. His face is stern, as though he were doing homework against his will just to please me, or to get me off his back. In a low voice, hoping to engage him with the scene, I whisper in his ear: "Look at the language of those feet"; "See that couple ... watch their total immersion in the moment"; "That woman — she seems to be in seventh heaven...."

Florencio says nothing. He does not even look at me, and he gets up to leave after 10 minutes. I get up and leave with him. Once in the street, I ask: "Well, what do you think?" With his face transformed by anger he starts yelling: "These people are conservative retrogrades; I know the type! They are the ones for whom tango started in the 1940s. Have you ever heard them talk about tangos of the 1920s, before it got contaminated by lyrics — before the music got relegated to background noise? They are the ones for whom Piazzolla does not exist. They are stuck in the same ol' same ol' poetry of the past."

"Well, how can you — "

"I did not see anything that felt good." (He is furious now.) "Just the opposite! How can you expose yourself to this environment? It was disgusting to watch men with their arms around the women, touching their breasts."

Wait a minute, I say, it looks like they are touching the breasts but — and here he interrupts me again. With his intense temper he has to have the last word before turning on his heel: "Well. This was not the temple you told me about."

And off he walks toward Corrientes, without even a goodbye.

In these milongas, these houses of the past, we live the eternal present of the dance. We do. I insist.

Alone, I walk down Corrientes. I don't know where Florencio is. It drizzles still, nostalgically. The thin rain shivers down into the puddle of my soul.

4

The Invisible Heart of the Dance

When I think about all my dances over the years, the most unforgettable ones are those I shared with strangers of different cultures, religions, languages and skin colors. In seamless moments with them, when they become instantly familiar, I feel that an invisible umbilical cord connects me with All.

When I dance connected to the earth ... when on rare occasions a part of me defies gravity and grows wings ... when music, lyrics, partner, and self converge in perfect harmony, I call this "my deliciousness." And when I dance in seamless oneness with a man from a distant place, despite the everyday boundaries that separate us, I call this experience "my primordial" dance. Moments like these are few and far between.

My tango is colored by my life story, by the child I was, by the woman I am. When I dance I am always aware of Mother Earth under my feet. Feeling that I'm a part of her intoxicates me. I get an instinctive pleasure from caressing her with my high-heeled super-sexy stilettos. I revel in feeling that I, too, am Earth moving as a woman.

Mother Earth? Stilettos? These two do not go together. A mismatch? Yes. One of the many mysteries of the tango. I enjoy the many apparent opposites that collide in the dance.

In the tango embrace, the child in me gets cozy in my father's arms. My head finds a nest on his shoulder. I hug him around his neck, feeling my small legs hanging down his chest.

As a woman who likes to be in charge of her own balance, neither clinging nor carrying anyone else's weight, I enjoy negotiating the ancestral

There are as many tango embraces as there are tango couples — some evoke energy, some a sweet surrender. ***Photograph courtesy of MicMac (Catania, Italy).***

man-woman dilemmas stirred up by this dance. Can we agree about who leads? Can we be one and yet be two? Can we both have a voice? How do we manage mistakes? Minute body movements introduce and resolve these perennial issues in a matter of milliseconds, and the middle ground of silence always comes as a kind of surprise.

I like the many emotions of tango music: they speak to me, some in a gentle voice and some screaming out loud at me. Sometimes I hear the soul and the innocence of its first humble homes, and I dance to what "home" means to me. Sometimes I hear the bellicose strains of its marginal stomping grounds, and I dance to everything that goes on in the streets of that "other" part of town: the fights, the danger, the life on the fringe of the law. Either way my dance makes me tremble; either way it is as real as my pulse and my breath. It can be as weighty as a heavy heart, or as light as young love.

When I find this harmony with a nameless stranger, I feel an awakening of my inmost core, and the truest part of myself dances this dance of dances. I gladly shed my everyday self and discover a more luscious me. I feel the awe of creating art in a zone beyond time.

A Conversation Without Words

This invisible heart of the tango was unknown to me when I went to Club Gricel in the late 1990s, one year after I began learning the dance in the United States. Having watched the dance at family events during my childhood and adolescence, but never having set foot in a milonga myself, I had a burning desire to enter the culture of the tango in Buenos Aires, the city where I was born. I was not an astute observer; but I had some knowledge of the dance's intricacies, and I had my own deep feelings about the tango. Full of expectation, feeling half North American and half porteña, I went to Gricel with an Argentine couple.

I was too much of a novice to even dream about dancing with strangers in this city of experts, but I had the nerve to ask my male friend to dance with me. Maybe he would praise me? Instead, he stated frankly that I had "a lot of salsa" in my hips and a long way to go.

With the wind out of my sails, I concentrated on the scene of the milonga. One couple in particular stood out: they made a deep impression on me, epitomizing the tango I remembered from my childhood. They were in my thoughts later that night in my hotel room as I wrote down my observations and intuitions, with my limited but already-growing knowledge of the dance:

> A man and a woman stand in front of each other on the edge of the dance floor. Gently, her left arm envelops his neck. Her right hand meets his left hand; they join together in ceremony. They do not smile. They do not exchange words. Closely embraced, they move to the music as an inseparable unit. Her eyes stay closed. His eyes look down and only rise to navigate the dance floor. In this inward gaze, they look as if they share a secret, a sorrow, a pleasure, a desire. They hold one another as if they are dancing the last tango of their lives. Their feet look like paintbrushes; their movements match the pulse of the music. When the song is over, they look each other in the eye; she walks to her seat as he follows her. When she arrives there, he turns back and goes to his table in a different part of the hall.
>
> They are complete strangers.

What I wrote after watching them was all I thought the perfect dance was: two people flowing effortlessly, with no need to think about what they

The tango embrace is a social ritual, as in this photo of a street tango show in Valencia, Spain. Often when stage dancers are about to present the tango in its social form, they magnify, in slow motion, the moments during which an embrace and connection is created between them, so that the audience can appreciate the genesis of the dance. *Photograph courtesy of Pablo Casal (Valladolid, Spain).*

were doing. But there was something profound in their inwardness; there was something intense about their expression: what was that "something"? Looking back, I understand that only they knew what that something was; only they knew if they shared a sorrow, a pleasure, a desire or something utterly different from all of these. Maybe they shared nothing but a little companionship while delving inside themselves.

To know what that tango was, I had to overcome the stage of combining steps like words in sentence. I had to experience the tango that my eyes could not see by watching others; the mechanics of the dance would have to become a part of me. But even with that taken care of, there would be a further complexity to master: becoming a mind-reader of sorts, and understanding the *intentions* of the movements — whether minute or

79

large — that the man constantly proposed to me. I had to become deft at answering clearly and holding up my end of the dialogue, the splendid skill of "talking" through subtle body clues and intuition — of having a conversation without words. We do not talk during the dance; words get in the way: they are major impediments to being in the moment. After learning this I would then be free to dance from my heart, and would finally partake of that shared "something" my intuition saw in the couple at Gricel.

Describing that wordless moment in the embrace is a challenge, too — not only because words cannot be part of it, but also because poetic language is all that remains to us afterward, when we have overcome our separate selves in the dance. To merge with another, we leave ourselves behind: all we have left, inevitably, are metaphors.

The Lightness of a Gazelle, the Energy of a Jaguar

I've just arrived at my first milonga in Buenos Aires, and I'm wondering, as the new face I am, when and if I will get invited to dance. I casually look sideways, and soon an imposing man is walking up to where I'm sitting. He's not necessarily good-looking; he's sun-tanned, with heavy mustaches, and dressed in black.

During the first 20 seconds of our embrace I learn a lot about him; something about him is reassuring and inviting. He is someone I can trust. I place my temple on his cheek. It is a tender sensation. Although the arm wrapped around my back holds me gently, it has a male possessiveness about it, as if he were saying, "You are completely mine for the three minutes of this dance."

His chest offers a cozy nest to mine. We are literally heart to heart.

I lean more on him than he does on me; and with this slight pressure between our upper torsos, my body and legs become lighter. Letting my ego dissolve, I take a deep breath knowing he will wait for me to completely exhale, no matter how long it takes. Exhaling and surrender go together for me; this is my signal. It says, "I am yours in this dance."

I can sense that he reads me, and I get ready to dance with all that I am, with all that is pure primitive emotion in me. In these few seconds we have sown the seeds of our dance, a dance that is ours alone, with its own energy and quality. Relaxed, I let him carry me. And he does, with confidence. With the lightness of a gazelle and the energy of a jaguar. He wraps me up and propels both of us forward and upward in a pendular motion that touches dear Earth, flies and returns to Her. This propelling has the intention of a wild cat chasing its prey.

Tango couples are usually depicted as moving slowly and melancholically. The dancers in this picture are moving with a zest and confidence that we do not observe in the other couples behind them. The body connection between them appears seamless. *Photograph courtesy of Jaime Montemayor (Washington, DC).*

> The slight swaying as we dance this set of milongas would not feel more perfect even if we had practiced it for a lifetime. During the last seconds we are holding still, dancing to silence.

With many other moments like this, I began to discover the real tango, the internal tango — the tango of those special, rare connections. It made me realize that I had not discovered the dance, as I thought I had, that night at Gricel when I was a novice and I watched with only my eyes. I did not have any idea about the exchange of energy that takes place between dancers. I did not know dancers could feel electricity, flotation, or the gliding sensations I had begun to feel in the arms of strangers. I did not know we could experience a melding of identity.

There's an element of surprise and of wonder involved, continually. When it's real, it can only be conveyed in a story, if at all. I had no idea it would take me years to begin experiencing the tango's infinite inner treasures; and even after I did, I had no idea that men could experience the same sense of transport that women sometimes speak of. Men, I thought, had to remain alert to their immediate surroundings, if only to navigate among the other couples. The personal account that follows, related to me by a seasoned male tanguero, opened my mind once more about the invisible heart of the dance.

Transport at El Corte

I'm in El Corte in the Netherlands, about 30 hours into the New Year's marathon, and I've probably slept for only four of those hours. I've danced all day and all night with old friends, and strangers, to favorite music, as well as to new surprises. I am sitting by the edge of the dance floor, and a woman approaches me. She is a close friend of one of my friends, but we've never danced before. She invites me to dance in a way that feels so completely relaxed. I say yes, in a way that really means, "yes, I would like to dance with you." Not as a formality, or a social ritual. Not as an embodiment of our roles in the milonga, but just as two people sharing something.

We dance a tanda of Canaro tangos, sweet, playful music. My mind is too tired to dance in a clever way — it's more of a dance of instinct by now; besides, the hall is so packed with other dancers, there is hardly room for cleverness.

The next set is slightly more energetic valses [tango waltzes] — De Angelis, I believe — and the whole floor is picking up momentum, sweeping and swirling; I have the experience that my partner is not just moving with me, but almost

82

Milonga in Italy. *Photograph courtesy of MicMac (Catania, Italy).*

moving for me. She understands the intention and gives energy to the couple; our movements feel sure and warm, and somehow true.

Four songs later, the music comes back to tango, Troilo, full-bodied, energetic, with a wide range of emotion, and now things are a bit fuzzy. I'm not sure where one song ends and the next begins, or where one body ends and the next begins. We just keep dancing, but now it seems artificial to release the embrace between songs. We hold each other and share our own rhythm in breath and heartbeats.

What I do remember is the music eventually shifts to a very rhythmic alternative piece, something unrelated to tango, fast, with Latin percussion and a jazzy bouncy feel, and suddenly we are awake and alive and full of power and play; our bodies move in a way that feels almost like puppets moved by the music; we are moving in a way that seems beyond intention, as if the music is creating the movements, and our bodies are just passengers. The music breaks in waves across the room and ripples through the bodies around us — it seems everyone is swept up in this current. It is unreserved and absolutely shared. I dance most of this song with my eyes closed, and I imagine others are dancing this way as well. We don't need to see each other — we are all together. The song ends; our hearts and our breath continue this faster pace for some seconds. The hall is buzzing, but not with discussion — just sound and feeling.

The next song is something totally different, an old, sweet tango that I don't remember by name. Our bodies start into this new pace almost without asking. And in this song, after all these layers and stories, all this connecting, I have the experience of dancing not just with the body in front of me, but something more whole, and difficult to describe. It is as if our axis extended well above and below our bodies and the space around us is part of our couple. I am less aware of pairs of arms and legs and more conscious of circles and columns and some sort of flow around and within our bodies.

And all of this is very concrete, very palpable; there are moments where we arrive together, and it is like basking in the sunlight; everything is beautiful, tranquil, together. As the song ends she holds me a little tighter for just a moment. There is a tiny shiver. And then we walk off the dance floor. There are no words, just gratitude and a sense of awe.

Luscious moments find us only rarely. When they come upon us, our thoughts recede or evaporate. Our naked selves are exposed. We are vulnerably close to people we do not know. We tremble.

Some dancers call these wonderful moments "mystical." Some compare them to being under a hypnotic trance or the influence of narcotics. Others feel adamant about staying away from romantic clichés, as the following dancer expressed.

The Moment of Creativity

The descriptions about connections and inner experiences I hear people talk about sound cliché to me. The standard cliché is when the man says that his dance partner has a beautiful embrace, or when the woman says she falls in love with her partner during the three minutes the song lasts. For me an embrace is beautiful when I am hugging my girlfriend, and when we are not dancing. When I dance, an embrace is comfortable or uncomfortable and nothing else. To have my best inner experience, three elements must be present: We have to share the same technique, and I must feel my partner is enjoying herself dancing with me; otherwise I become inhibited. And thirdly the muses have to be with me at the moment. When these three elements coexist, I feel free in the best possible sense of the word. I feel I am doing art. I compare this experience with Pollock's "action painting." For me it is "action dancing." The moment I seek is when I let myself be unconsciously carried ... and leave everything to what god or the muses want. In this sensation there is no past or future. When that moment ends I feel frightened. I ask myself, "Where was I?"

I have my own understanding of why some dancers compare special moments to being under a hypnotic trance or the influence of narcotics. I believe unusual sensations occur in tango because there is something in the corporality of this dance that allows us to enter a state of consciousness akin to the one between wakefulness and sleep — a state of transition, a vivid dreamlike zone with auditory, visual and tactile sensations different from those we experience during our waking hours.

The physical immediacy of the tango raises a question. Can we express our physicality and sensuality without sexual interest or desire? Tango is unquestionably sensuous, sometimes scrumptiously sensuous. It is among the most intimate and purest forms of human interaction that I know of. Whether the dance is sensuous or sexual has been a topic of intrigue ever since it was born. The debate is likely to continue, perhaps because there is no theoretical line that clearly separates one experience from the other. In the dance, however, the line is clear.

The Differences

Tango is a dance of men and women, a ritual dance of the genders. At the milonga men move and act manly. Women accentuate their femininity in behavior and dress. Men and women walk svelte, exuding confidence. No slouching posture, no shyness: pride instead. The man searches for the right woman, and the woman searches for the right man: they know the tango offers richer complexities, greater depths, and sweeter highs than nightclub bumping.

In the early stages of becoming a dancer, however, all of us have to learn to bypass or sublimate this to some degree. We don't fully know what the tango is until we dance it. Sometimes we get the wrong idea about the dance from its poster propaganda; sometimes it's a matter of sorting out the physical from the cultural. In any case, as the following story from an experienced dancer explains, the body is something we both use and overcome in this intimate dance — whether or not we "keep it on the floor":

> My first years of tango took place at a bar, and a few women my age danced with me there and brought me up as a tango dancer. With one of them I would sometimes begin to get aroused, and it always mortified me: it was an intrusion and a nuisance. Even then, at the beginning, I knew it didn't belong on the dance floor, but my body was still learning the difference between sentiment and sexuality. I wasn't even attracted to this girl; but the "proximity issues" of the tango simply required me to understand that physical closeness doesn't have to mean "lover" — it can mean "brother" or "protector," something

more properly macho. And once my body understood that — once it caught up to my heart — the dance became richer than ever.

There was, of course, another young woman there whom I did find attractive; but I never encountered this sexual/sensual problem with her. My body, in this case, knew better than I did; there was something about her that put me off when we got close. It wasn't anything weird; it was just a chemical mismatch, maybe an off scent under the conscious radar. So we just danced, and I never asked her out: no crime. Where I had to master my body before, here I learned to trust it.

I have no idea what these girls thought about me. We were all friends, and the (would-be) sexual stuff I'm describing was just my own moments of "lost focus." Now there was another woman I knew there, and I danced best with her, maybe because she showed up more often than the others. With her I encountered neither un-focus; we danced, close, open, whatever we felt like. Tones, not undertones. It was comfortable, cordial, natural. One night we were talking longer than usual after the milonga, and since it was late I walked her home.

Since we were still talking, I walked her up the stairs, too. We had some wine, and the next morning she scolded me for putting things off for such a long time: she'd been interested in me for a while. I felt pretty stupid, especially since by then I was set to move away in a matter of weeks. We had a brief, human romance together; she was sweet, which I already knew, and a little disorganized, which I didn't expect. And a little sad, which I could relate to.

Nobody cried when I moved. When I visited a year later, her apartment was still a mess. Our old milonga had shut down, so we went to a few others in the big city. Our sex was a little desperate, because we'd both been single too long. Our tango was better than ever, because the body was no barrier now; and because we had both lost something; and because we knew we weren't for keeps. It gave us something to dance about ... the kind of thing you're more likely to play down than show off.

A fully lived tango is all about the exaltation of a human connection at the primitive level of our senses, movements, and reflexes. It sublimates our basest instincts, which actually interfere with dancing, and draws out our memories, histories, sentiments.... As amazing as it may seem to an observer, tango is a social dance where people are not looking for sexual gratification, because to pursue that goal on the dance floor ensures that it won't be reached with any dignity: to dance about sex is to dance quite poorly. This is one of the paradoxes of the tango that lives on the edge. At the milonga, as in any group where men and women interact, each person may have a different agenda: some could be looking for friendships, and others might welcome romantic relationships. The vast majority of dancers look for the enjoyment of good dancing connections.

Sometimes in the transport of the dance, we might leave ourselves so far behind that we wind up totally disoriented, like someone unable to entirely awaken from a dream. Overwhelmed by the experience, we lose our sense of time and place, self and other, and even find ourselves unable to remember consciously what the experience was. We end up with a paradox — a vivid recollection of oblivion — as one female friend of mine described to me.

Where Did My Memory Go?

As the unmistakable rhythm of D'Arienzo's "El flete" begins to play, someone is passing by and, with an arm gesture, invites me to the dance floor.

His touch is so light, so imperceptible. His body feels so weightless. From the way he holds me, the gentle way he sways our bodies in place, I can tell, before taking a single step, that he is an experienced dancer. He is Anglo, at least 16 inches taller, and probably a decade and a half younger than I am.

As we begin to dance, I am not conscious of direction, or where we are on the dance floor. It feels as if I become energy, as if we are air. He has the intense focus of a cat watching a bird, making my legs move with utmost precision. The details of the experience evaporate. Where is my body? When the music stops, I have no idea of details. Were we dancing fast or slow? I was only conscious of what felt like circular motion, of swirling upward. Where did my memory go? Did we do complex figures? Did we just walk? What remains is the sweet sensation of having left the ground, embraced to a nameless other.

The unknown can descend upon us and leave us disoriented. Before we have begun to find our way to the inner tango, it can even confuse us or leave us terrified. But without the unknown, there can be no surprise and no delight. Dancers get to know it, because it's how every embrace begins: with a discovery of the other.

Some partners feel earthy, and others feel ethereal. We never know how a partner is going to "feel" until we meet in the embrace. In a few seconds we learn their "weight" — a concept totally unrelated to actual weight on a scale. He or she may be tall and sturdy, but once in each other's arms the couple may become "air." This is a kind of combinatorial chemistry: we become different dancers ourselves when we are with different partners.

The dancers' attention to each other, too, can have a curious relationship to the outward appearance of the dance. Sometimes an inward, tenuous beauty can become radiant, projecting the deep graciousness of the dancers' connection with each other and giving onlookers a glimpse

Sometimes in the transport of the dance, we might leave ourselves so far behind that we wind up totally disoriented, like someone unable to entirely awaken from a dream. Overwhelmed by the experience, we lose our sense of time and place, self and other, and even find ourselves unable to remember consciously what the experience was. We end up with a paradox — a vivid recollection of oblivion. *Photograph courtesy of Leone Perugino (Catania, Italy).*

at the invisible shadow-play enacted privately. So inward might we become, that it later comes as a mild surprise that our dance had been outwardly beautiful at all. A male friend of mine had an experience of this kind: absorbed by the interior act of listening to his partner and learning her, he was not expecting anything special to shine forth, and wasn't even certain that his partner was enjoying the dance.

The Pugliese Tanda

My teacher introduced me to an attractive, well-dressed woman who had traveled to the festival from another state. She was Argentine. We chatted. Soon a Pugliese tanda came on, and she remarked how much she liked "this 'Yumba' music." I asked her if she would like to dance, she said yes, and we went out.

The first moments on the dance floor with a new partner are full of listening: listening to the music, her "listening" to his invitation to the embrace, his "listening" to her way of responding. Eventually, the first movement; more synchronization; then a salida. Then another, until at some point the man

Two dancers in Moscow share an embrace of sweet intimacy, while the band behind them plays live music using instruments similar to those played in traditional tangos. *Photograph courtesy of Alexander Zabara (Moscow).*

gauges what kind of dancing he can try with her, to this music, on this dance floor, at this moment: and then finally the tentative sensing and evaluating of the partner disappears, and they both dance without thinking.

Neither partner knows how it will go at the beginning. And that's how it went with her. In my dancing I made a move, waited to see what she made of it, and then made another move, "listened" to see if it was all right. Walk to the cross, a little turn, some more walking, another turn, a little rocking. The Pugliese they played was from the 1950s, and had lots of dynamics. Even though the floor was not crowded, we paused often with the music, and sometimes did nothing more than swivel slightly on the spot and change weight once or twice. I felt in a way like nothing was happening, and worried occasionally that I might bore her, and wondered if I should do something more interesting. But I didn't, because I kept feeling the intensity of her attention to my movements. She was still listening to me as if we were taking the first step of the dance. And our little swivels in place were filled with a kind of density; she took a single pivot with an attitude of grave absorption, as if it were the most meaningful movement in the universe. Even if I could have thought of a stunt that would fit the mood we were sharing, I wouldn't have tried it because it would have broken our shared attention on each other.

After the first song, the next one was the same way: slow, minimal, absorbed in each other's movement, but not spectacular at all. I think the hard part is knowing whether she is in agreement. Once you know someone, then you know what she likes. Was she waiting for me to do more? That thought crossed my mind, but we held each other and continued feeling our way through the powerful dramatic music, barely making any progress on the floor. No matter how little we did together, I always sensed that her mind was with me, and every movement of ours was motivated by the phrasings of the violins and the bandoneóns. When the tanda ended, I looked at her eyes, and she was smiling. So was I. I thanked her and walked with her back to where we started from. At every table, my friends stopped us and asked me to introduce her. They wanted to know who she was, and said how beautifully we had danced. I thought, "Well, it certainly didn't look like nothing to them."

Sometimes we have a sense that the unique moments born in the embrace are mutual: we can see it in the other's eyes, or we feel it during the few instants when we linger in the embrace after the last notes of a song. Or when we do not break the embrace between songs, or when we gently squeeze our partner's hand at the end of a tanda. But we can never be completely sure about the reciprocity of the experience. At the milonga we do not talk about what we feel, no matter how amazing it might seem. And for good reason.

Good dancers, as they learn how to dance for real, learn to live with a degree of uncertainty. It's part of the transitory dream-realm in which we hold each other when we're on the dance floor. We have to be content with not knowing everything — content to dismiss the part of our ego that wants to decide and control everything — because there must be something unknown if there is to be discovery in the embrace.

Like the Faces of a Coin

The tango can have its moments of awe, but we don't choose when they happen: it does. As soon as we close our minds to uncertainty, and draw our conclusions too soon, the dance can show its flip-side and play tricks on us, as in the following account sent to me by a friend:

> I'm sitting in milonga Niño Bien, Thursday night in Buenos Aires around 3 A.M. There is a young man, probably European, perhaps Dutch, dancing with a beautiful woman whom I presume to be Argentine. I've seen her before, and I know her to be a very good dancer. The couple catches my eye because of the man. His face is animated, his movements very unusual. He is totally enthralled by the music, trying to capture every instant, every tiny morsel of expression from Pugliese's orchestra. They are traveling across the short end of the dance floor toward my corner table, and I can't take my eyes off them.
>
> I get the impression from his body language and his facial expressions that this is an absolute peak moment for him, a tango epiphany. Then the couple turns, and I see the expression on her face. She is bewildered and a bit flus-

tered by his unusual movements; she seems ill-at-ease, even disparaging. Enough that I wonder if something has just happened that I didn't see — perhaps they were just bumped by their neighbors disturbing her dreamy tango. And as they turn, right in front of my table, I witness this tragic scene, like opposite faces of a coin, or some mystical wheel of fate: their faces alternate, bliss and scorn. And it is clear that he is unaware of her critique. The tanda ends, he thanks her profusely, and she gives a coy smile and a reply that reveals nothing, and I can't help but wonder if this has happened to me, or to my partners, or perhaps to all of us who engage in this dance.

This man on the dance floor seems to have had a party by himself — at his partner's expense. This aberration of doing a "dance of the legs and not of the heart" is some distance removed from the tango's real center. Unlike this sad caricature, when we dance from the heart we engage in a pure form of closeness with the other that leaves us bewildered. This "invisible heart" is what utterly possesses us and holds us captive. It is no wonder we get addicted.

Or is it? A field of questions opens in front of me: why does the tango shake our very core? Where did this marvel all get started? Who searched it out, who set us on this path? In wonder, we must go to tango's stomping grounds to look for its old guardian spirits; they may tell us where the deep impact of the dance comes from, what lies behind the embrace, what potion they brewed at the heart of it all that makes strangers become so deeply and so instantly familiar.

5

La Boca:
The Rebel Embrace

I have read it countless times: the tango's parents were disempowered and terminally hopeless people with no other choice than to live on the city outskirts and die there. This is the official story.

Many suffered such lives, and we hear their sadness in the nostalgic music and relive it in the solemn inwardness of dance. But tango music is also self-confident and vibrant. Vulnerable as it is, this power and sweet self-confidence cannot come from sadness alone.

I must visit *La Boca,* the tango's legendary cradle. I shall see it, step on its soil, touch it with my palms, listen to it, smell it. I must get a feel for its people, and through them I must reach back to their ancestors' ways of being, their social circumstances, their everyday lives. If I find traces of what I feel in the music and dance, I will tune in my intuition and open my mind to memories. I trust that all of it will tell me the real story.

On the Way There: My Barracas

To drive across the city center via Nueve de Julio Avenue (the widest avenue in the world, the one with 19 traffic lanes) is to pass through a seismic core that sends quakes of energy throughout this entire metropolis. Pedestrians do not have the right of way in Buenos Aires; those who dare to cross the traffic lanes do it as fast as they can. Speeding vehicles crisscross lanes just for the sake of it, even if time is not an issue. Horns are a medium of catharsis. Brand names up on mega-signs remind me of our commercial globe.

Eventually I spin out of the riot and reach Montes de Oca Avenue, which at the turn of the century used to be named *La Calle Larga* (The Long Street). The car is on it awhile, and the world feels calmer here. There is a feeling of neighborhood. I am driving through the business district of Barracas, where I was born, just a zip code away from La Boca. My mother and I used to come to the big block-long market that was here once; today, not with my eyes and nose, but in my brain, I see the colors, and I smell the fruits, the flowers, the cheeses and spices that used to line the vendors' stalls....

Amid this pinwheel of sensations, something from still another time rivets my attention: the streetcar tracks. I have so many memories of them. Not far from here, I used to sit by myself on the white marble steps of our second house, admiring those old hippopotamuses as they lurched and swayed slowly down the cobblestones. I loved their clanging, their *talán-talán*. Which one would bring my dad home? *Talán, talán, talán ... pasa el tranvía por Tucumán.* We played games on the sidewalk singing these verses, which I did not know are Alberto Vaccarezza's lyrics to the tango "Talán ... talán...":

> *Talán, talán, talán...*
> *pasa el tranvía por Tucumán.*
> *"Prensa," "Nación" y "Argentina"*
> *gritan los pibes de esquina a esquina.*
>
> Talán, talán, talán...
> The streetcar rides along Tucumán.
> *"Press," "Nation"* and *"Argentina"*
> The newsboys cry from corner to corner.

At the 500 block of Montes de Oca, I see the church of Santa Lucía, much smaller than I recall it. An old exhilaration draws me back to December 13 and to my grandmother: every year on that day, we adventured together to the grand festivities held in the saint's honor. Our ritual started early in the morning. We cut some of the jasmines that perfumed our courtyard; we dressed for the festivity and walked twenty blocks carrying our bouquets to the church. We held them for hours while we waited in line, so we could pass by Santa Lucía's statue and touch her gown. This sacred act of touching was supposed to prevent illnesses of the eyes because she was the patron saint of the blind. (The legend says that Lucía of Sicily became a martyr in the days of persecution because she refused to marry

Tango broke the barriers of physical distance between man and woman as no other dance had done before. Today dancers enjoy the cozy "home" of the embrace — something invented by nostalgic people who had lost their sense of home in the New World. For many people nowadays, this close embrace of the tango remains as rebellious now as it was a century ago. ***Photograph by Beatriz Dujovne.***

a pagan suitor; the Roman authorities plucked out her eyes, but she miraculously recovered her eyesight before they burned her at the stake.) Believers, in bliss, with fingers purified by the gown, touched their own eyes. Yet the indoor spectacle was nothing compared to the afternoon crescendo of bells ringing, music playing, and zillions of white handkerchiefs dancing in the air as the statue of Santa Lucía was taken out of the temple. To see her young and beautiful, bigger than life, eight feet tall, standing on a platform carried by six strong men, was the most thrilling moment of the day. She wore a tiara with five golden rays and was dressed in a white robe partly covered by a purple cape embroidered in gold. Children in white communion uniforms followed her in procession; grownups did, too, and others watched in silence from their doorsteps and balconies.

At a certain point, we tossed our bouquets up in the air, and a white mist of flowers descended upon her: the air took on the same luscious aroma of our courtyard. We waited for Santa Lucía's return to a stage outside the church, and when she arrived amid a symphony of bells, praying, singing, and loudspeakers, it was earth-shattering. It marked the beginning of the 6 P.M. open-air mass. Patios, sidewalks, and streetcars, closeness with neighbors, and fragrances of early childhood — these are all recurring themes in tango poetry. Somehow they bring porteños' collective past alive in the present. I had passed by this church countless times without a tango presence in mind, and no memories had come to me. Until now.

Almost in La Boca, I do a quick mental survey of Argentine history. Buenos Aires and La Boca were born at the same time around the mid–1500s. Today's 20-minute drive south would have taken me much longer by train or streetcar in the 1880s, and I would have traversed flatlands instead of city blocks filled with uninterrupted high rises; back then I would have seen no buildings once I was out of the city center, until I finally reached the semi-urban outpost. And I could have parked my horse-drawn carriage wherever I wanted.

With pleasure I anticipate strolling around this riverside community, which is unique among the 47 districts of the city. Where to begin my tango mission? At the tourist spot on the port, or inland, where the residents live? At the outdoor museum Caminito, or at the Escuela Museo Pedro de Mendoza — which we know as Museum Benito Quinquela Martín? The last of these, yes, definitely. The celebrated painter Quinquela was the beating heart of La Boca.

The church of Santa Lucía during the festivities of December 13th, in the Barracas district of Buenos Aires (bordering La Boca). *Photograph courtesy of the Photographic Department, General Archives of the Nation, Argentina.*

The Waterfront Museum

I am no stranger to this working-class district, but my solitary goal this year is to absorb its character, its way of being. The luminosity of today's immense blue sky is perfect for the mission. I have with me a book full of old photographs, *Old Buenos Aires: Urban Changes 1880–1940*, and another one that contains many pictures of La Boca. They may come in handy.

I park at 1835 Pedro de Mendoza Street, near the museum, which faces the Riachuelo River. The houses here were built about five feet higher than street level; these used to be floodplains, and houses had to be elevated. The story goes that the *Boquenses*— inhabitants of La Boca — stubbornly built their homes close to the water even though they were expelled by floods time and time again. Their passion for the waterfront speaks volumes about the tenacious personality of this place.

Crossing the street takes me to a three-story neighborhood museum that blends in with the adjacent plain-looking buildings. At the entry hall

I browse books and pamphlets to get myself oriented. I learn that Quinquela was born in 1885, which makes him the exact contemporary of the early tango composer Juan de Dios Filiberto (which I had never realized before).

"Are there photographs of the two together?" I ask Vanita, who runs the gift shop. She tells me to come back on my way out: she might be able to dig up a photo somewhere.

The old-fashioned elevator lifts me up to the galleries on the third floor, and opens its doors on Quinquela's grayish-bluish melancholy art. The very colors remind me of his story: he was found outside an orphanage with a simple note stating his name and the fact that he had been baptized. His adoptive parents — coal workers — were perplexed when young Benito began drawing on the walls with coal. A priest who recognized the child's obvious talent brought him drawing materials and some paper. Encouraged by the barrio locals, thus began the career that eventually raised Quinquela to international renown.

I feel tension in the chiaroscuros' subject matter: shipyard workers of massive muscles with backs bent by the weight of the cargo, oil polluting the Riachuelo River. I feel the burden of the stevedores' lives. Quinquela painted these men in epic proportions, portraying them as having transcended the drama of their lives into a proud stoicism and honest ethics. At the opposite end of the central hall a small room displays paintings with a contrasting tone: ochres, reds and oranges, shipyards burning, undulating flames dancing their exotic movements as if ready to leap from the frames. The fire and heat of the industrial ovens project heat out into the room. These colorful oils are meaty and sensuous. Quinquela's brush was melancholic and proletarian but also vigorous and fiery. Quinquela's brush painted water, fire, work, and human will. His art does not fit any style; he traveled inside his heart to make it. It is so individualistic that it was called Quinquelism. This man who adhered to no school *was* the tango's personality, and he painted his canvases with it.

An older woman pacing around the central hall has a look of feeling at home and seems to be the one in charge. She tells me Quinquela lived here on the third floor. I know that but keep my mouth shut. We converse. Although his art was pricey, she says, he died poor because he had donated his money to fund hospitals, museums, schools, a theater.... He was a generous man who had done his share of activism in his youth. I ask her what she means. She tells me he participated in a strike that resulted in better working conditions for stevedores; he did that as a youngster, when he himself worked as one until age 20. He also worked in the campaign of Dr. Alfredo Palacios, who ran for a seat in congress. Our conversation soon drifts to Quinquela's death in 1977, which was ignored by the ruling junta during the "dirty war." This man, who began life without a family of his own, died in an embrace with his entire community.

It is my turn to share a story. As she shows me his private quarters, I tell the woman how Quinquela's art had always appealed to my melancholic and proletarian side. I came here in the early 1970s, wanting to meet him; I saw the inside of his spacious studio when he was in it. He opened the door himself and let me in, right here where we are standing now. He wore a charcoal-colored doctor's type of uniform and, in his calm and shy manner, showed me his work. There were several paintings in his atelier, from which he could see the Riachuelo river, its cloak of fog, its hungry monster cranes, and the many sweet bridges. He and I conversed awhile and then went outside to have a picture taken. The woman and I say farewell to each other soon enough; I stop by Vanita's gift shop.

She is happy to show me the photograph she found. What a treasure — the two men together, the lions of La Boca! Vanita's heart makes an impression on me: she did not have to bother to look for a picture. With Quinquela and Filiberto's picture engraved in my mind, I step outside trying to reconstruct those years that seem so close I can almost reach out and touch them. I cannot separate Quinquela's big heart from the solidarity and bonding I feel in the dance ... but what was it like around the turn of the century, when he and Filiberto were laborers? What was it like when they worked for the campaign to elect Alfredo Palacios to congress? I look to the far right, at the old port, and my mind goes suddenly blank.

Mist upon the Harbor

I stand in one spot, and I stand in one spot ... but I keep traveling back to childhood, watching the same view I saw as a child, the Riachuelo River and its network of drawbridges. This is the exact place where I used to stand with my father, after a short ride from Barracas on bus 45. We used to come here frequently. On this very spot I asked him to tell me about the streetcar that got swallowed by the river: he would tell me the

Quinquela Martín (left) standing before his mural "Cosedores de velas" (The Sail-Menders). Standing beside the painter is the director of the school he founded, Don Juan Marzinelli. *Photograph courtesy of the Photographic Department, General Archives of the Nation, Argentina.*

story two, three, four, as many times as I wanted to hear it. Each time I wanted him to show me the exact bridge where the accident had happened. I cannot feel my old emotions if I write the story in English ... I need to hear my father's voice:

> *Pasó una madrugada muy fría cuando todavía era de noche. Los pasajeros tenían que levantarse temprano para ir a trabajar a las fabricas. Hace mucho tiempo Beatriz. Fue en 1930. El tranvía se cayó en el río cuando el puente se estaba levantando, porque el conductor no podía ver nada. La niebla estaba muy espesa. Aquel puente que se ve alla. Lo ves? Se llama Puente Bosch. Fue una tragedia nacional. Todos murieron.* [It happened on a very cold morning when it was still night. The passengers had to get themselves up early to work in factories. A very long time ago, Beatriz. It was in 1930. The streetcar fell into the river as the bridge was opening up and rising, because the driver could not see anything. The fog was very dense. That bridge over there. Do you see it? It is called Bosch Bridge. It was a national tragedy. Everybody drowned.]

Now that I hear him with his way of telling the story, ... I feel so happy with my small hand in his!

Reluctantly, I let go of his hand so I can take out my picture book, and flip to the page that documents my morbid childhood obsession: "When in July 1930 tram 105 fell from Bosch Bridge into the Riachuelo

100

Painter and benefactor of La Boca, Quinquela Martín, with an unidentified friend dancing on a boat in 1926. *Photograph courtesy of the Photographic Department, General Archives of the Nation, Argentina.*

River (the river which marks the limit of Buenos Aires city), causing the death of 52 people, porteños felt deeply touched and the event remained in their memory as the Riachuelo tragedy." Four photographs portray different moments of the streetcar being hoisted up from the murky waters. (I'm a little in disbelief as I look more closely at the bodies drawn from the river. They were on their way to work at dawn, and somehow these "terminally indigent" people, as the usual history defines them, were raised from the water in business suits.) Could these pictures be the same ones my father saw in the newspapers back then?

Art in the Air

An enchanting sight, a mere block away, distracts me from the old tragedy. The sight tantalizes the teenager in me: it is a short street; we

A gathering of artists, June 1939. Pictured here are the lifelong friends and "lions of La Boca," the painter Quinquela Martín (center, in uniform) and the composer and orchestra leader Juan de Dios Filiberto (far right, with cap). The other artists in the picture remain unidentified. *Photograph courtesy of the Photographic Department, General Archives of the Nation, Argentina.*

simply call it *Caminito,* I walk ahead, humming the nostalgic lyrics of the tango with the same name, a song composed by Filiberto that every porteño knows by heart. The lyrics are by Gabino Coria Peñazola:

> Caminito que el tiempo ha borrado,
> que juntos un día nos viste pasar;
> he venido por última vez,
> ha venido a contarte mi mal.
>
> Caminito que entonces estabas
> bordado de trébol y juncos en flor;
> una sombra ya pronto serás,
> una sombra lo mismo que yo.

> Little road that the times have erased,
> that saw us pass here together one day —
> I've come back to you one last time,
> I've come back to recount you my woes.

5. La Boca

Little road that once was embroidered
with clover and flowering reeds,
you soon shall be naught but a shadow,
a shadow, the same as me.

Caminito today is a living open-air museum. It exists because, early on, when the land went up for sale, Quinquela dispatched a neighbor to plant a signpost here with the inscription "Caminito" on it. He then influenced the municipality to purchase the land. Soon thereafter, with scraps of old tenement houses, he designed a façade for this one-block little road, which is itself a testament to the lifelong friendship of Quinquela and Filiberto. Painter and musician inaugurated Caminito together.

"Caminito" — the song — occupies an eminent position in tango history: after 80 years it remains one of the three or four most internationally known tangos. Filiberto's inspiration is said to have been a certain woman's face: she would peek out of her window while he was on his way to work, and he always looked forward to engaging her eyes during the otherwise lugubrious trek.

Like Quinquela, Filiberto was of humble origins. Born in a tenement house, he dropped out of school at age nine, and found work as a manual laborer — bricklayer, shoe shiner, stevedore, mechanic — until he "met God" (referring to Beethoven) while working in the city center at the Teatro Colón opera house. At age 24 he began formal musical education and went on to become a noted musician and orchestra director. The ageless music he composed is still danced to all over the world today; and perhaps because he was the son of a Genovese father and native Indian mother, his music has a peculiar mix of tones, something of the city and something of the country.

Walking along Caminito, my thoughts transition to the 1970s, when on an outdoor stage here I saw the play *Chismes de las Mujeres* (*The Gossip of Women*). It was a joint collective magic, where authors, actors, technicians and (literally) the neighborhood itself worked together. It seems that art has always been in the air here, ever since Quinquela had the "Caminito" sign planted. When I saw the play, the houses looked exactly as they do today: no doors facing the street, only windows with flowers dripping down the colorful tin walls. Clotheslines crossed the street window-to-window, just like they do in the streets of Naples. Actors interacted from the balconies with those performing outdoors. What a natural stage! Of the many spectacular sets I was later to see on Broadway, not a single one surpassed Caminito's realness and natural charm. Cecilio Madanes, a well-known theater director, brought Shakespeare, García Lorca, Pirandello and other playwrights here for 15 years.

Something from a different time zone rings; my friend Celina's phone call summons me back to the electronic present. She knows I am on a tango mission. Celina is not as entrenched in tango dancing as I am; she belongs to the majority who never go dancing at the milongas; yet like most porteños she has a passion for its music and poetry. I ask her if she ever attended Teatro Caminito's functions: no, she never did. Did she know Cecilio Madanes? Yes, he was a distinguished director whose body rests in Teatro Cervantes, she tells me. We are unanimously hungry and ready to meet for lunch. Her suggestion: "Let's go to this restaurant down there, located a few minutes' drive from where you are, Beatriz. It's ten minutes to one o'clock; we have time, we can both get there by 2 P.M." (We are used to the porteño way of making last-minute arrangements.) Done.

Our relationship is defined, at bottom, by the childishness we bring out in each other. It starts the moment I set foot in Buenos Aires. Predictably, she picks me up at the airport. When we are done hugging and shaking with joy like grade-school kids, she stares at my comfortable shoes and insists on taking me shopping for a new pair — pronto.

We find our routine quite funny. (What she does not know is that I wear my most hideous shoes for the occasion.) "Ooops...." I am wearing the same ugly shoes right now! Will she insist on taking me shopping after lunch?

The Book of Old Photographs

I still have almost an hour to walk around. I browse my La Boca picture book to select where to go next, since time is limited. In one photo I recognize a huge rock monument with an inscription on it: "*República de la Boca.*" It commemorates the fact (or legend) of a time in the late 1800s, when the Genovese residents sent a letter to the king of Italy declaring the secession of La Boca from Buenos Aires. What ballsiness they had! Of course, the revolt endured for all of a few minutes: Argentine president Roca came here, *subito*, with a small army, and took down their flag — end of rebellion. Still, these must have been passionate immigrants with a proclivity for pushing the envelope. This irreverence brings to mind bits and pieces of La Boca's history around the turn of the 20th century: the formation of unions; the so-called "anarchist" movement; and the illustrious and respected citizen who came to be admired by all Argentines, Alfredo Palacios. A sign at the door of his law office read: "Dr. Alfredo Palacios does not charge the poor." He lived the social fairness he preached. The people of La Boca and Barracas, mostly immigrants, joined forces and asked him to run for office. Palacios accepted. He campaigned from tenement house to tenement house, giving speeches in Spanish, Italian, and Genovese dialect. With the muscle of the immigrants behind him, he was soon elected the first socialist member of the Argentine congress.

The immigrants and their children were shaping a new society. With Palacios in office, they were on the way toward achieving better protection, and earlier than in most countries of the Americas. This happened in 1904. Palacios, Quinquela, Filiberto — they all belonged to the same generation, in the same locality. Never before had I connected the dots — this was a generation of art-loving and empowered people that transformed the country's conservative ways and brought about a new social order, and a new person: the porteño, born from the fusion of the local and the European. They were feisty leaders. Their ways of being and motivations, so relevant to my tango mission, are signposts to the ethos of that era. Those immigrants must have been born outside the box, must have been determined to break the mould of poverty in their foreign villages; they must have had the courage to entertain a dream before they even set foot in Buenos Aires. Intrepid and unconventional, many settled in La Boca and adjacent districts and began shaking up the status quo. I cannot separate their way of being from tango, a dance that broke all the existing rules in the dance world. I cannot separate their way of being from the testosterone of today's tango dance halls. Nor can I separate the irreverent dance embrace from the context of these radical personalities.

It is 1:30. Before meeting Celina for our late lunch I have a few minutes for a stroll inland with a single destination: a legendary tango corner.

A Place Time Left Behind

I feel at home walking around the unpretentious homes inland. Unlike any of the other 46 districts of Buenos Aires, the passage of time is not as

Strikers awaiting deportation in police custody, 1902. Immigrants formed the first unions and organized frequent strikes. In 1902 various unions declared a general strike that paralyzed the country. The leaders were anarchists whose presence was strong in the districts where tango evolved. In the mid–1890s they edited a newspaper of regular circulation, *La protesta humana* (*The Human Protest*). *Photograph courtesy of the Photographic Department, General Archives of the Nation, Argentina* .

noticeable here. This residential area has preserved a certain intactness of character, an Italian character. No big chain stores here; no charmless McDonald's or Burger King. A feeling of barrio with small stores: beauty shops, cafés, shoe repair stores, greengrocers, bakeries, restaurants, butcher shops, pharmacies. Some people still speak their family's native old-world dialects. The residents have traditionally loved it here and have resisted moving away. I am surprised to see people living in tenement houses. I thought they were things of the distant past. Recently, a taxi driver warned me drug crimes were high in some parts of La Boca these days. I don't care; it feels safe to me. The mix of regular houses and tenements on the same block echoes the sociology of tango's beginnings: human mix.

A four-block walk along Lamadrid Street takes me to Necochea, an old tango street. One right turn, two more blocks, and I am at the legendary tango corner: Suárez and Necochea. Filiberto used to play guitar and harmonica here. Angel Villoldo, singer, dancer, poet and composer,

Cooks and waiters on strike, 1903. Many immigrants who came to Argentina with skills found employment and rapidly built up the country's working and middle classes. In the early 20th century, La Boca was a major center for the unionization and empowerment of this new section of society. *Photograph courtesy of the Photographic Department, General Archives of the Nation, Argentina.*

was part of the action. Just around the corner, there were three cafés where between 1905 and 1918 several of the tango's early musicians played: "El tano" Genaro from San Telmo; Eduardo Arolas from Barracas; Vicente Greco, Roberto Firpo and Francisco Canaro from San Cristóbal.... The first place for dancing was opened not far from here, on Olavarría street in 1878; the second one sprang up at the intersection of Suárez and Necochea, followed by two others nearby, one on Brandsen and another on Almirante Brown.... By the early 1900s, this was a dynamic, noisy corner, packed with stores, restaurants, bars, and multitudes partying and fighting to get into these small musical cafés. In these places, there was no dancing: only tango music, which inebriated the customers.

I find no traces of that era. It is so quiet right now. The old soul of this corner seems absent. The owner of a restaurant is sitting outdoors, straddling his straw chair, drinking mate. Could he be a bridge to what this place was a century ago? You are sitting in a historical tango place, I tell him: he doesn't seem to know what I am talking about. I tell him about tango and the musical cafés: he knows nothing but offers to go inside and ask the others. He returns shaking his head: "*Lo siento, nadie sabe nada de eso*" ("Sorry, no one knows anything about that").

Love for Lunch

Disappointed and now in a hurry to meet Celina, I get back to the car and begin driving, map in hand. I pass by a mural commemorating the tenement house where Filiberto was born, but do not have time to stop. I start getting lost around the non-touristic, non-residential streets with their impassable craters. It is 2 P.M.; the map shows me I am almost at *El Obrero*, the restaurant.

Outside, Celina tells me she chose El Obrero for a reason. Susan Sarandon, Tim Roberts, Bono, Wim Wenders, and other celebrities had eaten there. She is curious about why this humble place (its name means "the worker") in the middle of nowhere attracts Hollywood personalities. As she speaks she looks at my shoes, and I get ready. "Beatriz, you look ravishing with your fuchsia top, your hair looks fabulous, but" she pretends to cough, delaying the punch line; we both know what is coming next. "but when I look down and see your shoes, I think they belong to an old retired elementary school principal." We burst into laughter, and I agree to go shopping for shoes.

We inspect El Obrero's façade. Celina frowns at its brown nondescript walls. I like its starkness. Then we look at each other incredulously: right in front of this working man's restaurant there are Mercedes-Benzes and BMWs parked along the curb.

Once inside, my heart is warmed by the place's hominess. I can tell the food will be simple and real. Before we sit down, my fingers stroke the cement walls; they have a tiny floral print on a beige background. Is it wallpaper? It looks like it, but I get up and discover it is not. Celina says it is a painting technique and winks at me, redirecting my attention to a dark brown wood cabinet, about four feet square, standing between our table and the wall. Rushing waiters take bread rolls from it, place them in baskets and carry them to tables. Rushing waiters cleaning tables bring the baskets with leftover rolls and dump them on the same cabinet.

Bread in, bread out. The same bread. My North American side gets all shook up.

I look again at our basket of rolls, knowing where they came from; and I smile at Celina, take one and eat it. She does the same. Like Boquenses. Now I am really part of the culture. Content in this different environment, my feet draw small tango figures on the concrete floor. Now the place becomes a little bit mine.

Feeling at home, we wait for our food and watch the mix of local and tourist patrons and the Spanish waiters who are moving fast, except for one who looks to be in his 90s and has a folded napkin hanging from his shoulder. We keep observing him with curiosity. He keeps himself busy, changing plates from one pile to another, going from table to table, moving bread baskets a little bit this way and a little bit that way. Celina comments that his eyes look rather vacant, that he seems to act without thinking. She mentions how comfortable he seems to be, doing routines he knows well. We cannot keep our eyes from following this sweet old man.

Our waiter intrigues us, too, and not because of the way he brings our orders. He behaves like he's part of this place, as if he somehow owns it, or it owns him, or they own each other.... Although quite busy tending tables, every few minutes he goes to the back of the restaurant where the open grill is and takes a puff from the lit cigarette waiting there for him. He also sips red wine from a goblet. A smoke and a sip of wine. This is atypical behavior for a waiter in Buenos Aires. In one of his trips back to our table, Celina tells this man in his late 50s that it is a pleasure to eat a simple meal as good as our grandmothers used to cook at home. When I ask him, "How long have you worked here?" he answers, "Forty-five years." He is *simpatico*, so I keep the conversation going:

"Where do you live?"

"Here. I love it here."

"Do you still get floods when it rains heavily?"

"Not anymore — we have had sewers for many years."

"Is it true that Boquenses do not want to move away from La Boca?"

"Of course, where would life be better than here? Well, I must say things have changed lately. The new generations are not like the older ones. There are problems of safety now; you can get in your house, and someone behind the door may be pointing a gun at you."

I could not resist asking him, "Who owns this restaurant?"

He hesitates, shakes his head, and with tearful eyes says, "Do you see that man there [pointing to the old waiter]? He was the original owner, Marcelino, my boss, but now his family runs the business. He has Alzheimer's. We keep him busy here because we are afraid to lose him."

These last words, *"tenemos miedo de perderlo,"* stick with us. He doesn't say, "We are afraid he would get lost." He says he does not want to lose this man he loves. How lucky Marcelino is, puttering around, surrounded by people who care about him so much. The waiter's bond to his former boss is thick. And so is the caring family who lets him be in his familiar environment feeling useful. In this bond, in this embrace, I feel the warmth and humanity of the tango embrace.

Once outside the restaurant, still feeling moved, Celina and I decide to drive separate cars to the touristic north end of the waterfront, which is where we go every year. When we reunite a few minutes later, we leave the cars behind, take a breath of fresh air, and walk at leisure with arms behind each other's waists the way schoolgirls do.

A Different Cafecito

We are in La Ribera, the waterfront port area immortalized in the tango "Aquella cantina de la ribera," dedicated to Quinquela Martín in 1926 by the poet José González Castillo and his son, the poet-composer Cátulo Castillo. The lyric evokes the old, deserted port at night, and compares its cantina to a lighthouse that calls to souls who have lost their way on the sea and have no harbor: "It seems like a sad, strange canvas Quinquela Martín might have painted."

We stay away from the mobs of visitors buying tango and soccer junk, cheap souvenirs, Gardel and Maradona T-shirts.... Dancing couples in fedoras and fishnets perform for tips. Tourists line up to pay for tours of the recycled tenements. Our eyes soak in the waterfront's houses, painted in patches of vibrant greens, loud blues, screaming yellows and burning oranges. They are urban architectural quilts. They look like a meeting between Cubism, Italian street art, and the Caribbean windward island home colors, all painted on one- and two-story houses made of tin and wood. How old could these houses be? A tour guide on smoke break is standing by; I ask him. Some of them are about three hundred years old, he says. Shipyard workers used to take home bits of leftover paint from their jobs to paint their homes: when they ran out of one color they used another. That is how the tradition of painting houses in patches began. (I whisper to Celina that if these houses are that old, they must have been witnesses of the early tango scene, and these colors tell me tango was born from unquestionably vibrant, categorically non-phlegmatic personalities.)

An outdoor table with full view of the harbor invites us. What would this area have looked like a century ago, a century and a half ago?

Celina says, "Let's look at this book of old photographs; maybe we'll find one of this exact place."

"We flip through the pages ... nothing of "la ribera." Instead we find an old photograph of the river taken from the shore; it shows three medium-size ships ("Riachuelo. Vuelta de Rocha. La Boca. Witcomb Collection. Year 1889"). Another one shows a large group of people ("Newly disembarked Italian immigrants, Year 1907."). There is pride in the way they dressed: the men and even the boys are wearing suits. Celina and I keep looking and find a photograph of women, girls, and boys in a circle around a man who is giving out candies ("From Russia to Buenos Aires. Handing out titbits. A conventillo of the Russian community. *Caras y Caretas* magazine. Year 1900."). The women wear long skirts; their hair is up in a double bun. Men wear hats; one of the girls has a babushka, and one of the boys an old newsboy cap. While Celina is waving at waiters and being ignored, my mind drifts over the legend (never documented) of the German seaman who brought the first bandoneón through this very harbor.... The story has it that the bandoneón came straight from the churches of Germany to the bordellos of Buenos Aires.

The bandoneón — the soul of tango music, the only instrument about "whom" many tangos were written — is a diatonic reed instrument related to the accordion but with buttons instead of piano keys, and is notoriously complex to master. I give a big fantasy smile to this fantasy man; tango music would not have its gravitas without the moaning voice of "his" excellence, the bandoneón. I say, "thank you," out loud and share my fantasy with Celina. We become sentimental about the bandoneón, not unlike the night before when we were at her house. Last night she had suddenly gotten up, mid-conversation, and come back to the kitchen hefting an old, heavy box. It was the case of her father's bandoneón, which had been locked up in silence since his death. She had not looked at the instrument ever since. I had never been so close to one myself; all I knew was that it had a human throat, breathed like a person, and expanded and closed like a human lung inhaling and exhaling. We touched hidden red designs inside its wrinkly body; we caressed the wood, leather and silver. Celina was re-bonding with her father as we counted its 72 mother-of-pearl buttons and caressed the yellowed sheet music inside the box, perhaps from the 1940s. It was like an archeological find, harboring the mystery of a time unknown to Celina.

But that was last night. Now we are taking an interlude at this café to do what we always like to do: play-act, get childish, and giggle. Today's theme has to be tango.

"Celina, let's pretend it is 1895. Do you realize that we are sitting in a former nightlife district with lots of drinking establishments? Look! A ship is approaching! Men from faraway places will soon be strolling around looking for fun. They would want to dance *el tango* with us."

We pretend to wear long inexpensive dresses, double buns with a red rose on top, and extremely high heels. Our imaginary male cast is composed of free-spirited, muscular, cigar-smoking, curly-mustached, fun-loving, foreign men. We join them singing contagious rhythms from their lands. We like the habanera from Cuba and the *tanguillo* from southern Spain. Celina and I sing the habanera (from Carmen) with a sun-tanned sailor from Havana. We dance a tango as it was done then, with figures called *cortes* and *quebradas*. Not minding what people at other tables might think of us, we get up to do those cortes, holding our bodies frozen through several beats of the music, and quebradas, bending back from the waist up. The time to say goodbye is dramatic, tearful, and full of promises. Paper napkins dry our imaginary tears. I recite some lines from "Ave de Paso" (which wasn't written yet), which would express what our transient friends are saying to us:

> *Ha llegado el momento querida,*
> *de ausentarme quién sabe hasta cuándo.*
> *En mis labios se asoma temblando,*
> *una mueca que dice el adiós...*

> The time has arrived, my love,
> for me to leave until who knows when.
> On my lips there appears with a tremble
> a grimace as I say my goodbye...

Getting up and sitting down, and waving our goodbyes, brings our play to an end. Not once do we get out of role; only afterward do we laugh with gusto. In Buenos Aires I feel free to be silly in public; people at other tables don't seem to judge. Our reconstruction was as delicious as the last sips of our second cafecito. Somehow the spirit of the place, of La Boca, brought it out. We looked around: there were no remnants of the former taverns, nothing. As at Suárez and Necochea, it's like the history I feel such a connection to has evaporated with the harbor fog ... or was our playfulness and togetherness fueled by the same inspiration? Was it a one-time thing, that recipe for tango in the belly of this suburb, with its unique genetic pool, its ethos of social change and solidarity, its fertile artistic soil? Or do all the human emotions we have in our hearts find a freedom from restrictions here, in this place where the streetcar tracks remain while the roads themselves are always vanishing?

The multicolored cubist houses with their old tin siding catch our eyes again, as if a curtain before them had just gone up. The 1895 "la ribera" fades into the background behind us.

"Celina, those heels are not fit for the streets of Buenos Aires. Shall we go to Santa Fe or to Palermo Soho and get you a new pair of shoes?"

6

San Telmo:
Improvisation in the Wilderness

I look up from the back seat of the cab, taken aback by a huge red sign in the fifth-floor balcony window of a French-style apartment building: "*Me alquilan*" ("They're renting me"). Certainly not the usual "*Se alquilan*" ("For rent") sign. This is tango poetry! An inanimate object is suddenly sentient and saying, "Poor me, I'm getting ditched." Where am I? I read the street names at the intersection: San Juan and Defensa. No wonder....

"Chauffeur, let me off here to take a picture of that helpless apartment."

My shoe hits the pavement, and I have reached imagination territory. I stand in San Telmo, the oldest district of Buenos Aires, and another cradle of the tango. It's Sunday. That means I'm in the middle of the sprawling outdoor *feria* (street fair), a celebration of bohemia and nostalgia, which has been a city tradition for 40 years.

I have been here many times but never on a tango mission. Will ghosts from the past be roaming around? Will I find tango in the air as I did in La Boca? There are no tin houses painted in loud colors here; no junk for sale either. Here stand a few sumptuous mansions (abandoned when the yellow fever struck this area in 1887) interspersed with some colonial dwellings and many plain old houses. Together they give this heart of San Telmo its atmosphere of extinct nobility mixed with working-class earthiness.

I enjoy stepping on the gray *adoquines*, the original cobblestones here. There's nothing like looking down at their eroded surface to get a feeling

Street mural of the tango singer Tita Merello (1904–2002) in San Telmo, Buenos Aires. The painting was done by Grupo Muralista Ricardo Villar, circa 1990. "Se dice de mí" (the words partially visible in the background of the composition) is the title of both the mural and the 1943 milonga that became Merello's signature tune. *Photograph courtesy of Mónica López (Buenos Aires).*

of the past in the pit of the stomach. Tango poets know their evocative power and use the adoquines as a symbol of the bygone times. Looking from side to side, I see the past guarded in fine antique shop windows and in many collectors' booths, where old jewelry, watches, outmoded household paraphernalia, out-of-print books, yellowing sheet music, and old musical instruments wait to be taken home by an enthused nostalgic shopper. The heavy atmosphere of the past that pervades this district echoes with the same intense nostalgia that beats at the heart of the tango.

Going with the flow in the middle of the pedestrian streets here is best. The narrow colonial sidewalks, with just enough room for two people to walk side by side, are totally unsuited to the more than 10,000 visitors who come here on weekends. In this district, the indigent immigrants of the late 1800s had to invent how to live from nothing. With the same imaginative gifts our ancestors had, porteños have survived many economic catastrophes and reinvented themselves many times over the past hundred years. Nowhere else in the city do I find imagination and creativity in such concentrated doses as I do in San Telmo. Nowhere else do I find the human flora and fauna I see here. As I walk, I look to the right, to the left, ahead of me, and even behind me, so as not to miss anything; I encounter surprise after surprise. One afternoon can barely take in a fraction of it.

I begin my walk watching the healers. I am intrigued by the wide variety of treatments: Egyptian Tarot, Reiki, Reflexology, Aromatherapy, Angelical Numerology, Graphology, Coffee-grounds Readings, Solar Revolution.... Some have their own shops; others sit outdoors at tables covered by handcrafted tablecloths that compete for attention. I like the psychedelic silk lavender; but the crochet one conjures up for me the generations of grandmothers who spent their hours doing things that are too slow for today's frenetic pace. Today's grandmas are busy working out at the gym, dancing salsa or tango, sending text messages....

Oops! Something interrupts my walk: a truck is suddenly blocking the way. In a flash, the instruments of a tango orchestra — a piano, two violins, three bandoneóns, two basses — get unloaded from the back. A group of professionally dressed and proficient musicians starts playing immediately, before the vehicle even vanishes. Why is this operation done at the speed a bank robbery? Aha — a truck on this exclusively pedestrian street must be violating city regulations. Anglo-looking tourists begin to gather around the musicians. They begin to dance tango without knowing how. The ebullient energy of the street artists vaporizes the usual inhibitions of onlookers.

Over there — what's going on over there? People are forming a group around something; whoever the artists are, they have a large audience. Curious, I break through the circle. Incredulous, I see a small stage, a two-by-three platform, where a couple performs stage tango with fancy leg ornamentations. How can they dance on such a tiny piece of wood? Dressed in mythical pimp and prostitute outfits, they do their number in silence, without soliciting tips. They do it for *amor al arte* (the love of art), an expression porteños use when anyone does anything without monetary interest. The dancers' movements are impeccable.

Further down the street I recognize the older man to the left. Yes, the one who has no audience. Yes, the one in a suit and tie, who wears powder on his face to look good in pictures. He is trying to imitate Carlos Gardel, our legendary singer who in 1917 invented how the tango was to be sung. A sign next to him says:

> "I am the famous Gardelito
> $1 to see the tie Carlos Gardel used
> in the movie Cuesta abajo"

This man does not talk, smile or sing. To appear taller, he stands atop ten-inch-high adoquines (cobblestones)—strategically hidden by the guitar propped up in front of him. Impeccably dressed in a brown suit, brown bow tie, brown hat and shoes, he remains completely still, his left hand resting on the headstock of his guitar, with a cigar between the index and middle fingers of his right hand. From a boom box Gardel's perfect voice sings the tango "Volver." The scene has a pathos to it if one compares the young, tall, handsome singer who died in 1935 with his deliberately mute impersonator. Rumor has it that Gardelito makes more money than real singers in Buenos Aires, from the generosity of those who want a photograph with him, or from the gullibility of those who believe that he actually is famous. And in a way, he is famous for his non-act: I have seen him here every Sunday for years. On Saturdays, I usually see him at another feria, the one in the park in front of Recoleta cemetery.

Looking to the left, I spot my favorite artist. He dazzles a large audience that keeps renovating itself without shrinking. He does it without histrionics or drama. He is the puppeteer I watch year after year: with a colorful and beautifully handcrafted miniature stage, he moves the strings of a drunken puppet and makes him walk without balance, falling, getting up, falling again, getting up again and finally holding onto a street lamp for some rest. Charmingly the puppet's every move follows the music and lyrics of the tango "Esta noche me emborracho" ("I'm Getting Drunk Tonight"), which drowns the porteño's heart in nostalgia.

Pochi and Osvaldo are the most widely photographed icons in Feria San Telmo. For more than 26 years they have performed their compadrito and milonguita spoof, having as much fun as their audience of passersby. A small wooden platform on the cobblestones is the "pista" (dance floor). *Photograph by Beatriz Dujovne.*

What's that happening further down the street? A multitude is laughing and clapping at something. I maneuver through the crowd to get a peek of the show: dancers again. Unlike the ones we just passed, this couple dances as regular people do in the city's dance halls. They have a much larger audience than the other dance acts do, and a six-by-twelve area rug

118

on which they move as though it were a wood floor. Their natural movements make it look easy to dance on carpet. He, a natural MC, solicits tips so creatively that people give with pleasure: "All currencies are accepted, dollars, euros, cruzeiros. I offer a better exchange rate than the banks. But do not leave if you do not want to tip. This is a free show." He announces that he and his wife will perform "a macho tango, because *el tango* is macho, and so am I. At home I clean the floors, make the bed, do the dishes and iron my shirts. Not because my wife bosses me around. *I* want to do it."

Further down there's an artist all alone. Like Gardelito. How unusual. She is pacing up and down the three-foot-wide sidewalk with a stern look, making sure no one takes her picture without paying. She does not do her art for the love of it. She is intimidating. People do not gather around her but watch from afar, with curiosity, feeling *verguenza ajena*, an expression that means "shame about what another person does." Indeed she looks pitiable. With her long, bleached blonde hair and excessive makeup, she acts like the owner of the sidewalk. Her heavy body hardly fits in her tiny miniskirt, holey fishnet pantyhose, obligatory garter and high heels that complete the look she's going for (and not achieving). Next to her a sign reads: "Rubia Mireya" ("Mireya the Blonde"). This name, the memorable character depicted in a famous tango, was immortalized in lyrics all porteños know by heart. This other Mireya of San Telmo makes her money when a daring visitor takes her picture from afar, or when someone dares to stand next to her.

Sitting close to Mireya, a conservative-looking woman, a homemaker-type in her 80s, is totally absorbed in the noises she improvises with an assortment of gadgets. She seems totally fulfilled. She takes no breaks to feed her neglected tipping can. Once in a long while she covers her face with a sign written in English: "Show me your money." Nobody tips.

A few meters down the street, a large group is watching something I cannot see until I get very close. On the marble step of a home, in the space between the outer wall and the recessed door, a man in suit and hat —á la *compadrito*— holds a life-size woman doll wearing a green dress, red fishnets, and black gloves, which is tied to him at the feet. Tango music plays. They dance, but he frequently stops to neck with her, moving her leg a little closer to his, letting her hand caress his face. One has to be a porteño to know why he is on the marble step and not in the middle of the street as most of the street performers are. He and his woman doll are actually where couples used to neck, outside the house but in the certain privacy of a space a bit removed from the street. He is a consummate actor; and while he dances with the doll, he wastes no time putting on his secondary act — seducing real women in the audience with hilarious facial expressions.

After a good, two-hour dose of singers, dancers, people-statues, storytellers, magicians, photographers, makers of intriguing objects and pet-monkey owners during my walk, I arrive at Plaza Dorrego. Fifteen years ago, the extended Sunday *feria* used to occupy just this area. At that time, former upper-class women came here dressed in époque gowns and elbow-length gloves, to sell expensive family heirlooms. Today common people sell nostalgia at high prices. Someone tells me the merchants arrive around six o'clock in the morning with trunks, boxes, tables, baskets and everything necessary to set up their almost three hundred contiguous display booths. When they arrive here, they cross paths with the dancers leaving the milongas at dawn.

It is now time to navigate the maze of narrow corridors in Plaza Dorrego, where there's no option but to bump or touch others as you move around. As I inevitably do, no one gives me the "you are intruding on my space" look that I get in my other culture; but the thought of those unnecessary spatial boundaries reminds me: there are invisible artists at work in these plazas as well. The human currents that pool around the various street attractions make this place a pickpocket's paradise. Their art evolves constantly as they devise new and creative tactics. When a street artist passes the hat, the pickpocket eyes the men and notes where they tuck their wallets. Sometimes they work in teams, with a decoy bumping into the victim while another removes the bounty; and sometimes a restaurant menu conspires against the unsuspecting target, whose purse has left her armrest by the time she's ready to order.

But these are the amateur methods. More sophisticated and daring than the bump-and-swipe is the thief who spills mustard on you by accident and then ostentatiously busies himself with helping you clean your shirt cuff. By the time you stop trying to figure out why he was carrying mustard to begin with, he's long gone, and it's no use looking for your jewelry back at the hotel. You squeeze your purse under your arm? Squeeze harder: invisible hands with an invisible razor blade are emptying it from below.

6. San Telmo

Like the bank heist and the Tommy gun in American popular culture, which have associations with the jazz age, the petty thief and the dagger are stock images in Argentina, and for many they evoke the early fictions of the tango, outside the confines of the law. The variations on them seem almost endless; in a way, they are by now part of the porteño imagination, and they supply it with its antiheroes. For many young Argentines, it remains a point of pride that when in 2006 one of President Bush's daughters was dining here, at a San Telmo restaurant, some silent and anonymous thief managed to snatch her purse without Secret Service knowing a thing.

Unperturbed myself, I visit a few more booths. "The Pirates' Dames" are two refined and perky elderly women with nicely made costumes; they wear floor-length red dresses and elaborate head adornments. I ask one of them why she chooses this identity, and she replies that San Telmo is filled with caves where English and Spanish pirates once hid: "We are their former girlfriends." We share a good bit of laughter over that; but it eludes me how they make a living with their number. They probably do not need the money and do it just for fun. We, the audience, come here for entertainment; they, the artists, pay good money to rent a hard-to-acquire booth, so they can entertain themselves with us. What an interesting way to spend a Sunday! It sure beats sitting in front of the TV, or visiting virtual friends on Facebook, or being hooked up with Bluetooth, iPod, and cell phone, or Tweeting, or messaging, or Skyping...

Another stand displays a Colonial virgin with a silver crown; she sits on a throne that itself rises atop a table; and an enormous gold picture frame around her makes her look like a painting. Since she is yawning and unattractive, I am not inspired to talk to her. (Is she trying to look gross? Maybe that's her own entertainment....)

So what about this booth with the two men of the "Thousand and one nights"? Their sign reads "*Las mil y una fragancias*" ("The thousand and one fragrances"). What an imaginative *mise en scène* to sell perfumes.

Who is that man a block away, holding up a sign with the words in red? Is it a political statement? A sign of protest? I get closer and read it: "Free hugs." As I approach him he seems well groomed and looks happy, so I dive upon him with open arms (like an airplane), and we hug. Other men passing by, who are neither *cortos* nor *perezosos* (expressions that mean "inhibited" and "lazy"), say to me: "We give free hugs, too!" We all laugh. "Where did you get this idea?" I ask the man with the sign; he tells me it is done all over the world and that I could check it out on YouTube by looking up "free hugs." The throwback to cyberspace on this nostalgic afternoon taints the mood of my heart.

With over-stimulated eyes, I sit down in the first row of an outdoor café to keep up with the incessant action from the sidelines. I've hardly taken my seat when a man standing next to my table says to me, "*Vendo sueños*" ("I am a broker of dreams").

We chat. He is well dressed and articulate. He is neither crazy nor asking for money. Within a few minutes he has engaged someone else; I hear him say: "*Soy abogado. Trabajo para los pobres y desposeidos.*" ("I am a lawyer. I work for the poor and the dispossessed.")

Suspicious at first, after watching him for half an hour I conclude he is playing with words and imagination without any ulterior motive. He's a conversation inventor. Overhearing his repartees with various people passing by was like being in the absurd normality of an Almodovar movie.

At 4 P.M. there is a tango show at Plaza Dorrego. It is run by Pedro Benavente, nicknamed El Indio (the Indian). When he is not teaching in Europe, he puts down a large mat here in the plaza to make a dance floor on top of the pavement, which is otherwise unsuitable for dancing. How inventive! He was the mastermind of outdoor tango dancing; his vision inspired the milonga *La Glorieta* in Buenos Aires, as well as others mushrooming throughout the world, like the one in Central Park, New York and at Freedom Plaza in Washington, DC.

This tall, well-built man with Indian features and a classic nose profile is not here just to provide a place for dancing. Today he performs with Sofía Saborido, and we learn she is a descendant of the famous composer Enrique Saborido. I seat myself at the edge of the dance floor, cross my legs like everybody else, and listen to his passion for tango culture. He is a pedagogue who uses the history of tango to raise social awareness. Honoring neighborhood solidarity, he solicits applause for teachers, firemen and public servants whose work is essential for the community's wellbeing and who are yet always so poorly paid. Osvaldo Pugliese's life supplies some of his favorite stories. The famous tango orchestra director was jailed often for his leftist activism during Perón's regime. Sometimes during performances he wore pajamas beneath his black suit and tie, when he had been tipped off that he would be arrested that evening. When he was in the lockup, his piano remained silent onstage while the orchestra played without him, stationing in his place a vase with a single red carnation to let porteños know that their beloved maestro was in jail.

Will El Indio accept an invitation to be interviewed over a cafecito? He does. We find an outdoor table close to his milonga and musical equipment, and he orders a beer. He tells me that in 1955 he was sitting on a plaza bench close to where we are sitting now. "I was sad," he says, "but I looked at the Plaza that was desolate, and at sky and the stars, and I had a vision of people dancing the tango. I conceived this milonga out of sadness, after losing a love," he adds. He reminisces about that moment with dreamy eyes as he sips his beer. After our conversation, I thank him for his generosity and depart to lose myself once more in the sea of people.

I'm seized by a craving to visit a former *conventillo* (tenement house). The majority of these old communal dwellings were cheaply built to house people in subhuman conditions during the massive wave of immigration between the 1880s and the 1920s, but some were converted from upper-class manors. Immigrants used to hold parties in these tenements on Sunday afternoons; and this Sunday, a short walk takes me from the grand fair to the old-world façade of this once-abandoned mansion.

Conscious of entering not just a different place but the time zone of a bygone world, I traverse its huge doors, imagining myself a guest arriving at the Sunday party. A wide hallway (*zaguán*) leads me to an open courtyard (*patio*) framed on several sides by bedroom doors. In the center of the open courtyard stands a tall tree, two stories high, sprinkled with specks of sunlight drifting down to its leaves and branches from the sky. Could its unspeaking, aged bark have witnessed the earliest tango dances, back before tango had enchanted the entire city? I can see a second patio further down, but I stay here, observing, thinking, musing.

I watch the vendors who sell arts and crafts in the small rooms here that used to house entire families, and I watch the hundreds of people who wander around from table to table, shopping with their eyes bent down at the merchandise. They do not know the immense role that a patio like this played during the infancy of the tango. My eyes are raised up, inspecting, trying to connect with the place around the turn of the 20th century, thinking that courtyards like this, a world ago, gave impetus to the dance in the *orillas*, the outskirts beyond the city center. The periphery of this barrio, San Telmo, back then, was one of those orillas.

It only takes me a fraction of a second to squint my eyes and blur the scene into an unkempt place, with the unbearable stench of a single latrine for all the residents. As I squint, the hundred shoppers darken into silhouettes with the faces of the immigrants on the block where I was born — Don Francisco and Don Felipe (Italian), Doña Margarita and Don Manuel (Spanish), El Polaquito (Polish), Doña Segunda and her two daughters (Italian again), Don Isaac (Turkish).… Transfigured in my imagination, the shoppers as these old immigrants exit their rooms and join the afternoon dance, to enjoy what is probably the highlight of their austere existence. They step from the shadows into the courtyard with their best clothes on, as in the tango "Oro muerto" ("Dead Gold"):

> *El conventillo luce su traje de etiqueta*
> *Las paicas van llegando dispuestas a mostrar*
> *Que hay pilchas domingueras, que hay porte y hay silueta*
> *A los "garabos" reos deseosos de tanguear.*

> The tenement looks dashing in its formal attire;
> The local dolls are showing up, ready to show off
> What Sunday clothes they have, what silhouettes, what bearing
> Before the "grownup" rascals raring for a dance.

Children make noise and jump rope, play marbles and hopscotch. In the second courtyard, I imagine a Russian grandfather reading to a group of children sitting around him, just like I saw in yellowed photographs of those times.

Some Italian residents play guitars, flutes, mandolins, accordions. They play tangos, mazurkas and waltzes. Promising musicians drop by — a young Francisco Canaro with his violin under his arm, a young Vicente Greco with his bandoneón in its case. Everybody dances with everybody, adults with adults, children with parents, uncles with neighbors, just as I danced with grownups when I was a child. Italians dance with Poles, Spaniards with Russians, Germans with Japanese, immigrants with creoles, blacks with whites, mestizos with Anglos. Young men, full of expectation, are searching for "the pink princess with blond curls who might be looking for her Romeo." This romantic ambience of "Oro muerto" keeps forming a backdrop for my fantasy:

> *El fuelle melodioso termina un tango "papa"*
> *Una pebeta hermosa saca del corazón*
> *Un ramo de violetas que pone en la solapa*
> *Del "garabito" guapo dueño de su illusion*

6. San Telmo

The melody-rich bellows ends a tango "proper";
A pretty little mistress pinches from her heart
A boutonniere of violets, and pins it to the lapel
of the handsome "chap" who's now the owner of her hope

Immigrant parents, introducing their daughters to tango, are afraid a pimp in disguise will seduce them and talk them into leaving home. They are also suspicious of wealthy youngsters (*niños bien*) who come in groups (*patotas*) in their slumming adventures. They're suspicious of the creoles (*criollos*, also known as *compadritos*) who flaunt their skills on the dance floor, much to the admiration of the women. These compadritos are the innovators of the dance and the kings of the dance floor.

Heavy-set men patrol the floor, ensuring "light" between the bodies of the dancers. My imaginary ear hears them shouting, "*¡Que haya luz!*" ("Let there be light!") My imaginary eye sees someone at the door screening outsiders, separating the admissible from the undesirable. My imaginary antennas sense that in spite of the friendly atmosphere there is conflict in the air. Local men seem resentful of the immigrants and call them "gringos" or make them the object of their derogatory jokes (*cachadas*). The gringos, in turn, are suspicious of the young natives.

I open my eyes. The party is over. I am still receptive to ghosts from the past. One descends upon me as the sounds of Francisco Canaro's tangos emanate from a nearby music shop. They make me vibrate biologically, and Canaro's story unfolds in my mind like a movie. He was born in the late 1880s; I see him growing up in utter poverty, in a conventillo much worse than this one. I see his neighbor, maestro Giovanni, who helped the six-year-old Francisco build a shoeshine box so he could work. At that young age, the boy also sold newspapers to help his parents raise his 10 brothers and sisters. Francisco's father, like many immigrants, was an inventor of how to live on nothing. When a new baby was born, there being no room for another bed on the floor, he would hang a homemade bed from the ceiling. Although his children had to work during the day, father Canaro hired a teacher to school them at home in the evenings.

In his teens, Francisco found an oil can in the trash; with it he made a mock violin and got passable sounds. With this homemade Stradivarius he began entertaining at parties, not knowing that he stood at the beginning of an illustrious musical career. At age 18, he began traveling to the interior of the country with a trio he had assembled, without any inkling that he would be playing in Paris and touring the world with his orchestra in the 1920s, or that someday collectors would debate whether his discography amounted to 5,000 recordings or only 3,500. Nor did he foresee the vast commercial success that awaited him, a future of such affluence that it made him ever after a byword of wealth for today's porteños, who often turn to the phrase "*Tiene mas guita que Canaro*" ("He has more bucks than Canaro") to describe a person of substantial means. And surely he had no idea whatsoever that a new world would still be dancing to his music today.

Once this evocation of Canaro's life came to my thoughts, it got stuck there like a song and left me with a need to get closer to this prodigious musician. I wanted to touch something, step on something he may have touched or stepped on. Why don't I go to the tenement house where he grew up? I know the address by heart because another great musician, Vicente Greco, lived next door.

Without a second thought I wave at an approaching cab. "Chauffeur, please take me to Sarandí 1358." I am internally busy; he can sense that and leaves me alone. It is only a short drive, he lets me know, to neighboring San Cristóbal, where that address is located. We arrive, and I look out the cab windows; I ask the driver to wait. I get out and go across the street, look at the numbers again, and it's certainly the one I was looking for. I pace up and down the sidewalk before a relatively new building with the number 1358. There's no conventillo. I keep pacing as if waiting for it to suddenly appear.

After about five minutes I hear the driver's voice: "Señorita, what are you looking for?"

"The conventillo where Canaro grew up."

"Señoooorita, if you want to see conventillos, I can take you to La Boca. I can show you as many as you want. Most of them are in Lamadrid street — they are made of tin and wood and have 1 bathroom for 30 people. Can you believe that? People are lazy. They do not want to better themselves," he muses. "They prefer to live without dignity. The other day, a 40-year-old man asked me for money. He told me he needed to eat. I have a job for you, I offered. He told me I could go to —"

I accept to go back to San Telmo instead. He makes me laugh. He is Italian. During one of his trips home, he informs me, he was appalled by the women's "permanent" underarm hair.

6. San Telmo

"I want to live here … with the noise … with the cement … with the Sunday *asaditos* (barbecues). Ah, and with the women of Buenos Aires. Do you know that young men from other countries come here and do not want to leave because of the girls? I do not know why they are so beautiful. I guess it's the mixture of races."

He drops me off in front of the helpless apartment with the "Me alquilan" sign. I sit down for my last cafecito of the evening and re-live my afternoon.

Strolling through San Telmo, participating in my imaginary Sunday party, reflecting on the creativity and drive of Canaro, thinking about his father's ingenuity—all tells me that the improvisation and imagination infused in tango are still palpable in the culture of San Telmo's Sundays. The "dream broker" and the "pirates' dames" are their direct descendants. These are life's animators—the opposites of those with bland personalities and an adherence to routine. These are life's perennial fresh arrivals, whose days are unpredictable, whose riches begin in their creativity, and who need to reinvent themselves if they are to survive. Perhaps somewhere on Iriarte Street as a child I picked up the end of a thread, not knowing it would later lead me to those who, after all, are made of the same emotional fabric as I am, the same fabric that wove together the people I grew up with.

When I feel, in my own immigrant heart, how much those highly emotive immigrants of the past must have missed their homes, I entertain a new vision of the tango embrace as something they adopted and nourished—or maybe something they just found, and cherished as a substitute for the home to which they could not return. Thinking of them dancing in the welcome of each other's arms helps me understand how the dance, contrary to common myth, could not have been the creation of lonely men who danced behind closed doors. There were masses of men and women that needed this sense of home. The warm embrace of the tango is a projection of that need, a creation of that need.

There's a reason why it caught on, and a reason why it endures. Perhaps in our Information Age, where gadgets keep us "in touch" without touching, and more connected to a virtual void than to a living person, we need it even more than ever. And perhaps that is why those of us who are hooked go out of our way to find it, in whatever corners of the globe keep the spirit of San Telmo alive.

127

7

The World Milonga: Tango Gypsies of the 21st Century

At my first festival out of town, a dancer from Istanbul sat down next to me in the midst of the gala milonga. After a moment we began to chat and soon discovered that we had visited each other's cities of birth. When he asked me to dance, I said yes to the depth of his eyes: they reminded me of the soulfulness of the bandoneón and of the warm Turkish people I knew. As we walked to the pista, in my mind's eye I watched the breathtaking view of the port of Istanbul, the smells and colors of spices in huge open burlap sacks at the Grand Bazaar, the minarets at dusk letting out their lamenting chants....

These memories vanished quickly when he and I faced each other on the dance floor. Our initial embrace told me he felt very much at home in this dance: it suited his essence. I felt an instant affinity. With skill and presence he led me through four heartfelt tangos. At the end, as we lingered for a couple of seconds when the music was over, I tilted my head and rested my cheek against his hand. No words were necessary to communicate how moved I was. In the European tradition, he raised my hand to his lips. Then Istanbul and Buenos Aires went their separate ways.

We never danced or saw each other again.

Life on the Tango Road

For me, tango travel began with the experience I just described. What lures me to other places is the same thing that came to the surface during

The beginning of a festival milonga at the Roman theater in Jerash, Jordan, September 2010. *Photograph courtesy of Jerzy Dzieciaszek (Stockholm, Sweden).*

my tanda with the man from Istanbul: for me it's about coming face to face with the soul of people of different ethnicities and ages, through their dancing bodies. I feel myself at home amid the cultural mixture of festivals: I feel I am back on the block where I grew up in Buenos Aires, the 2700 block of Iriarte Street in Barracas, surrounded by immigrants.

I have traveled for dance not only within the United States but also to Buenos Aires for 10 years. This always highlights for me the double life I lead, in a specific way: in both lands, I am both a citizen and a foreigner. In Buenos Aires, porteños frequently ask me where I am from, as if they can instantly tell that I have not always lived there even though I look, dress and speak like a porteña. I have asked them many times, but they won't always tell me how they know — they just do. My fellow dancers in the States hear my accent and also see me as a foreigner. Dwelling between the two cultures used to make me uncomfortable, but now it fits me quite well. I enjoy belonging and not belonging at the same time. I get a unique perspective of the two worlds I inhabit. And there is no better vantage point to perceive the soul of another culture than on the dance floor, next to another dancing body, mind and heart.

For all that, though, I treasure the relative anonymity of festivals, which brings an enticing mystery to things. I like that formal introductions are not customary; that we do not wear name tags; that we really get to know people, but not through what they say. This is the way of Buenos Aires; in the States we perhaps engage in conversation a little more and often introduce ourselves by name, but still the non-verbal dominates.

Many dancers find special connections at out-of-town festivals, and often it's an initial moving experience of that kind that propels new seekers to hit the tango road. Tango gypsies of the 21st century have become an anthropological phenomenon; it is hard to know how large our group is because we are constantly on the move, and we are always spreading throughout the world. But if 120,000 dancers attend a single yearly festival in Sweden; if 800 descend upon Portland twice a year for festivals; if contingents from nearby cities and suburbs flock to special events almost every weekend of the year in the United States; and if unknown hundreds meet at yearly festivals and summer camps throughout the world, it would appear that our itinerant community is well over a hundred-thousand, and growing.

The Inside World of Festivals

U.S. tango festivals were created in the early 1990s by pioneer organizers who were nostalgic for the feeling of Buenos Aires, where hundreds of people gather to dance on a daily and nightly basis. Large numbers of dancers on the floor intensify the energy in the room and enhance our tribal feeling.

Nostalgic organizers created "weekend cultures," which take place all over the country; they come in a variety of prices, sizes and styles. The most expensive ones set up in high-profile venues, while others might take over a university ballroom or a large arts space off the beaten path. At a typical festival we commute to the city of destination, check in at the hotel, get our registration packets, and unpack the excessive amount of clothes we carry to make sure some would match the mood of the moment. We split up to attend different workshops during the day and then come together at night for the social dances. Regardless of where we are, we feel exhilarated to be with hundreds of others who share the tango lifestyle — the same codes, the same passion, and the same amazement at the inner richness of the dance.

The individual stories of tango gypsies began to intrigue me many

At the "Yo soy milonguero" annual meeting in Crema, Italy, couples move on the floor in one kinetic mass. The collective energy of the group often energizes the night, leading to a dynamic experience of shared collaboration that knits together the individual, the couple, and the room as a whole. *Photograph courtesy of architect Giuseppe Bianco (Piacenza, Italy).*

years ago. But there was no time to get their tale at large festivals, because during the daytime we were either concentrating on workshops or resting between them; and at night, at the milongas, it seemed anticlimactic to sit down and conduct an interview. The focus we need for tango dancing admits no compromises; distractions break the mood. After several years on the road, I managed to collect a few snatches of conversation. What I learned surprised me several times over.

The Abducted: Tim, Mike, Umeko

At a West Coast festival I learned that Tim, a dedicated U.S. dancer and university professor, had quit work for tango. He listed the communities to which he had traveled, solely for dancing, within a single year: Minneapolis, Denver, Aspen, Champaign (Illinois), Chicago, Mount Vernon (Missouri), Pittsburgh, New York, Providence, Atlanta, Portland, Seattle, Ann Arbor, Albuquerque.... "I have not been to Buenos Aires this

131

year," he added, "but in the past few years I have been to Buenos Aires, London, Brussels, and Istanbul." He traveled about twice a month, sometimes more. Unexpected: people quitting jobs for dancing? What can possibly move them to do so?

Mike, another U.S. dancer, had not really quit his job, but when he found himself in the market for a new one, he decided to postpone the search and dance instead. By nudging him a little bit, I learned that in one year he crisscrossed the United States, then went to Spain and England just for dancing, and finally visited Buenos Aires, where he stayed for one month. He made sure after the break that his new job gave him more than the standard amount of time off, so he could maintain this tango-centered lifestyle.

At a festival in the southern United States, I had a brief conversation with Umeko, an elegant businesswoman who had traveled from Tokyo for the three-day festival (from Tokyo, for a three-day festival!). She's a gypsy with resources: her latest adventures included festivals throughout Europe as well as two tango-themed cruises in the Caribbean. Since we were just watching a workshop when I spoke with her, she seemed amenable to talking some more. I asked her what moved her to travel such distances to festivals, and she replied, "My mother used to take me to tango concerts in Japan, so I started liking the music a long time ago, when I was a child.... I watch dancers [she points to couples on the dance floor] and can see their life, their history in the way they move."

Still intrigued by the power in the heart of tango, which I could only glimpse in the individual stories of gypsies, I sought assistance from a festival organizer in my own community. I wanted to get the inside story, and to do that I would have to arrange several interviews ahead of time. The plan required that this organizer and I break the tacit code of anonymity, learn the dancers' names, and obtain a way to communicate with them prior to the event. Fortunately, this event was an alternative festival, where life is less anonymous.

Community Round-the-Clock

What is an alternative festival? Usually the number of registrants is restricted to facilitate the development of a sense of community by sharing life around the clock. I went during the daytime to get a feel for it. It was hard to find the address in this silent ghost town of an area, unknown to me despite being in my home community. I found myself walking down a street with no people in sight, no open stores; only the passing train's whistle reminded me that I was not alone on a movie set. Across the street I could make out a homemade sign: "Tango."

I cracked the scraggly door open, peeked inside, and saw a stairway: I could hear nothing. Was I in the right place? I tiptoed my way up the stairs and stepped out onto a large wooden floor. I saw some movement at the far end of the space, which quickly leapt together in front of my eyes as dancers carried beds, mattresses, sofas and tables. The space began to take on a casually artistic look with white rectangles of draped, undulating fabric hanging from the ceiling.

The beds were to be used by the 20 instructors who planned to live and bond on the premises over the four-day weekend. Some noises from the kitchen area caught my attention; people were beginning to cook. Others sat around on couches; some conversed, and some slept. I learned that "urban camping" was available in the vicinity. I had never heard of it: this was the name for a large shared room with one bathroom and one shower, where at the far end of the night, sleeping bags would await tango gypsies who were on limited budgets.

Gypsies were hanging around all day and evening, and were more available for and amenable to conversation. The organizer introduced me to the people I had made appointments with. I talked with six of them at length and got behind the lifestyle to the motives and the meanings on the inside.

The United States: Kevin and His Special Connections

Kevin is a rather tall and handsome tanguero who wears his long curly hair in a pony tail. He's a talented dancer who lives globally with a U.S. passport. I asked him to tell me about the gypsies he had observed throughout the world.

> There's a few of us, extreme cases, who just give up entirely on the idea of work and become tango people and try somehow to make a living from tango in order to do it as much as possible. And actually that group is not as small as one might expect. I think most of us in this group, in this country, gave up

good careers. We're bankers or lawyers or photographers, people who had another career and got hooked on tango.

We are seekers of some sort. This seems to be true of a group of people who work in order to dance; they will have non-tango jobs that are disposable. They will have a service industry job, and they'll work for six months, and then they'll take off and dance for three months, and then they'll come home, out of money, and they'll work for another six months. Maybe their job is less of a career and more of a job; waitressing might be a good example. There are some people whose jobs are mobile, like information technology or massage work. Some spend as much time as they can in Buenos Aires and support themselves teaching Pilates or working from their computers.

This resonated with what I had encountered before: the work-dance compromise. I asked him what was behind it, what drives people around the world's dance floors.

Special connections in the dance are fairly rare. The first time you connect with somebody that was a relative stranger … that's magical. There's something about that discovery moment, where you say, "Oh, you like this, too." "Oh, you want to move like this, too." "Wow, you hear the music like this, too." That's really precious. And in anyone's community, that happens a limited number of times. So it seems very natural, then, that we would move around seeking those connections. I think this is the part that sustains our traveling lifestyle. If we were to stay in one place, we would have that special feeling maybe a few times a year. And that's not very satisfying. It's not probably a conscious motive for people, but it's something that encourages them to keep doing it. Well, I also believe that if any of us could say exactly what it is that makes us do this, we wouldn't need to do it anymore.

Russia: Millie and Her Sense of Family

By the time I got to her, Millie had been a hardcore gypsy for eight years. In her late 20s, she was a petite woman with the figure of a ballet dancer who dressed in unique and exotic clothes.

Following standard tango procedure, we conversed over a cafecito. She had started dancing in Moscow nearly a decade ago and took to the tango trail only a year after she started. Her first outings took her to the Netherlands, and then to two other festivals in Europe; during her third year she went to Buenos Aires for the first time.

I asked her what moved her to travel for tango.

A traveling community gets formed as I keep meeting the same people in different countries, at different festivals. This is true of the United States and of Europe. I became friends with people who travel as much as I do; I go to the next festival looking forward to seeing them. We begin to sit together, to dance with one another. We become like a family. I feel part of a secret group. The more I travel the more of an insider I feel; the more I feel like an insider, the more I have command of a secret language, and the more I want to stay with tango.

Buenos Aires is a different story. I like the mystery there. Other big cities like Moscow or San Francisco do not have this mystery; I know what people are all about. It is different in Buenos Aires. There are so many people there — many are locals; many pass by. It is impossible to know everybody, as I do in my own community. This mystery of dancing with strangers is 50 percent of the attraction. You never know what will happen at any given dance in Buenos Aires. I dance more sensuously there; I even let myself be flirtatious. People are personal there, but there is no expectation of taking things outside of the milonga. South American men are more flirtatious than their North American counterparts. They give compliments. It is so nice to receive them!

I go to Buenos Aires, and I have to keep going back. Gradually I build a family there. I consider it my second home. Every time I go, there are people who recognize me. I like the feeling of being recognized. Even waiters at milongas recognize me.

Turkey: Asli and Her Tribal Family

Tall, earthy, and extroverted, Asli teaches political science at a U.S. university, saves money for tango travels, and gets to them by plane or by sharing rides with friends. To control expenses, she tries to crash at the homes of local dancers — a practice many enjoy, which underlines the inclusive feeling that often develops among tangueros.

Asli began our conversation by giving me her background: she felt most proud of it.

I was born in Izmir, a beautiful city on the sea, in the Aegean culture. Throughout history many cultures lived together there — Jewish, Greek Orthodox, Turkish, Circassian — so you have a sense of mortality when you live there, because you have these incredible ruins everywhere, and you feel so small and yet so proud to be living there. Part of my family is Circassian, which is a small tribe from the Caucasus. Even though you're so small in that big time span, you're still part of it. I always wondered, Why am I so attracted to tango? It's not Turkish; it's not European necessarily; it's not Middle Eastern. Maybe it's the sense of melancholy that I find in it.

Asli is among the minority of married tango gypsies; she travels solo. I asked her how she manages.

I met my husband after I started dancing tango. He didn't have any interest in it. So I said, "I love this dance. Who I am today is partly defined by my

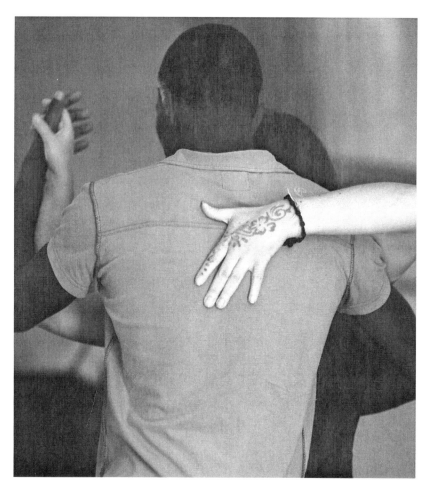

The tango couple finds an ideal form in its community of two. *Photograph courtesy of Jerzy Dzieciaszek (Stockholm, Sweden).*

tango experiences. I really discovered myself through them. I can't ignore this part of myself." He said, "If you love it, do it."

I do travel a lot for tango. It is my favorite thing to do. But I wouldn't say it's the center of my life. My life has multiple centers: my husband, my teaching, and my family in Turkey. I don't go to every festival out there. I didn't always travel like this. Before, I could not afford to go to festivals because I was a student, but I did not feel the need to go because I was in very good communities. I was in Montreal, for instance; the community was so rich that I felt that I did not need to travel. Then I realized that traveling is not necessarily just for dancing. Festivals have a little culture of their own. There are people who consistently travel, even though they live in great communities like New York, Montreal, or San Francisco. I run into them in the oddest places, like Minnesota and Kansas City. If it was only about dancing, why would these people travel to these small communities?

Well, what happened to me is that the more I went, the more affinity I developed. With some people I still do not know their names, but I know their faces. It's almost like a traveling village for me. I also enjoy traveling because not only does it have this culture that's very interesting, but also it's the same people you know and yet you don't know. You're connected somehow through tango; it draws you together.

We are drawn to it like moths to a street lamp. This is why we travel, for what I call the process, the maturity, the growth that we experience as we continue to dance. I also like to travel because of the cosmopolitan lifestyle. I'm okay living in the Midwest now, but I can go to Kansas City; I can go to Montreal: it's just a flight away, just a car ride away. The tango community has diverse cultures coming together; I'm sure there are many different nationalities in this group right now. I know I can get diversity in tango. And I do not have time to build that where I live.

Asli was very willing to keep talking, so I asked her what it was about tango that appealed to her so strongly — what does she get out of it? What is the burn in that street lamp?

It's a very quick, intense burst of energy that I need to go on with the rest of my life. It stimulates my emotions and my intellect — not "intellectual" in the sense of talking about world issues. I do that in the classroom every day. I meet interesting people at festivals; emotionally I feel a great affinity with them. And in society you don't feel that affinity often. In the spring when it's sunny outside, my senses become very sensitive; I can smell the air better; I can feel the wind; I can taste the pollen. And I want everyone to feel that. So I'm walking down the street, and I see a tree that's just incredibly green like the greenest tree you'll ever see, and I wonder how many people are seeing it. And I want to stop people and say, "Look at this tree — this is just beautiful." But nobody does. At that point I yearn for affinity. This is what happens at festivals for me. I'm surrounded by people, and we're all seeing that tree. And we're giddy — we're saying, "Did you see that tree?" Of course, there is no tree — it's tango. That's what happens but not every time. Successful festivals achieve that. That's what the tango high is, and it's something that transcends the steps, transcends the music, transcends the clothing. It's all of it and more, much more.

I asked Asli what was "the more." Her answer was simple:

Tango. That's what tango is for me. When people referring to tango say, "Oh, I've heard of that dance," it's almost offensive to me. It's not just a dance.

Germany: Hanna and Her Bigger Self

Blonde and petite, with a personal style of dressing, Hanna belongs to a large group of intellectual gypsies who live on a tight budget and know how to go from festival to festival, making miracles happen with little money. She even knows what resources to use in a new city to get transportation from the airport without charge. She is working on her PhD in comparative literature and teaches at a German university. She offered yet another interesting perspective on the tango gypsy phenomenon.

> I started tango in a traveling experience when I was living in Cordoba, Argentina, teaching German at the University. It was by chance—I didn't look for it. None of the foreign visitors caught the fire, but I did. And it has never ceased.
>
> Now I live in a small town in Germany. To really challenge my dance, I have to travel to other cities for a weekend, for some days, like to Hamburg or Berlin. I go to other countries too, I choose festivals that are not expensive. I have been to Oxford, Croatia, and the Netherlands. Once a year I go to Buenos Aires if I can. With tango you can go to any place. You can go to Africa; you can go to Japan, to the States. And if you go to a milonga and find a dancer, you don't have to talk—you just dance. And isn't that the most fascinating thing about tango? Tango for me is a language, and it's spoken by so many now that it's more globalized than English. It is a bigger language than English. I mean if there were life on Mars, I'm sure I could go to a milonga there and have a dance, and it would work.
>
> I'm not always happy with tango; sometimes it drives me crazy. I have evenings when I go home and think, why I am wasting my time? What for? I ask myself those questions when those things I'm seeking are not working—if the communication doesn't work, if expressing myself doesn't work, if getting together is a catastrophe, if dancing is awful, if my back hurts, and I'm not able to take my frustrations graciously. Now, when I feel an evening is going badly, I choose to stop it and I go home.

I asked Hanna about "belonging to the tribe," and what her take on that topic is. She had introduced the topic of how we sometimes have "off nights," so I expected that her insights about our sense of community might be a little different than what I had heard so far. She didn't disappoint:

> I have to talk about something that's a delicate issue. We have an idealized image about tango that's about being social, connecting, and nice. But sometimes the tango world is really cruel and can be exactly the opposite. So this makes me feel frustrated. That happens to people who travel to Buenos Aires

for the first time. They have the illusion that, "Oh, in Buenos Aires, I will dance the whole evening; I will get the best dancers; it will just be great." And then they sit on the margins, and they cry because they feel humiliated waiting to dance for hours. Nobody invites; the good dancers all turn away. If they don't like how a woman dances, she gets one dance, and that's it. They will never ask again. They can tell you are a tourist. The way you enter the room, the way you look, how you present yourself. We cannot idealize tango as a communicating social panacea. But I feel here in the United States tango is too social. And that's kind of nice; but I would like it to be in the middle. If it's too social I feel obliged to be nice, which I also don't like, because I like the possibility to say no.

I asked her about on-nights, and what makes her seek out new places to dance.

What I'm seeking in tango? This finding of myself. But not the self of daily life. A self that is bigger than me. A self that's just being, existing, a very generous and gracious self. You see some beginners with a capacity to communicate, even if they are only able to do just a few steps; they are already creating. And it's so satisfying. When that happens, it's the deepest satisfaction I can get, not only because it puts me together with the other person and the music, but also because somehow this connects me directly to myself more than anything else.

Have you heard about a chemical process applied to old writings? The chemical makes the writing visible. And somehow tango is like a chemical you put onto life, and you suddenly see the things — you see the beauty in it, but you also see the jealousy and fighting and struggling, and the desires that are not fulfilled. But also you see the nice things, the generosity, the creativity. So actually, tango is like a study of life and a study of human beings.

Lithuania: Nick, Connecting through Time and Space

As an independent practicing professional, Nick belongs to the minority of gypsies who have the financial means to support a tango-centered lifestyle on the road. He has been a gypsy for three years within the United States, Canada, and Europe. He also danced in the small tango community of his European hometown. When I spoke to him, he was all about the positives.

To me, tango is pure joy. Tango music has that appeal to deep emotion. Tango becomes an overwhelming force in your life, so that's what you do — you travel for it. And for me it's been a really strong temptation to just fall into tango fully and just do tango.

You know, there are times when you dance, especially in these festivals, and it doesn't matter actually where: there is this music, the other people dancing, and your partner. And you move, and you feel this sense of oneness. And it's not just oneness with the partner. You feel one with thousands and thousands of people who danced to the same music 50 years ago, 30 years ago, who danced to that music then, and who will dance to that music when I am gone. And it's amazing when you realize there's a connection there through the past, the present, and the future. It's magical. They felt and will feel the same, exactly the same, as you and I.

Since Nick made it sound like the tango comes to him, I asked him what draws him out on the road so much.

Going to festivals satisfies my need to search. I am like a pilgrim always searching for something. It's a way to continue to be inspired. It makes my life wonderful, because I have these moments from the last event, and I know I will have them again. I also like the community. I know half of the people here; I met them in other festivals. We become a big diverse family traveling from place to place and seeing the same people.

I want to know how the people I'm dancing with now will be 10 years from now, 20 years from now. I want to be dancing with them when I'm 60 and 70 and see how we have developed. At some point, to become a tango dancer or to make tango your own, you have to dance who you are. And often we don't actually know who we are. We don't really have much to say when we start because we don't really know our body. You have to discover this as you grow. You become a dancer when you say, "This is who I am no matter what anybody says."

So if time and space are no obstacle, what is? I asked him if there was a catch to all of this.

Tango offers a big temptation to live tango life and actually avoid real life. You see a lot of people in tango that don't necessarily have long-term working relationships. There's a feeling of impermanence. Maybe that's part of the attraction. You have a moment you share, and you move on with very little responsibility. You may get the delusion of connections. This is the dark side of tango.

Tango is a distilled essence of life in some way. Life's whole spectrum plays out in the milonga setting, the best and the worst. You can be in a very bad space and still dance beautifully and enjoy it in some way. That's the beauty of tango. Because you realize this is the energy — this is who you are — and you can dance that. You don't have to be always nice and loving. There's room for negative energy as well, like anger, jealousy, and insecurity.... Well, insecurity undermines your dance.

The United States: Misty, in Pursuit of the Perfect Moment

Misty is an attractive, single, professional woman, born and raised in Boston. She moves with the lightness and gracefulness of a ballet dancer.

She is a serious student of the dance, music, poetry, and culture of Buenos Aires at large — not just the culture of tango. Naturally, she came up with many reasons for being a tango gypsy.

> I love doing tango more than just about anything else, and in this case, more is more. A tango festival or dancing anywhere away from my home community is both an adventure and a safe, familiar place even if I've never been there before. It's interesting to see how all us addicts start basing decisions about professional or family travel on "Hmmm, I can dance there; I hear there's good tango there!" Like the way some people for whom religion is important want to make sure they'll have access to services or a congregation if they travel or move somewhere new. In this day and age, it's a wonderful feeling to experience what is truly a universal language, a language of bodies, souls, hearts ... not a language of words, except for the glorious poetry that's part of so much of the music.
>
> Last week, while floating blissfully in crystal-clear turquoise waters in the Caribbean, it struck me that there are incredible similarities between my yen to travel for tango and my endless quest for perfect beaches. You lie on the beach waiting for the right moment to get up and walk into the embrace of a delicious sea, just like you sit at the table, waiting for the right moment and the right music to bring you onto the pista [dance floor], into the embrace of tango. Maybe we are a little like tango surfers, carrying our boards around the world, riding the same sea on different coastlines, looking for the perfect wave.
>
> Financially, I can't really afford all these trips, but somehow I do. After all, being single, it's not like I'm taking money away from my children's education. When I think about how financially irresponsible it is, and how I'm going to end up a bag lady in my old age, I also think about how I don't want to end up old without having done this!

Coming Ashore Again

By Sunday night, tango gypsies all over the world typically are beginning to head back home. Kevin, Millie, Asli, Hanna, Nick, and Misty will be home, too.

Festivals do come to an end. As long as we can afterward, we try to preserve the *oomph* of having lived in the "be" mode. The *oomph* of lungs filled with great quantities of oxygen that happens when we exist for the sole purpose of self-expression and aesthetic pleasure, when we live in the moment with no thought of before or after. The *oomph* of having lived in a temporary "home."

Going back to the daily routines requires switching to the "do" mode of regular life, where we tend to lose the self that just *is*. We go back to the schedule mode, the planning mode, the lack-of-time mode, the do-

People from all over the world created the tango together in Argentina and Uruguay over a hundred years ago, and now the tango is danced around the world, as at this milonga held in the "Galleria Meravigli" in Milan. *Photograph courtesy of architect Giuseppe Bianco (Piacenza, Italy).*

not-look-at-other-people mode. Seekers are aware of the resurrecting power of festivals. Many leave taking with them a warm feeling of home, a renewed bond to the tribe, to the secret group, to the village connected by the passion for tango.

It is delightful to think that, just as businesspeople increasingly travel internationally to serve the global-competitive values of anonymous corporations, so, too, there is an ever-growing caravan of tango lovers zigzagging the international airspace, moved by passion, self-expression and bohemian zest. We live an alternative lifestyle by the mere fact that we spend time and energy playing, seeking joy and growing new "cells" of our selves. Corporate travelers carry leather briefcases and check in at four- or five-star hotels; most tango travelers carry shoe bags and stay at inexpensive hotels, urban camping spots, or the houses of local dancers who are always ready to embrace their fellow nostalgia-tango peregrines.

They remind me of the Gypsy. The real Gypsies presumably emigrated from northern India around 1000 AD, and had established their presence in central and western Europe by the 1400s. They were intelligent people who made an impression on the local communities with their invented titles, introducing themselves as lords or dukes. They concocted elaborate stories about having been expelled from their homelands; various monarchies were duped into protecting them, sometimes even treating them as important foreign ambassadors. Following the Road of Santiago, they eventually reached northern Spain; they were permitted to stay in the region under the so-called "Peace of the Road" law, which stipulated that they could move within the country as long as they didn't stay in any one place for any length of time. Their forced itinerancy precluded them from owning land or becoming regularly employed. If a gypsy was caught disobeying the law, one of their ears was forcibly removed; a second offense was punishable by deportation or death. Thus, the gypsies had to be constantly on the move.

We tango gypsies of the 21st century have stationary homes (for the most part) and hold jobs (for the most part). Like the real Gypsy, we do our share of migration, not to avoid punishment but to seek fulfillment. Our destination is not Santiago but the next tango festival and ultimately the city of Buenos Aires, where the culture of tango is on around the clock, overflows the limits of the dance floor, and pervades every aspect of life. And whether we realize it or not, the history of that culture — the history of the tango — is alive and well in the poetry of the music we dance to, whose very syllables as we hear them knit together our Virtual Age with the shifting sands of the past.

8

The Conversation of Song

In Buenos Aires, we have a high institution for conversation: the café. They are such an important part of daily life that we celebrate them on October 9th, the day of the city's historic cafés. In them we linger, sharing our life with friends, or just meditating about our favorite preoccupations: life, relationships, and our place in the world. And in this metropolis of gazes, it is easy to find a pair of inviting eyes saying, "Do you want to converse? Come, sit down, let's talk a moment...."

This nonverbal rapport guarantees us safe passage from strangeness to familiarity. Since the people of Buenos Aires tend to be self-disclosing, and to engage in personal conversation with friends and strangers, the style of tango lyrics, naturally, is as inviting and conversational as the inhabitants of the city are. This is what the poet Horacio Ferrer meant when he said that the lyrics were a way of talking before they became poetry.

In a tango embrace of sorts, skillful lyricists draw us close to their hearts with the language of the common person. As a gracious hostess would, the poet-composer Eladia Blázquez converses with us as if we were brothers and sisters. In her tango "A un semejante" ("To Someone Like Me"), she invites us to sit down with her, as if she were opening the front door of her home. She calls me crazy, a term used with affection in Buenos Aires. I have an inner dialogue with her: Eladia, are you going to open my eyes about a current tragedy? Or are you going share an allegory about the human condition? She has prepared me to listen to something important, and then she tells me, "We can't go looking for God on street corners anymore — they've carried him off, and nobody paid his ransom!"

Blázquez's parable: we are on our own. We have to look out for each other. She wants us to be conscious of it, and she delivers the news in this directly personal way.

This confidential attitude, written into the lyrics and brought to life by the singers, is part of the intimacy and closeness of the tango. When I dance, I feel *las letras* in my body, and I move to them as much as I do to the music and to my partner's inspiration. When not dancing, I hear them in my mind through the singers of my childhood or renditions that speak to me on some special level, usually in that particular friend-to-friend way.

Into the Confidante's Arms

Tango lyrics do not just pad out a melody: most of them are stories with a beginning, middle, and end. They are not lukewarm either. We can think of them as highly dramatic mini-operas; if the tango dance has been likened to "a three-minute romance," then when it comes to these lyrics we should interpret "romance" with the literary sense of "short novel." Such is their subject matter. The texts are conversations with everybody and everything. Objects and places grow ears and voices in the poets' imagination. And in the blink of an eye, the poetic imagery sneaks into our hearts and transports us back to smells, sights, textures of our lost childhood home.

In "Nostalgias" (1935), Enrique Cadícamo talks with a generic other he calls his brother, and with the bandoneón. I want to be part of the conversation, so I hear "sister." I know he is about to bare his soul. As I listen, I imagine Cadícamo and I walking, his arm around my shoulder, along the mythical Corrientes Avenue. He tells me he can only think of drowning his sorrows in alcohol. He wants to get his heart so drunk "that it will quench a crazy love that, more than love, is agony." I cannot listen to his pain with detachment. I empathize with his thirst for vindictiveness: "And here I've come to this: to wipe out old kisses with the kisses of other mouths." Cadícamo portrays emotions we know; he is talking about you and me. And he is eaten up by jealousy and regret:

Nostalgias
de escuchar su risa loca
y sentir junto a mi boca,
como un fuego, su respiración...
Angustia;
de sentirme abandonado

146

Horacio Ferrer (b. 1933), today's "poet of Buenos Aires." Ferrer is an active writer, historian, and performer. His surrealistic poetry began to revolutionize traditional lyrics during the 1960s when he wrote lyrics for Astor Piazzolla. Ferrer's lyrics no longer dwelled on nostalgia, discontent, or anger, but became a celebration of life, love, and dreams. His protagonists may be real people (Aníbal Troilo, Woody Allen), or inhibited parts of our beings. He invented words and departed from traditional formats by alternating rhythmic narration, speaking, singing, and even yelling. *Photograph courtesy of the Photographic Archives, Buenos Aires National Academy of Tango.*

> *y pensar que otro a su lado*
> *pronto … pronto … le hablará de amor…*
>
> Nostalgias
> of her mad laughter in my ear,
> and feeling my own mouth so near
> to the fire of the way she breathed…
> The anguish
> of feeling that I've been abandoned
> and thinking next to her another man
> already … already will be talking of love…

The mood shifts here are fast and keep gaining momentum. I can feel him driving himself crazy until he gets worn out, his emotions turning back on themselves until his regret cancels itself out. Venting, he escapes into an image of loss that at least is beyond the storm:

¡Hermano!!!
yo no quiero rebajarme,
ni pedirle, ni llorarle,
ni decirle que no puedo más vivir...
Desde mi triste soledad veré caer
las rosas muertas de mi juventud...

My brother!
I don't want to stoop before her,
or to whimper, or implore her,
or to tell her that no more can I go on...
From my saddened solitude I'll see them fall,
the withered roses that were once my youth...

The subject matter of this tango is not "high" or refined literary matter, and neither is the voice. Clearly, it is a street-level lament. The text is not over anyone's head, and the singers bring it even closer — so close that you can move into the voice and hear it physically expressing your own angst, or feel that just by listening you are helping the other get through something serious. Although there are recordings more preferred by dancers (like the one by Francisco Lomuto with the singer Jorge Omar), "Nostalgias" for me is connected with the voice of Hugo del Carril because I have fond memories of his old movies. He had a reputation of being a good man, protective of young singers; he would go out of his way to help them, even monetarily. That, for me, only reinforces the personal delivery here, and the connection it brings about.

Tango poets converse with God in the same manner they converse with people of flesh and bones, or bandoneóns, or the city. They ask questions that have no answers. In the tango "Decime Dios ... donde estas?" ("Tell Me God ... Where Are You?") of 1965, Tita Merello — a singer and movie actress I remember from my childhood — is looking for God as one looks for somebody around the house, maybe downstairs, or outside in the backyard raking the leaves. In her raspy, *rea* (bad-girl) voice she presents the case of her existential dilemma. We empathize with her easily, as we all know how much we struggle to figure out life's paradoxes. Tita's quandaries are not different than yours and mine:

Le di la cara a la vida
Y me la dejó marcada
[...]
Si sos audaz te va mal.
Si te parás se te viene el mundo encima.

8. The Conversation of Song

Decíme Dios ... Dónde estas?
Que te quiero conversar
[...]
Decime, Dios, dónde estás?
Que me quiero arrodillar.

I turned my face to life
and it left me with a mark
[...]
Audacity does you no good.
If you stand still, the world crashes down on you.
Tell me, God, where are you?
I want to talk to you
[...]
Tell me, God, where are you?
I want to kneel down.

Her predicament is dramatic, and she ends the story on a tragic note: "So now I am sitting down bleeding, waiting for the final judgment day."

Tita Merello became a legend for singing tangos like this one, which were such a fine match for her style and personality. She is truly *arrabalera*— from a tango neighborhood. In her first theatrical debut, when no one knew her, she was introduced as the *vedette rea*— the bad-girl diva. She never pretended to be other than who she was, a woman born on the other side of the tracks who grew up in utter poverty, who felt most comfortable playing the roles — in films — of the poor and marginal. She was always Tita the "rea"— and also the highly respected "dame" of Buenos Aires. Like Gardel's life, Tita's early life was shrouded in mystery; only on her 80th birthday did she reveal that she had lost her father when she was four months old, spent part of her childhood in an orphanage, and worked as a maid before coming to Buenos Aires. "I was sad, poor, and ugly," she said about her childhood. Her longest lasting relationship, with actor Luis Sandrini, lasted eight years. Tita and Sandrini played central roles in the 1933 film "Tango," which is considered the first official Argentine film with sound. The film's cast includes the singers Libertad Lamarque, Azucena Maizani, Mercedes Simone; the legendary dancers José Ovidio Bianquet ("El Cachafaz") and Carmencita Calderón; and the notable musicians Juan de Dios Filiberto, Osvaldo Fresedo, Edgardo Donato, Pedro Maffia, and Ernesto Ponzio. Merello died at 98. For her 90th birthday celebration, the modern singer Cacho Castaña wrote her the song "Tita de Buenos Aires":

Part III. The Poetry

Te pintaron las cejas con dos pinceladas de asfalto caliente
y quedó Buenos Aires dibujada en tu frente.

They painted your eyebrows on with two strokes of burning asphalt
and left Buenos Aires pictured on your brow.

Tita's impact shows us how entranced we can become, listening to singers' outpours of high drama. And she shows us how dramatic lyrics easily turn into confessions. Not the kind meant to be whispered in someone's ear. The kind meant to be screamed out loud! And as we hear confessions of personal shortcomings, we, too, confess! In their acceptance of life's frailties, tango lyrics accept everybody's humanity. The poet's confessing heart could be our heart; the feelings disclosed are not strangers to us, even if they are feelings of failure, shame, or regret.

This is because these tango confessions inevitably turn reflective, whether it's the audience or the poet who reflects. No one brings this home quite like Enrique Santos Discépolo in his later lyrics. In his 1948 tango "Cafetín de Buenos Aires," he speaks to this locale, a mixture of café and tavern, where solitary men gathered regularly for company and to "philosophize" about life. The *cafetín* brings back memories of older friends who helped the young man grow up. In those small, sweet worlds he learned the good and not-so-good facts of life, and shared his dreams with men of all ages and from all walks of life:

> *En tu mezcla milagrosa*
> *de sabihondos y suicidas,*
> *yo aprendí filosofía ... dados ... timba...*
> *y la poesía cruel,*
> *de no pensar más en mí.*
> *[...]*
> *Sobre tus mesas que nunca preguntan*
> *lloré una tarde el primer desengaño,*
> *nací a las penas,*
> *bebí mis años,*
> *y me entregué sin luchar.*

> In your miraculous hodgepodge
> of know-it-alls and suicides,
> I learned philosophy, gambling, dice,
> and the cruel poetry
> of thinking of myself no more.
> [...]
> Over your ever unquestioning tables
> I wept one afternoon in my first disillusion,

150

was born into pains,
drank down my years,
and surrendered without a fight.

I wonder.... Today's virtual realities.... How can the young learn "the cruel poetry" of no longer thinking about themselves? How do children learn how real people of flesh and bone feel and think? The version of this moving tango that comes to me is the one recorded by Edmundo Rivero, whose full baritone voice had a wide range of expression. His name reminds me of how respected he was as a human being. At a time when orchestras hired handsome singers to dazzle women, Rivero succeeded without looks, only with human quality and voice. It is fitting that he rendered this particular tango, which is so centered on the human ties of the individual life.

Talking the Tango "Ethic"

But hang on one second.... The poet is saying he grew up in a tavern? That he learned philosophy and gambling, from know-it-alls and suicides? What kind of a place was this? This broaches a topic that is not so well understood outside of Argentina. Tango people, for the most part, tend to embody an alternative ideology and the unspoken cosmology embedded in it. It is a certain something, sometimes hard to define, that defied institutionalized barriers regulating expression of the erotic, approved speech, and aesthetic codes.

In the most popular poetry of the tango, certain values are endorsed; others are condemned. Frivolity, hypocrisy, wealth, elitism — these are consistently mocked. Freedom, subjectivity, self-direction, individualism, disregard for the external — these are consistently endorsed.

Freedom is tango's first name; it starts with dance improvisation, play in the present, imaginativeness. *Lunfardo* (the slang of Buenos Aires), one of the languages of tango, was also born as an expression of freedom, rebellion, and affirmation. Its intention at birth was not to be understood by outsiders and to confuse "the authorities."

Subjectivity and introspection are tango's middle names. These clash with philosophies that interfere with self-expression and inner direction. They clash with forces that want people to look outside for decision-making and entertainment.

A certain disregard for the superficial is part of the tango's value sys-

Enrique Santos Discépolo (1901–1951), the "Schopenhauer of the tango." With a string of hits at the end of the 1920s, Discépolo brought a new, ironic dimension to the tango lyric by inverting its conventions and deepening its sense of human character. His opus as a lyricist was small but intense (fewer than 45 songs) and has remained greatly influential not only within the tango world but also within Argentine music and culture as a whole. *Photograph courtesy of Ricardo García Blaya, director, archives of www.TodoTango.com (Buenos Aires).*

tem. There is an implicit code, more prevalent among Buenos Aires' dancers, of not asking questions about what a person does for a living. This relegates the societal position of individuals, such as class or occupation, to irrelevancy.

Tango, as music, dance, and poetry, is the voice and expression of the masses. Never did tango aspire to be upper-class. Most of its early musicians were born in utter poverty and rose above it. Angel Villoldo was a typographer; Eduardo Arolas, a billboard painter; Francisco Canaro and Vicente Greco, newspaper boys; Augusto Berto, a decorator; Juan Maglio "Pacho" was a mechanic; Ricardo Brignolo and Juan de Dios Filiberto were bricklayers; Roberto Firpo was a metallurgical laborer; Agustin Bardi and Francisco Lomuto, railroad workers. The landscape changed in the mid–1910s, when young middle-class musicians joined the ranks of tango: they had a higher educational level and, in particular, a solid academic musical knowledge. This was the case of the De Caro brothers, Osvaldo Fresedo, Juan Carlos Cobián, Enrique Delfino, and others. Regardless of their backgrounds, many became affiliated with working-class political parties by choice in the early 1900s. Many grew up hearing so-called anarchist ideas at home.

Early lyrics consistently affirm the connection between tango's humble origins and proletarian values. The usually exaggerated speech and coarse voice of the singer, who aspires to sound like the working person, further seals this identity with the masses. No matter how educated musicians and singers were, or how wealthy they became, they have unquestionably identified and resonated with the working districts of *Sur* (the Southside) and its people.

These working-class ties and attitudes fill in the cultural background of "Cafetín de Buenos Aires," and they are constantly reaffirmed by tango lyrics generally. Many of the characters portrayed in lyrics up to the 1930s were working-class, such as the well-known "compadrito" who typically scorns the upper classes with a self-aggrandizing posture. A good example of this is the 1927 tango "Niño bien" ("Socialite Boy"), by Victor Soliño and Roberto Fontaina. It flaunts a tone of a defiant mockery throughout, putting down wealthy youngsters by calling them pretentious and stuck up, and mocking their use of elaborate two-part surnames and ridiculing the way they hold court in fashionable bars.

This makes it abundantly clear that when it speaks as the macho compadrito, the tango — and "Niño bien" is typical in this sense — embraces the cultural underdog and has no qualms about clashing with the elite. On this count, the lyrics come from precisely the same source as the dance.

Up through the 1920s, "compadrito" was a style of dressing adopted by the men of the outskirts: black fitted pants and jacket, high-heeled boots, neckerchief, and gray hat. This was the skillful and macho dancer of the suburbs outside the city center. By the mid–1930s, he had long disappeared from reality, but poets continued to use him as a protagonist.

The 1942 tango "Así se baila el tango" ("This Is How to Dance the Tango"), with its lyrics by Elisardo Martínez Vilas (aka "Marvil"), lets us see an example of this that achieved extreme effects. The most popular recording is by Ricardo Tanturi's orchestra with the voice of Alberto Castillo, who with his cynicism and bravado provoked fights from the stage by targeting certain "niños bien" on the dance floor and spouting in their faces:

Alberto Castillo (1914–2002), the tango's *reo* singer who for many fans embodied a reinvention of the *compadrito* in the 1940s. A licensed doctor before his fame grew as a singer, Castillo on stage was always on the edge. His long career included numerous tours throughout South America, and even crossover work with a rock band in the 1990s. *Photograph courtesy of Ricardo García Blaya, director, archives of www.TodoTango.com (Buenos Aires).*

> *Qué saben los pitucos, lamidos y shushetas;*
> *qué saben lo que es tango, qué saben de compás.*
> *Aquí está la elegancia, ¡qué pinta, qué silueta!*
> *qué porte, qué arrogancia, qué clase pa' bailar.*
>
> What do the highbrows know, the affected and the fops;
> what do they know about tango, what do they know of its beat?
> Here is the elegance for you, the look, the silhouette!
> the arrogance, the bearing, the class it takes to dance.

From time to time the aggressive singer would inflame so many in the audience that he had to be carried off-stage, lifted up above the crowd by several bodyguards. Castillo's *reo* (bad-boy) speech was not congruent with the medical professional he was: until he quit his practice to devote himself to his singing career exclusively, he was a licensed gynecologist.

But on the stage, he was a born provocateur, not just in his actions but also in his way of dressing, as he frequently wore suits out of fashion, a handkerchief in his coat pocket, the top button of his shirt undone, and a loose necktie, as if to purposefully transgress the accepted fashion codes of the day. With his provocative sex appeal and his mocking swagger, he was the compadrito reincarnated.

Castillo was a radio figure of my childhood; as "reo" as Tita Merello, except that Tita was actually from "the other side of town," while he was upper-middle-class enough to have earned a medical degree. His ways, in any case, were unpalatable to many, although he was wildly popular among his fans.

This, as I said, is an extreme case. The same tango, with its "boasting underdog" attitude, was also recorded by a very different singer: Ada Falcón (the Garbo of tango), who reached the pinnacle of her singing career to suddenly disappear in 1942. Her career and her subsequent vanishing is intertwined with her relationship with the richest man in tango: Francisco Canaro. He managed her singing, acting, and recording career, and their stormy relationship endured for 10 years. Ada was Canaro's lover, the diva with a red convertible, furs, expensive jewels, and a three-story mansion in exclusive Palermo Chico, despite being rather reclusive in her downtime. (As in the jazz and hip-hop worlds, to make it to the top is not the issue; what matters is who you belong to and what you stand for. What tango lyrics show contempt for is the person who was born with privilege, the person who remains ignorant that others do not have it so easy.) Ada was at the top: and then, abruptly, she just wasn't on the scene anymore. Her whereabouts were unknown until she resurfaced 70 years later and gave permission for an interview and a documentary, "Yo no se que me han hecho tus ojos" ("I Don't Know What Your Eyes Have Done to Me"— the name belongs a tango waltz), which I watched in the early 2000s. In 1942, she had entered a convent in the province of Córdoba and had never sung again: this woman left the center of the scene and a hugely successful career for the voluntary seclusion and poverty of the convent. The speculation is that she gave Canaro an ultimatum to divorce his wife and marry her. Realizing he would lose half of his wealth if he went through with it, he refused her, and so she vanished.

Ada Falcón's story helps us understand why tango values are what they are. There's always a flipside to material success. It can be attractive and seductive; but not falling for the outward glamour of the surface is part of the tango ideology. We know better because we know the words of "Tristeza de la calle Corrientes" ("Sorrow of Corrientes Street"), the 1942 tango by Homero Expósito, and one of the many tangos inspired by Corrientes, the Broadway of Buenos Aires that was lined with nightclubs during the 1940s and 1950s. With seasoned artistry, the poet talks to this street about the grittier realities that go hand-in-hand with its glittering matinees:

> *Calle*
> *como valle*
> *¡de monedas para el pan!...*
> *¡Río*
> *sin desvío*
> *¡donde sufre la ciudad!...*
> *¡Qué triste palidez tienen tus luces!*
> *¡Tus letreros sueñan cruces!*
> *¡Tus afiches carcajadas de cartón!...*
> *¡Risa*
> *que precisa*
> *¡la confianza del alcohol!...*
> *¡Llantos*
> *hechos cantos*
> *¡pa' vendernos un amor!...*

> Street
> like a valley
> full of pennies meant for bread.
> River
> with no exit
> where the city suffers on...
> What a sad pallor there is in your lights;
> your billboards dream of crosses;
> your posters cackle in cardboard!
> Laughter
> that requires
> the confidence of alcohol.
> Weeping
> made into songs
> so as to market us a love.

With these animated images, the poet exposes the other side of glitz and tuxedos: the poverty lurking underneath billboards, the self-confidence puffed up by alcohol, the sordid underworld of the commerce of women. The attitude here is pensive again, intense, realistic: the tango "ethic" of being real. I hear this song in the tenor voice of Raul Berón, sweet, never exaggerated. But I also hear it in the voice of Libertad Lamarque, the strikingly beautiful singer and movie actress whose old movies and recordings I grew up with. Her delivery, in a 1942 recording, is provocative and strong, arresting the listener. Her response to the images in the lyric modulates from tenderness and pity to outrage at the way things are. Her rendition draws you in and takes you on a ride: it confronts you with the hard realities of Expósito's poetry and demonstrates the captivating effects she could achieve as a singer.

Libertad is also the only tango singer, to my knowledge, who wrote her memoirs — and she had a lot to put on paper. During the Perón years, she had to flee Argentina and take up residence in Mexico, due to an old quarrel she had with Eva Duarte, the woman who soon became Perón's wife, Evita. The two women had been rivals, and both were loved by the people; but Libertad had not left things on amicable terms. She knew it was time to make herself scarce when Perón was in power with Evita at his side. Despite this period of exile, Libertad was so loved by all Latin Americans that she became known as *la novia de América* (the bride of America); she did not suddenly vanish the way Ada Falcón did, but found a new people to sing for. On the occasion of an emotive performance I attended in Los Angeles some years ago, the Spanish audience who filled the auditorium begged her, shouting from the balconies: "Don't you ever die, Libertad!"

Her rendition of "Tristeza de la calle Corrientes" makes clear another aspect of many tango lyrics: their use of impressionism and imagery to involve the audience. No tango poet was more impressionistic than Expósito, and Libertad responds emotionally to what she relates as she delivers his spare lines, adding a charge of meaning to images that might seem very bare and minimalistic on the surface. Many tango lyrics of the golden age — especially in the 1940s — employ this approach, drawing singer and audience closer to each other by presenting poetic symbols that are not entirely explained, and don't always need to be: they carry a subjective and cultural value that South Americans and indeed all Spanish-speakers recognize and have in common. This "shorthand" of the lyrics often creates a kind of aesthetic solidarity by speaking in a shared code, which acts as a parallel to the "ethical" attitude the lyrics were made with.

The Conspiring Audience

Much classic tango imagery has meanings that resonate in a special way with porteños, but most lyrics transcend the realm of local reference and prove surprisingly universal. Themes like loss, nostalgia, and heartache are not culturally specific, and many dancers I've spoken to have said that the way they dance to this music became richer when they learned what the lyrics are about. They draw us together in a shared experience, just as the singer does, even in cases when a singer like Castillo might seem to create an incendiary divide. The lyrics represent not some other world, but us, by giving voice to our own inner experiences.

The imaginative act of completing a broken phrase, or responding to the bare coat-hanger of an image, involves us further in this expression. It shows us that we are united, on the inside, despite the empty space that a lyric can seemingly leave on the surface. This is the tango's interior, subjective mode. The symbols summon up something inside us, and that interior response prevents us from remaining detached, mere spectators or consumers. We participate; we are involved: the more impressionistic lyrics leave room for us to enter into a dialogue with them — a dialogue as silent and as deep as the dance. The impressionistic passages of tango lyrics bypass our "left-brain" logic. In "Tinta roja" ("Red Ink"), Cátulo Castillo's protagonist returns to the barrio of his birth and finds it changed; he becomes distraught. He tells this story after verbal paint-strokes of textures and colors set off memories and stir up moods:

> *Paredón,*
> *tinta roja en el gris*
> *del ayer...*
> *Tu emoción*
> *de ladrillo — feliz —*
> *sobre mi callejón,*
> *con un borrón*
> *pintó la esquina...*

> Bounding wall,
> red ink amid the gray
> of yesterday...
> Your emotion
> of happy brick
> over my alleyway
> with a blot
> painted the corner...

These initial verses are like a collage of mixed media. Red, black, and gray may create different associations and moods for different listeners. A single brushstroke (*paredón*, a large, thick cement wall) stands in my visual path, as in real life: it places me in tango territory. I could be in La Boca, San Telmo, Pompeya.... The word evokes images of decayed structures surrounding unsightly housing, children playing soccer, couples looking for privacy at night, gray cement, graffiti, multiple small writings: "Juan loves Sara, Viva Boca, Muera Cualquiera, Vote for This Person." And what is a happy brick doing in this painting? Is it the happy heart of childhood? The poet does not resolve this: he makes room for us to fill in what is fuzzy with our inner stories.

The ambiguity of the poetic language invites us to become co-creators as we complete what the poet left unsaid. The fuzziness of the unfinished is highly seductive. In the 1948 tango "Sur" ("Southside"), the great tango poet Homero Manzi reminisces about former landscapes and past times. He bombards our senses with aromas of childhood, the unique smell of the blacksmith's shop, of alfalfa, mud, and herbs:

> San Juan y Boedo antiguo y todo el cielo
> Pompeya y más allá la inundación.
> Tu melena de novia en el recuerdo
> y tu nombre flotando en el adiós.
> La esquina del herrero, barro y pampa,
> tu casa, tu vereda y el zanjón
> y un perfume de yuyos y de alfalfa
> que me llena de nuevo el corazón.
> [...]
> todo ha muerto, ya lo sé.
> [...]
> Nostalgia de las cosas que han pasado,
> Arena que la vida se llevó.

> Old San Juan and Boedo and the entire sky,
> Pompeya and beyond, the floods.
> Your hair, long and loose like a bride's, in my memory
> and your name floating in the farewell.
> The blacksmith's corner, mud and pampa;
> your house, your sidewalk and the gully,
> and a scent of herbs and alfalfa
> that fills my heart all over again...
> [...]
> everything has died, I know...
> [...]

> Nostalgias for things that are no longer,
> for sands that life has washed away.

The poet, sitting at a corner café on the intersection of San Juan and Boedo streets (according to the legend), writing this poetry, was probably thinking about nearby Pompeya, the barrio where he grew up. Today the café at this intersection is an historical landmark, "Homero Manzi Corner," which commemorates the poet and this famous tango. The aura of this café, with its dark wooden walls, the brass, and the aprons of the waiters' uniforms (thin red stripes on black), is reminiscent of the ambiance of the 1940s, as I imagine it. Pictures of tango personalities from that era make it feel even more so.

At the end of 1947, Manzi showed "Sur" to the famous bandoneón player and orchestra director Anibal Troilo. The beloved maestro confessed a lack of enthusiasm about what he felt was a monotonous poem. After that conversation, Manzi added the words "Sur, paredón y después" ("Southside, bounding wall, and afterward")—three words that touched something elusive in the collective unconscious and that have kept porteños hooked on this tango ever since.

With the title ("Sur") and the names of the intersection (San Juan and Boedo) and the barrio (Pompeya), I know at once that I am in tango territory: my heartbeat changes. Manzi leaves us up in the air with the expression "and beyond, the floods." This incompleteness makes my imagination run wild: "floods" makes me think of the tears that went into the veins of the tango. (I like this meaning better than thinking about the actual floods in the lowlands of nearby Pompeya.) In my mind I co-construct the poem with the meaning I feel at this moment. Maybe another day my mind would conjure up the actual "floods" that turned Pompeya into a Venice of sorts.

I hear "Sur" in two voices: one version is the sandy voice of Roberto Goyeneche, the singer who made history with his free phrasing, the creator of a style known for giving weight to words and silences, to periods and commas. I never saw him sing, but he recorded the tango with Aníbal Troilo. (On a side note: Troilo's bandoneón has "resided" since his death at the Museo Mundial del Tango of the National Tango Academy in Buenos Aires. I heard this most famous of all tango instruments played, as is done periodically to keep it in good condition, by maestro Raúl Garello, with all in attendance standing respectfully on their feet.) The other version of

Homero Manzi Corner in San Juan and Boedo, Buenos Aires. This building, built in 1927 and renovated in 2000, has been declared an historical landmark. The paintings on the awning are by the artist Hermenegildo Sabat. Like other cafés in barrio Boedo, this one gathered talented poets during the decade of the 1940s; the legend says that Manzi wrote the poetry of the tango "Sur" in this bar. *Photograph courtesy of Café Esquina Homero Manzi (Buenos Aires).*

"Sur" that runs through my mind is by Susana Rinaldi, whose hand I held as this book was being written, on the day of the historic cafés of Buenos Aires. People wanted autographs; I just wanted to touch her hand. She opened her electrifying performance in the corner of San Juan and Boedo with the tango "Sur"; nostalgic reverberations traveled through a crowd of over five hundred people standing in front of the black stage built across Boedo street where a piano, 12 strings, and 3 bandoneóns accompanied her, under the direction of maestro Guacci. Twice during this song she turned the microphone toward the audience, and we sang with her this moving poetry we know by heart. With snow-white hair and commanding presence, she received shouts of love from all of us in the audience.

Words are sometimes also used for the distinct effect of marking time. In another lyric by the great Discépolo, "Martirio" ("Martyrdom," 1940), they are like drops falling from a dripping faucet matching the beat of the music. The first word, "alone," followed by ellipses, takes me to a zone of dense isolation and bereavement, where a second lasts a century. I like to recite this poem, to take more time delivering the words, to prolong the wait for the next word, for the next verse, to better accompany the protagonist in his agonizing stay:

> *Solo...*
> *(¡increíblemente solo!)*
> *vivo el drama de esperarte,*
> *hoy...*
> *mañana...*
> *¡siempre igual...!*
> *[...]*
> *¡Solo!...*
> *¡Pavorosamente solo!...*
> *como están los que se mueren,*
> *los que sufren,*
> *los que quieren.*

> Alone...
> (so unbelievably alone!)
> I live the drama of expecting you,
> today...
> tomorrow...
> always the same...
> [...]
> Alone!
> So terrifyingly alone!
> the same as those who are dying,
> those who suffer,
> those who love.

I hear Virginia Luque's voice in my mind. A beautiful singer and movie star idol of my childhood, she popularized this song, changing the masculine *solo* to the feminine *sola*. Just hearing "sola" makes my chest cave in. Virginia was in the cast of *Café de los maestros*, a recent film that gathered tango singers, musicians, and composers from the 1940s, most of them in their 80s and 90s now. As this book was in preparation, I watched her in person at Teatro Rex in Corrientes Avenue, where she gave an emotive performance and sang with the same *polenta* (spunk) and passion I remember.

It's Amazing to Have Your Shoulder

At the beginning of this chapter, we saw that a tango lyric can tell us, with a close and personal voice, that we are on our own. Where was

Susana Rinaldi is a beloved artist who frequently sings in private and public performances. She received a Latin Grammy award for musical excellence in November 2010. At a recent performance on the day of the historic cafés of Buenos Aires, she began her program with Homero Manzi and Aníbal Troilo's famous tango, "Sur," and continued with a selection of tangos whose lyrics were penned by Cátulo Castillo. *Photograph by Beatriz Dujovne.*

the poet going with her parable? In a world poor in human values, a friend's ethics and supportive shoulder may well be cause for amazement. It is not too late; we can change; we can still save our souls "as soon as possible."

Tango poetry is as conversational as the dance is. The songwriters make self-awakening possible when they bare their souls and we see ourselves in their image.

The lyrics are about high emotion, about the good, the bad, and the ugly of life. They are about what happens to us when we are alive, as opposed to dead, in life. Herein lies their universality.

We can be islands or break the circle of isolation and comfort each other as brothers and sisters. We can be complacent or wake up and change in a world of loose ethics.

Conversation warms our lives. We can converse with everything and everybody, as tango poets do. Porteños, the contemporary descendants of the poets, are still conversing with Carlos Gardel, dead since 1935.

9

Milonguita:
A Thread of the Tango Epic

Shortly after the turn of the century, a certain type of woman left the poor *orillas* (outskirts) of the city to escape poverty and a fringe existence, and to seek out a better life. She came to the metropolis, where the night lights and the money of the cabarets offered her prospects and opportunities that would be unthinkable back home in the outskirts. She got a job at the cabaret, fell for a man, sometimes fell for a rich man (*bacán*) — and my question is whether this was a fall up or down.

Hers is the immigrant story all over again: but she doesn't tell the story herself. The tale is always told by a man — the man she left in the suburban margins of the orillas, the man she left for a better one in the city, the man she left in her pursuit of free will and social mobility.... We get her story, such as it is, through the man's lament over her abandonment and betrayal. If tango lyrics, taken collectively, can be read as one sprawling epic, then this is one of its major female characters: the prodigal daughter, Milonguita.

Not all women in tango lyrics are represented this way; I am picking out one thread from the vast carpet, and I want to make that clear. Not all themes of the tango center around Milonguita, but some major ones do, and for better or worse she is one of the "main characters" of the story as a whole. It is tempting to see her particular story as one plagued by chauvinism. Time and again, male poets give us a glimpse of her enjoying the high life, only to relate that she came to a bad end: this became so much a convention of tango lyrics in the 1920s that some authors began to satirize it. We still dance to many of these Milonguita tangos today;

and if today's free-spirited women from other countries knew what these lyrics were about, they would probably be more irritated by the words than delighted by the music. Except that it's a good story!

Here is a famous example, and one that set the tone for future lyrics: Celedonio Flores' celebrated 1920 tango, "Mano a mano" ("Now We're Even"). The final stanza is the most famous:

> *Y mañana cuando seas descolado mueble viejo*
> *y no tengas esperanzas en el pobre corazón;*
> *si precisás una ayuda, si te hace falta un consejo,*
> *acordate de este amigo que ha de jugarse el pellejo*
> *pa' ayudarte en lo que pueda, cuando llegue la ocasión.*

> And tomorrow when you're an old, broken-down piece of furniture
> and you haven't got a hope within your poor heart;
> if you need a bit of help, if you can use some advice,
> remind yourself of this friend who is going to risk his hide
> to help you as he can, when it's the time for that.

This is hardly a "philosophical sympathy for women," as Yale professor Robert Farris Thompson calls it. Hearing "Mano a mano" inflames me: I identify with the woman, of course! In one and the same breath, this poet reduces me to an old piece of furniture, while from a cushy stance of moral superiority he offers me his "help." I tell him to take a hike and to stop predicting catastrophes for my life. And I add: Well, bigshot that you are, you cannot offer me a better life?

Tangos like this reflect the history of their times in a particular place: the outskirts of the Sur (southside) area of Buenos Aires. Let's keep in mind that some women in the sophisticated *Norte* (northside) were already writers (Petrona Rasciende de Sierra, Juana María Gorriti), poets (Rosa Guerra, Alfonsina Storni), educators and journalists (Juana Manso), actresses (Trinidad Guevara), doctors (Cecilia Grierson, graduated in 1889), attorneys (María Angélica Barredo, graduated from law school at age 19), and artists (like the sculptor Lola Mora). Tangos like "Mano a mano" reflect the social circumstances of the old Sur in particular. But they also rouse us today. We become these characters, I become Milonguita when I hear her tangos. And despite Flores' degrading and macho stance, he still seduces me with his beautiful metaphors. Before he arrives at this final stanza shown above, he shows off his skills at portraying the lives of the poor people of the outskirts. His brushstrokes are brilliant as he paints her struggle with the language of soccer ("*cuando vos, pobre percanta, / gam-*

165

beteabas la pobreza en la casa de pensión," "when you, poor broad, / were high-stepping poverty's tackles back in the flophouse"), and puts Milonguita's manipulation of men into sadistic animal terms ("*como juega el gato maula con el mísero ratón,*" "as the crafty tomcat toys with the miserable mouse"). Animated touches like these give Flores his place among the tango poets and do something to neutralize his chauvinism.

Many tango lyrics were written in bars and cafés during the bohemian nights of Buenos Aires. Here the photographer evokes the atmosphere of the tango with a composition alluding not only to nightlife and the cabaret but also to the downtown center of Buenos Aires, where the majestic obelisk rises amid the widest avenue in the world. *Photograph courtesy of German Luongo (Montevideo, Uruguay).*

I said that tango lyrics reflect the history of the times. They also reflect the psychology of the times in the not-so-remote orillas. The generation of indigent immigrants in the 1880s was nostalgic for the homeland, the European villages they left behind — more so because their dreams of becoming rich overnight did not come true, and most of them could not go back. Their children, the poets, were bred with that nostalgia; but unable to long for a place they never knew, the emotion was transferred to a new "object" — the woman who was (often) as unavailable to them as the motherland was for their parents. With so many hundreds of authors, no general statement can be absolute; but certain themes and attitudes do seem to belong to certain decades, and to get passed around from songwriter to songwriter. Real-life portraits become conventions and characters that get reused and refreshed. Incrementally, as history and creativity played off each other, attitudes changed, and the characters grew into new roles. Since the poets were almost entirely men, characters like Milonguita always seem to be portrayed with a male bias. But this character was also symbolic, functioning poetically as a scapegoat. The images and stories of women in tango lyrics may use them as symbols of the motherland — lost, longed for, or found — and may represent male experience in an exaggerated or biased way; but they also reveal the fears and anxieties of men in a world where they vastly outnumbered the women of their age in the population. Men had to compete with many rivals both for work and for women. The previous static colonial economy with the power in the hands of the elite had become more competitive, and more materialistic. Tango lyrics, then, were not just a reflection of the world people experienced; they were also a projection onto it, driven by the resentment or envy of men in reaction to the greater mobility of the few women there were — even if these women did not get any farther than the cabaret. Most men could not get that far themselves; they were stuck in the pauper outskirts. This symbolic and psychological complexity is what gave the lyrics their edge, and what gives them their shadows today.

I wish to trace the evolution of this one major character, Milonguita, through the tango epic. Her story, as the tango evolves, is a story of rising from nothing. And through her we come to see another character, the Adam to her Eve: the "Compadrito" of the outskirts, the man she left behind and is always leaving behind. He emerges as a voice — to get his revenge, to cry for his losses, or sometimes both. I like his voice because it is not politically correct, but real. He lets it all hang out: his fears, his tears, his failures. He is the loser that, by voicing his vulnerability, gives reality and expression to universal anxieties.

The Setup for Shortcomings

On the surface, Milonguita is like the North American flapper of the jazz age: she's a social butterfly, mobile, flirty, attractive, possibly dangerous. Unlike the flapper, she has a backstory in the suburban margins of the city. And there is another woman of the outskirts who always makes her a failure in the eyes of men: La Morocha.

"La morocha" ("The Brunette") of 1905 is widely considered the first tango to cross the Atlantic. (It was not: by that year, there were tangos in

Cover of the sheet music for "La Morocha," published in 1905. This was the most popular tango of the "Guardia Vieja" (Old Guard) period of tango (1880–1909), and many singers recorded the song: among others, Linda Thelma, Lola Membrives, Ada Falcón, Mercedes Simone, Libertad Lamarque, Virginia Luque, Lolita Torres. There are numerous instrumental versions, notably by Juan D'Arienzo and Carlos Di Sarli. *Photograph courtesy of Ricardo García Blaya, director, archives of www.TodoTango.com (Buenos Aires).*

circulation that had been recorded by Gramophone in London by the Royal Military Band.) A 1928 interview in the magazine *Caras y Caretas* reported it was written in praise of a real woman. According to the article, the composer and violinist/pianist Enrique Saborido and a Uruguayan dancer named Lola Candales were habitués of a certain *Bar Reconquista*: taken with her beauty, the musician went home at dawn, sat at the piano, and after 90 minutes had finished the tune. A few hours later, Saborido took them to Lola along with the lyrics penned by his collaborator Angel Villoldo, and she sang it for the first time. These are sweet, "clean" lyrics, written at a time when tango lyrics did not play the important role they found later, which nonetheless became an all-time favorite of porteños:

> *Soy la morocha argentina,*
> *la que no siente pesares,*
> *y alegre pasa la vida*
> *con sus cantares.*
> *Soy la gentil compañera*
> *del noble gaucho porteño,*
> *la que conserva el cariño*
> *para su dueño.*

> I am the Argentine brunette,
> who has nothing to weigh her down
> and gladly goes through life
> with the tune of a song.
> I am the kind companion
> of the noble porteño gaucho,
> who saves up her affections
> for where they belong.

This is sentimental, but was it ever more than a fantasy? It is hard to say. What is clear is that La Morocha was an ideal woman. This is definitely not a cityscape she inhabits: the lyrics are pastoral. We are miles outside the city center, on the fringes of the suburb where the infinity of the pampas begins. At break of day, she is already up and about, ready to serve her countryman his *cimarrón* (unsweetened mate). We are in a world of natural instinct and innocence, which was all about to be ruptured by the 20th century.

La Morocha inaugurates an ideal, and she stands as the predecessor that Milonguita, for all her champagne glasses, can never measure up to. La Morocha's key attribute is that she has "nothing to weigh her down" ("no siente pesares"). Barely a generation later, the symbolic presence of this ideal woman throws a deep shadow over the already-dark interior of the urban nightclub. The world had changed since the time of La Morocha in 1905. In the 1920s, tangos like "Mano a mano" portray the prodigal daughter as a sad opportunist, who left true love and good family values behind and now is unable to love or find fulfillment. In "Milonguita" (by the lyricist Samuel Linnig), the poet begins by evoking her early days in the outskirts:

> Te acordás, Milonguita, vos eras
> La pebeta más linda 'e Chiclana,
> La pollera cortona y las trenzas,
> Y en las trenzas un beso de sol,
> Y en aquellas noches de verano,
> ¿Qué soñaba tu almita, mujer,
> Al oír en la esquina algún tango
> Chamuyarte bajito de amor?

> You remember, Milonguita, you used to be
> the prettiest girl in all Chiclana,
> with your cutoff skirt and your braids,
> and in your braids a kiss of the sun.
> And in those summer evenings,
> what did your little soul dream of, woman,
> at the sound of some tango on the corner
> with its low voice talking of love?

Chiclana was an avenue in the suburb of Boedo — which later became the crib of the great poets of the golden era. With this evocation of her early days, the speaker opens by reminding this young woman that she could have been La Morocha, the ideal archetype. Instead, seduced by a tango — an image of the cabaret highlife — she stepped out of her social class (and his) to become a character in this new tango, and different world, of the 1920s:

> ¡Estercita!...
> Hoy te llaman Milonguita...
> Flor de lujo y de placer,
> Flor de noche y cabaret,
> ¡Milonguita!...
> Los hombres te han hecho mal,
> ¡Y hoy darías toda tu alma
> Por vestirte de percal...

> Estercita,
> today they call you Milonguita...
> flower of luxury and of pleasure,

170

> flower of nights and cabarets.
> Milonguita,
> the men have treated you wrong,
> and now you'd give up all your soul
> to dress in percale again.

Percale was the cheapest grade of cotton there was; for this reason it became a symbol of family values and the old-fashioned simplicity of life outside the city center. The poet here wants us to believe that Milonguita would trade in her soul "to dress in percale again," but this is a double condemnation: he depicts her as a sell-out for having moved to the city in the first place, and that move (it is implied) is the cause of her unhappiness:

> *Y entre el vino y el último tango*
> *P'al cotorro te saca un bacán,*
> *¡Ay, qué sola, Estercita, te sientes!*
> *Si llorás ... ¡dicen que es el champán!*

> And between the wine and the final tango,
> some bigshot takes you out to his crib...
> Ah, Estercita, how alone you feel!
> When you cry ... they say it's the champagne!

What is Milonguita's situation, in the eyes of her male creator? — not being La Morocha, and betraying her own social class. When I hear "Milonguita" I identify with Estercita; I want to scream at the lyricist for not understanding my predicament. In my mind I shout, "I had no choice but to work at a cabaret — it was the only way out of the conventillo! No, I do not want to go back to hunger and mice. I do not have to go back where you are! I like the taste of the *jailaife*."

In any case, with this tango the theme was clearly established, and other poets used it throughout the 1920s: the situation it portrays had the convincing details as well as the fear-fantasies of real life. This made these songs extremely popular. Milonguita is a creation of the poet's psyche as much as a reflection of the times, a projection of men's own failures in life and love, a symbol of reality's disappointments. This is not to say that women did not really experience what is described in the lyrics: certainly many of them did find disillusion and worse (many of them died of syphilis and tuberculosis). In the end, they were real women who made choices — and that, it seems, is precisely their crime in these lyrics. For the male authors, they stand for the betrayal and frustrations of the real world. In

171

a way it is fitting (from the male perspective) that they should suffer the same fate they bring upon others.

We think of the 1920s as a time of prosperity and frivolity in the city. And compared to what came after, maybe they were a time of relative excitement in the urban center; but they also were a period of great transition and major social changes (such as the formation of a large middle class), along with further expansion of the city. It was an increasingly materialistic age, all opportunity on the surface. But promises didn't always come true.

With the election of the popular president Hipólito Yrigoyen in 1916, for the first time the new middle class felt like part of the political process. But by 1922 Yrigoyen's term was up, and the oligarchy regained power. Under the new administration, many of the recent gains were lost. Yrigoyen was elected to a second term overwhelmingly in 1928, but then the Great Depression set in, people were dissatisfied, and a military coup ousted him from office in 1930, beginning the so-called *Década Infame* (Infamous Decade), during which time electoral fraud, corruption, and political repression made their way back into Argentine politics.

This dissatisfaction is what these "milonguita" tangos of the 1920s and 1930s record, even when the political is absent: a people's reaction to lost gains and broken promises, the nostalgic dream of better values and a just society. The lyrics were a way of confronting the truth, not escaping from it. And as the 1920s wore on, Milonguita got farther away from La Morocha, and male poets began to portray her character less as a sentimental symbol and more as a scapegoat for the anger and frustration of the times. On the one hand, the art was developing; on the other hand, the new social order was getting highly politicized.

From Imagery to Irony

At the end of the 1920s, tango lyrics begin to wake up into a literature. With the arrival of Enrique Santos Discépolo, the tango lyric as a poetic genre becomes a fully self-conscious art and takes on a new dimension of irony and universality.

Discépolo had a gift for sensing and expressing the pulse of the people. "Chorra" ("Thief") is an early tango of his from 1928, and one not often discussed very closely, perhaps because it is predominantly comic. It has

been called "the tragedy of the man who believes"—but it is basically a
farce. He believed in her love, when all she wanted was his money:

> *Por ser bueno, me pusiste en la miseria,*
> *me dejaste en la palmera, me afanaste hasta el color.*
> *En seis meses me comiste el mercadito,*
> *la casiya de la feria, la ganchera, el mostrador...*
> *¡Chorra!...*
> *Me robaste hasta el amor...*
> *Ahura,*
> *tanto me asusta una mina,*
> *que si en la calle me afila:*
> *¡me pongo al lao del botón!*

> For my being good, you put me into misery,
> you left me up the palm tree, you stole even my color.
> In half a year, you cleaned me out at the corner shop,
> the booth at the street fair, the meat hooks, the display...
> Thief!
> You even ripped off my love...
> Nowadays,
> a dame gives me such a fright,
> that if she flirts with me in the street
> I go stand next to a cop!

This exaggerates the Milonguita theme to an extremity: she is still false to
the speaker of the lyric, but now he is the total victim, and she gets away
with it. As in his other early tangos, Discépolo goes overboard with the
conventions of tango lyrics, releasing anxiety with a burlesque that is making fun of art as much as reality. The main inversion is the character of
the speaker: now he, for a change, is the broken-down furniture.

Discépolo's early tangos are certainly not kind to women, and in that
sense they continue to play with the image of the young woman as a "fallen
angel." For us today, the Compadrito and the quasi-flapper Milonguita
are part of the show-poster mythology of the tango; but at the time of
these tangos, both characters were shown in a derogatory manner. They
were tango's losers, around whose failures the epic takes its shape. What
Discépolo develops thematically is the male protagonist, by undermining
or inverting the usual tango attitudes. Through this we see an upside-
down portrait of the Compadrito, the man from the outskirts who in
reality was becoming the working-class city guy. And in that light, it is
very tempting to read "Chorra" as an allegory of how the political system
betrayed the common man's values, and left him with no work. (In the

1930s the first shantytowns appeared near the city center; one of them was called *Villa desocupacion*, "Unemployment villa.")

In the 1928 tango "Muñeca brava" ("Tough Doll"), another great lyricist, Enrique Cadícamo, gives us an updated portrait of Milonguita in this new social and economic environment. Now she is in a competitive market, and not faring well by any means. The 1920s were times of massive illegal prostitution: international mafia organizations brought women to the increasingly prosperous and overwhelmingly male-populated Buenos Aires by the thousands, selling them first to bordellos and later to those hotspots of acceptable evening entertainment which everyone enjoyed, the cabarets. There, they worked side by side with local women as waitresses, dancers, or singers. As hired *coperas* ("shills" might be an approximate translation), they induced men to live it up, buy drinks, and spend money in the venues. Many of the "imports" came from France; men sought them out more than the locals, who soon had to pretend they were French, too. Another story says that the Milonguitas picked up French manners from the wealthier young men (*niños bien*) who traveled to and often studied in France. Cadícamo's aggressive lyric unmasks these pretenses and puts the local girl down like a kind of false article, addressing her sarcastically as "*madame*" before calling her a cookie with long eyelashes and a second-rate toy.

With its bitter sarcasm mixing French and *lunfardo*, this lyric knocks Milonguita down a notch on the scale for betraying her origins once again, with a language that is not hers, and for her moral frailty: now there's no way to feel sorry for her, but pure condescension. The macho Compadrito, speaker of the lines, takes a stance of unadulterated mockery. For all that, we see her climbing up in the world. As in Discépolo's "Chorra," she is guilty not of her failure but of her success.

From Satire to Romance

The attitudes of tango lyrics in the 1930s continued to vary these themes and conventions: the two main characters, Milonguita and Compadrito, often no longer labeled as such, continue to clash with each other, him trashing her, her leaving him. This is the almost infinite cycle, even in the love songs, which by the 1930s came into greater prominence not only through the great fame of Gardel — whose songbook began to include Hollywood-driven hits by himself and Alfredo Le Pera — but also as a kind of "poetic antidote" or release from the political preoccupations of the 1930s in general. Gardel himself had been a kind of male Milonguita, a defector of the lower class who made it big in France and the United States, who got away with it and was even admired for it. By the 1920s and 1930s he was always at the cabaret, always in black tie, always with a glass of champagne in his hand. No one wrote songs about his defector condition (he was, after all, a guy), and in a way his enormous success enacted a change in the songwriters. He was getting too rich and too "foreign" to give voice to social tensions, and songs of romance were on the way in.

José María Contursi emerged in the 1930s as the love-song lyricist *par excellence*. The situation in his lyrics still is very similar: it is a case of love lost, of someone abandoning someone else. Often the roles are reversed, and the male speaker sings his regret for having moved on to some other lover. These romantic tangos lament a situation that could be summed up by these climactic lines from Contursi's 1940 tango "Toda mi vida" ("The Whole of My Life"): *"¡soy un pasaje de tu vida, nada más!"* ("I'm just a station in your life, nothing more!")

Contursi worked alongside the best songwriters of the day, writing classics of the genre for the famous orchestras of Troilo, Laurenz, and Mores, among others. These romantic tangos present love at a crossroads of recognition, where the male protagonist confronts and deepens his sense of loss. Some lines from his tango "Como dos extraños" ("Like Two Strangers," 1940) illustrate the difference between the harsh, gritty lyrics of the past, with all their social tensions, and these scenes that unfold in the personal sphere:

> *Y ahora que estoy frente a tí*
> *¡parecemos ya ves … dos extraños!*
> *Lección que por fin aprendí,*
> *¡cómo cambian las cosas los años!*

> And now that I'm standing before you,
> already we seem two strangers!
> A lesson I have finally learned:
> The years, how they make things change!

Gone is the blame and the condescension: all that remains at this point is reality's hard lesson and a very large dose of nostalgia. And the nostalgia is neither for the homeland of the immigrants nor for the *pampas* or outskirts of the earlier tangos, but rather for a love affair.

175

By this time, Milonguita has largely disappeared as a character, along with the Compadrito. The fact is that they had vanished from the real world, too: the outskirts of the past were gone by the 1930s, as the suburbs were becoming connected by urban expansion and were no longer semi-urban pockets isolated by empty land. But the Milonguita theme persists in one sense: even if he does not reproach her for it, or predict some dead-end "old furniture" destiny for her, she remains the cause of his sorrow. The big difference is that he can now keep her warmly in his heart even after their departure.

Contursi's famous tango "En esta tarde gris" ("In This Gray After-noon," 1941) offers a fine example of this new "sentimental" lyric, which had come to the foreground with the rise of Gardel and later dominated the 1940s:

> *Qué ganas de llorar en esta tarde gris...*
> *¡en su repiquetear la lluvia habla de ti!*
> *Remordimiento de saber*
> *que por mi culpa, nunca*
> *vida ... nunca te veré.*
> *Mis ojos al cerrar te ven igual que ayer,*
> *temblando, al implorar de nuevo mi querer...*
> *¡Y hoy es tu voz que vuelve a mí*
> *en esta tarde gris!*

> How much I want to sob in this gray afternoon!
> With its repeating drops the rain speaks of you...
> Remorse of knowing well
> that never, on account of me,
> life, never will I see you.
> I shut my eyes and see you just the same as then,
> all trembling with the plea to have my love again...
> And now it's your voice that comes back to me
> in this gray afternoon!

This tango takes an interesting turn in the chorus, as the male protagonist sings the plea he remembers her making. His voice becomes hers: it incriminates him in the present, since he evidently did not return to her. That is his lament: no blame of her, no reproach, only a crushing sensitivity for his own guilt. What a far cry from the tangos of the 1920s!

The woman here is still, however, the source of his woe. She is still not La Morocha, who speaks with pride and makes him happy. In the ongoing story of the tango, this woman is still, if in very diluted form, the abandoning Milonguita. Yet the tango epic had a further development for this theme, which in 1942 was born from the pen of the great Homero Manzi, who with Discépolo, Cadícamo, Cátulo Castillo, and Homero Expósito occupies the poetic summit of tango lyricists.

The Portrait of a Colossus

If Discépolo is the tango's greatest ironic poet and social critic, then Homero Manzi is its supreme portraitist. And a single portrait of his surpasses all others: Malena.

Malena is a final fusion of La Morocha and Milonguita, a cabaret singer who is also above the reproach of the male speaker, and who is responsible for what she gives and not for what she takes away. She emerges like some kind of supernatural giantess:

> *Malena canta el tango como ninguna*
> *y en cada verso pone su corazón.*
> *A yuyo del suburbio su voz perfuma,*
> *Malena tiene pena de bandoneón.*
> *Tal vez, allá en la infancia, su voz de alondra*
> *tomó ese tono oscuro de callejón...*
> *O acaso aquel romance, que sólo nombra*
> *cuando se pone triste con el alcohol.*
> *Malena canta el tango con voz de sombra.*
> *Malena tiene pena de bandoneón.*

> Malena sings the tango like no one else
> and in every line puts a heart of her own.
> Her voice has the scent of grass in the suburb,
> Malena has the blues of the bandoneón.
> Perhaps long ago, way back in her childhood,
> her skylark voice took on this dark, back-alley tone...
> Or maybe it was the romance she only ever names
> when she gets to drinking, saddened and alone.
> Malena sings the tango with a voice of shadow,
> Malena has the ache of the bandoneón.

For once, the man can only guess at her past: he does not know where she came from or what she has been through. There is an escape from nostalgia here: the past serves only to characterize her immense presence.

The huge difference here, too, is that Malena has a voice — literally and figuratively. We saw a woman's words quoted in Contursi's "En esta tarde gris," but still — what a change for a woman in a tango lyric! And yet how can a voice have an aroma? What is a "voice of shadow"? What *is* Malena?

A better question might be: who is the speaker? Here, the man is totally effaced: he does not exist except as a record-maker, a witness of Malena's presence. In this tango's chorus, we again see that he can only speculate about her, because as present as she is, she remains a mystery, an evocative power:

> *Tu canción*
> *tiene el frío del último encuentro.*
> *Tu canción*
> *se hace amarga en la sal del recuerdo.*
> *Yo no sé*
> *si tu voz es la flor de una pena;*
> *sólo sé*
> *que al rumor de tus tangos, Malena,*
> *te siento más buena,*
> *más buena que yo.*

> Your song
> has the cold of a last encounter.
> Your song
> Becomes embittered in the salt of memory.
> I don't know
> if your voice is the flower of heartbreak,
> all I know
> is that at the hum of your tangos, Malena,
> I feel that you're better,
> much better than me.

Clearly, this personage has overcome the tango conventions we encounter elsewhere. She is not the possession, not even the lost possession, of the speaker or of any man. She brings him no sorrow. Malena seems to be so much more than a singer: she is a woman with her own life. She carries and seems to dramatize wounds; to me these seem like the battle scars from other tangos, all the put-downs and degradations that were heaped on Milonguita. And not only does the male speaker lay off, but he again admits that he can't describe her, and — startling for a tango — raises her to a level above himself. He is about as big as the caption under a photograph or next to a painting.

If we consider that Malena was a real person, there is clearly a generation gap between her and the women who "were" Milonguita (just as there was a gap between Milonguita and La Morocha). I have been treating these recycled appearances like consistent characters, half-fiction, and calling tango lyrics collectively a coherent epic; but with the figure of Malena

this takes a new turn. She is too solitary an image, too much an icon, to
be repeated in other lyrics of the day:
she seems to arrest the cycle of woe
that created her. And her symbolic
value in the lyric as a female character — like a single free-standing
sculpture in a city of relief carv-
ings — has led to an interesting situation:

Every real-life woman, it seems,
identifies herself with Malena.

My friend tells me a story about
a painting he made, a picture of a
woman's face with brown hair and
brown eyes. It was a distorted image,
but every brown-eyed brunette who
saw it in person, and knew my
friend, thought that she herself was
the "real" subject. Something of the
sort has happened with Malena:
numerous female tango singers have
claimed that they inspired Manzi's
lyric, and numerous others have
been suggested. Names and dates
and locations seem to multiply
around her. One candidate, Malena
de Toledo (stage-name of one Elena
Tortolero) had been suggested a long

Homero Manzi (1907–1951), author of
the lyrics for "Malena." A prolific lyricist, some of his many other hits
include "Sur," "Barrio de tango," "El
últmo organito," "Mano Blanca,"
"Esquinas porteñas," "El pescante,"
"Milonga del 900," "Milonga sentimental," "Milonga triste," "Disce-
polín," "Mañana zarpa un barco,"
"Romance de barrio," and "Recién."
*Photograph courtesy of Ricardo García
Blaya, director, archives of www.
TodoTango.com (Buenos Aires).*

time ago by Lucio Demare (who wrote the music for Manzi's lyric), and
then her date of birth came loose: assumed to be 1916, the anecdotes that
substantiate her indicate it might have been 1906 instead. Nelly Omar,
the great woman tango singer, claims that she was the inspiration for
"Malena": she had a long love relationship with Manzi, but some believe
the affair began a little while after the tango had already been premiered.
(She herself once said that she prefers to keep the details of her relationship
with the poet private, and that certainly it was written for her.) Acho

179

Manzi, the poet's son, said the singer Tita Merello once expressed her belief that it was written for her.

Nobody, meanwhile, has volunteered to be Milonguita.

Women still identify with Malena because she is an image of artistic and creative power, who bears her wounds and puts them into song triumphantly. She has an existence independent of any man; she is autonomous. In the second verse of the lyric, Manzi describes her with a sequence of similes that seems like a variation on Renaissance love poetry:

> *Tus ojos son oscuros como el olvido;*
> *tus labios apretados como el rencor;*
> *tus manos, dos palomas que sienten frío;*
> *tus venas tienen sangre de bandoneón.*

> Your eyes are in darkness like something forgotten;
> your lips in a grudge that tightens to bone;
> your hands, two shivering doves in the coldness;
> your veins have the blood of the bandoneón.

Metaphors seem to be rushing in from every direction in this surreal description, which is entirely fitting for this evocative figure whose "voice of shadow" has an aroma. Visually, these lines conjure up a dramatic picture of the singer in a spotlight on stage. As the portrait concludes, she seems to become something else entirely, and her voice is revealed to be godlike, emanating beings that take over the entire city:

> *Tus tangos son criaturas abandonadas*
> *que cruzan sobre el barro del callejón*
> *cuando todas las puertas están cerradas*
> *y ladran los fantasmas de la canción.*
> *Malena canta el tango con voz quebrada.*
> *Malena tiene pena de bandoneón.*

> Your tangos are children orphaned, abandoned
> to the mud of the alleys they run through alone,
> when the doors and the windows are bolted and shuttered,
> and the ghosts of song wail on their own.
> Malena sings the tango with a voice that's shattered.
> Malena has the ache of the bandoneón.

Here the lyric escapes reality altogether, and the images become entirely mythical. Malena's voice takes shape, and her singing goes out to haunt the city like street urchins: again, things multiply around her. Now there are ghosts, too: are they the battered Milonguitas and the vanished La Morochas? Are they the Compadritos who were always getting left behind?

The photo montage used on the "Malena" cover, featuring the orchestra of Lucio Demare with singer Carlos Miranda. The eleven musicians are shown without their instruments in the lower center of the montage. *Photograph courtesy of Ricardo García Blaya, director, archives of www.TodoTango.com (Buenos Aires).*

These pieces of Malena's voice (I think of the antique gramophones that used to be sold "as pieces of the voice of Gardel"), these tangos go back to the alleys where she found them — here is our nostalgia, at the end of the lyric, in a different form than we have ever seen. Malena gave them that form. These pieces of her voice are now abandoned creatures — here is our Milonguita theme again, once more transformed by this strange character, this Mona Lisa of the tango, this colossus, this breeder of shadows.

A Backward Glance, a Country Dress

Malena belongs to the cabarets of the 1940s, which with their focus on entertainment and dancing were a very different scene from the opportunistic 1920s. But if Malena transcends the unlucky and maligned Milonguitas of the tangos that came before her, she represents them as well. Her imaginative presence is a sign that tells us: *The old times are over, and we*

have survived them. Malena inaugurates a new character: the fully independent woman, who carries the wounds of the past into a spotlight beyond
guilt.

This forward poetic evolution makes me read "Percal" ("Percale"),
the beautiful 1943 tango with lyrics by Homero Expósito, as a kind of
receding wave that washes the old themes into the past. As with most of
Expósito's lyrics, the words are highly impressionistic and contain much
ambiguity even as they create a definite mood: this is because even more
than other tango poets, he generated his effects from the symbolic value
of certain key words and images that already had a resonant history in
tango lyrics. Here, we encounter a symbol we have already seen — the cheap
grade of cotton that by the 1920s had come to represent life outside the
city:

> *Percal...*
> *¿Te acuerdas del percal?...*
> *Tenías quince abriles*
> *anhelos de sufrir y amar,*
> *de ir al centro, triunfar*
> *y olvidar el percal...*

> Percale...
> Do you remember the percale?
> You'd seen some fifteen Aprils,
> had dreams of suffering and love,
> of going to the center, making it big
> and forgetting the percale.

Expósito's language here literally echoes the words of "Milonguita," which
we saw at the beginning of this chapter. In that earlier tango, the poet
compared her life in the city to her more pristine beginnings, and the old
fabric of her past was mingled with a sense of blame and guilt over her
decision to leave it:

> *Te acordás, Milonguita, vos eras*
> *La pebeta más linda 'e Chiclana,*
> *[...]*
> *Y hoy darías toda tu alma*
> *Por vestirte de percal...*

> You remember, Milonguita, you used to be
> the prettiest girl in all Chiclana,
> [...]
> and now you'd give up all your soul
> to dress in percale again...

9. Milonguita

Two decades later, Expósito has removed all the guilt and the sense of longing, the symbolic resonance, the pure power of the images and tones:

> *Percal...*
> *Camino del percal,*
> *te fuiste de tu casa,*
> *Tal vez nos enteramos mal,*
> *Solo sé que al final*
> *te olvidaste el percal...*
>
> Percale...
> The way of the percale,
> you put your house behind you...
> Perhaps we heard about it wrong.
> All I know is in the end
> you had forgotten the percale.

I read this as a traditional tango written in the age of Malena. Here the speaker is not in the city, but in the place this woman left: as in Malena, his knowledge of her life is partial, and "perhaps we heard about it wrong." He expresses his sense of loss, not only or even primarily for her, but for the times he associates with her. As the lyric proceeds, the rhymes repeat like sobs, and the image of the dress recurs obsessively:

> *La juventud se fue...*
> *Tu casa ya no está...*
> *Y en el ayer tirados*
> *se han quedado*
> *acobardados*
> *tu percal y mi pasado...*
> *La juventud se fue...*
> *Yo ya no espero más...*
> *Mejor dejar perdidos*
> *los anhelos que no han sido*
> *y el vestido de percal.*
>
> Youth went away...
> Your house is now not here...
> And in yesterday, cast aside,
> they're left behind,
> terrified,
> your percale and my past...
> Youth went away...
> I now no longer hope...
> Better to give up for lost
> the hopes that haven't happened
> and the dress made of percale.

The man here, lamenting his memories as permanently bygone things, admits a crucial point: the past is actually over. We do not even visualize the woman of this tango, because she is no longer there for the man. Having left not only him but also the entire world he dwells on, she has escaped the cycle of possession and blame. Only the poetic symbols remain.

"Percal" seems like a deliberate answer to "Milonguita," not only in its evocation of the same symbols but also in its totally different treatment of the same situation. Milonguita was said to be unable to love, and it used to be that when she cries over her empty life, "they say it's the champagne." For Expósito that irony is gone. Even with tones of regret and loss, he affirms that she has lived a real life, whatever it may have been:

> Llorar...
> ¿Por qué vas a llorar?...
> ¿Acaso no has vivido?
> acaso no aprendiste a amar
> a sufrir, a esperar,
> y también a callar...
> Percal...
> Son cosas del percal...
> Saber que estás sufriendo
> saber que sufrirás aún más
> y saber que al final
> no olvidaste el percal...
> Percal...
> Tristezas del percal.

> To cry...
> What are you going to cry for?...
> You think you haven't lived,
> you think you never learned to love,
> to suffer and to hope,
> and to fall quiet too?
> Percale...
> They belong to the percale...
> To know that you have suffered,
> to know you'll suffer even more,
> and to know that in the end
> you didn't forget the percale...
> Percale...
> The sorrows of percale...

By the end of this lyric, the symbolic value of "percale" has been deconstructed and turned inside-out. For the poet, the old dress is tied to his memories; this is more or less the conventional meaning it had in lyrics. In his imaginings of her experience, however, it comes to be associated with everything intense she must have gone through — as the stimulus to keep going, to leave the past behind. This is a huge difference! Expósito appears to be saying that for her, percale represents everything worth getting away from. And although the tone is sardonic and possibly even resentful, he validates her experiences as real. In the course of its development, this tango voices a process of coming-to-terms with her independence. Its obsessions give shape to the reality of the speaker, who is living in a state of consequence. Its atmosphere and its deliberate echoes of a past tango — "Milonguita" in particular!— suggest that this recognition of her liberty was long overdue. "Percal" in its way offers closure to the theme: it puts Milonguita to rest.

10

Four Weeks and a Lifetime
with Alberto Podestá

The first time I greeted Alberto Podestá I moved toward him extending both my arms and feeling warm as if I had known him all my life. He took my hands into his hands.

I had never introduced myself to anybody in this manner before. I usually either extend my right hand or give a kiss on the cheek. Why was I greeting him in this way?

From the meeting of our hands, a chain of different and related events would soon be set in motion in various parts of the world. Serendipitously that small circle became symbolic of an even greater circle that took shape around Alberto Podestá. Two months after I first approached him in this strange way in Buenos Aires, the legendary singer held in his hands the last link of the chain, and a circle was made complete.

The Interview

"It is adoration I feel for our music, and for the people of this country." With these words, this man of enormous presence and sunny smile stood up at the end of his interview with Horacio Godoy, at Club Armenio before the milonga at La Viruta took place close to midnight. That was the moment when I moved toward him, but even at the start of the program I had already attached myself to him with an invisible umbilical cord, holding an earthquake of emotions within, basking in his candid and humble light.

Throughout his two-hour interview with Godoy, I learned about the life of this man who had been singing for over half a century under the major orchestra directors of the tango's golden age. As a child growing up in the province of San Juan, he worked selling candy at a movie theater to help his mother. Between shifts, he could slip into the darkened theater for free; and one day he chanced to see a film by Carlos Gardel, the first and most famous tango singer of all time. It changed his life.

In 1939, when he was just 15 years old, he moved to Buenos Aires with the dream of becoming a singer. As a teenager he started performing with a magnificent group of musicians, the Orquesta Miguel Caló. Under that maestro's baton in 1941, Podestá inaugurated his now six-decade recording career with the tangos "Dos fracasos" and "Yo soy el tango," and the vals "Bajo un cielo de estrellas."

While still a minor, he got picked up by the most prestigious orchestra of the day, that of Carlos Di Sarli. He told us, with the same awe and delight in his eyes that he must have had at 17, that this orchestra had four bandoneóns, four violins, the maestro's piano, a bass — and more than one singer. Unfortunately his happiness was short-lived. Roberto Rufino, the major singer in Di Sarli's lineup (himself barely older than Podestá), would tell him, "You go sing, kid," only when he wanted to take a break or avoid straining his voice.

"Usually Di Sarli asked me to sing 'Alma de Bohemio' [Bohemian Soul]," remembered Podestá during the Godoy interview. "One day I started extending the 'a' in the word *cantar,* so that it sounded *cantaaaaar.* Gradually I stayed a little bit longer with the 'a': *cantaaaaaaaaar.* This song gave me my own signature as a singer; I became known for it."

Godoy played the song (which Podestá recorded with another orchestra a couple years later) for the audience of about 50. I appreciated Podestá's tenor voice, his phrasings delaying the arrival of the end of the word.

Podestá: "I was jealous of Rufino. I cried so many nights. I was mad about not having the chance to sing more." I enjoyed his candor, the way he accepted and shared his jealousy, frustration, and anger.

He left Di Sarli and joined another major orchestra of the times, that of Pedro Laurenz. His new boss was "the best-dressed director of the times," he said: as the band's singer, Podestá had to have his suits and shirts made where his boss and the members of the orchestra dressed, at *Spiro y Demetrio*, one of the most expensive tailor shops in Buenos Aires. He told the story without any airs and with much delight, as the kid from San

Juan who sold candy at the movies and was discovering the expensive world of the big city. He continued telling us anecdotes and conversed with Godoy as the audience gathered in a circle around him.

When the program came to an end, there was a moment when he stood up: it was then that I, too, stood up and moved toward him, feeling warm as if I had known him all my life. I remembered at that moment that, during my childhood, Podestá's voice filled our kitchen and living room when my father listened to Radio El Mundo. The memories of those programs were like ripples of connection between Podestá as a young singer and myself as a young child, like bridges between me, my father, and the tango.

Singer Alberto Podestá (b. 1924). Active as a tango singer since his debut during the Golden Age of the 1940s, Podestá began traveling internationally again in 2009, with performances in Chicago, Bogotá, Berlin, São Paulo, Rome, and Bologna. *Photograph by Beatriz Dujovne.*

When he took my hands in his hands, in that tango enlace of sorts, I timidly asked if we could meet at some time convenient for him, to talk about lyrics. Generously, he asked what was convenient for me, and we arranged the time and place. I was too moved to recall what else we said; I just remember a feeling of gratitude over having met such a voice of my past in the form of a sweet, fatherly human being. I also remember thinking: "My dear Buenos Aires, you offer so many opportunities to connect with others without complicated transactions, even with icons like this singer. Thank you, Buenos Aires!"

The Café in the Fog

The morning of our meeting opened with the foggy type of rain we call *garúa*. I walked from my apartment to *Confitería La Biela*, my favorite place in the world. I was not thinking about people-watching or reading the newspaper, which are my daily routines there. I was single-mindedly focused on meeting Podestá and getting as close as I could to the spirit of the golden age of the tango. In my habitual camaraderie with the waiters there, I engaged them to help me spot his arrival. They seated me strategically, with a view of all three doors. The waiters' enthusiasm and my own was gathering momentum when Podestá arrived with his friendly and paternal smile. I asked if he preferred to sit in the nonsmoking section; with a mischievous smile he turned his hand over and showed me the cigarette he was smoking. With laughter, we ordered our cafecitos and began what became a 90-minute string of sweet and tearful moments for me.

When we sat down he offered me the *piropo porteño*: "I have to tell you that you look very pretty this morning," and then we conversed leaning forward the way old friends do. Overjoyed, he reminisced about the 1940s when dancing was everywhere in the city, when Corrientes was lined with confiterías where the big orchestras played.

"The 40s was the golden age of tango and football in Argentina," he told me. "We used to get together with Cadícamo, Manzi, Expósito, Discépolo, in bars that no longer exist. Francini and Pontier were brothers to me. If you had come years ago, I could have introduced you to them so you could have talked with them about the poetry."

Just imagining being in the presence of those giants overwhelmed me. Then I asked Podestá what was it like, as a kid of 15, to work with older men at cabarets. He reminisced: "I was protected in the Caló orchestra. The musicians were about 10 years older than me, but I thought of them as being much older. When Caló was about to hire me, he asked for my date of birth, to fill out the contract. When he found out I was a minor he could not believe it and refused to hire me; the city would close the cabaret if an underage person worked there. Stamponi, Expósito, Francini, and Pontier, who were his musicians, begged Caló to reconsider. They promised to hide me if the inspectors showed up." Podestá was in fact hidden every time the buzzer rang three times. That was the code.

In this sunny winter month, I had selected the lyrics of the tango

"Garúa" the night before, not knowing it would match the morning weather. When the moment felt right, I placed the poetry on the table and asked him to tell me what he felt when he sang it.

"I have to ask myself: What has happened to this man? Once I understand him, I can sing what I feel he is feeling," he told me. "This man lost his love. He is expressing his profound love for her. 'Garúa' cannot be sung loudly. It is about a man deep in thought, feeling sad, feeling down, living a tragedy."

As he was reading the lyrics, he sang them *sotto voce* close to my ear. At the end, with teary eyes, we looked at each other and said at the same time: "Ah ... what a tango!"

Next I placed on the table the poetry of the tango "Nostalgias." He sang parts of it next to me, telling me again what he was feeling as he sang it.

"This man feels bitterness about a love gone badly. Wow! It's an unhappy love affair, big-time! [*¡Ah! Es un desengaño amoroso barbaro!*]" With the most generous of smiles, he opened his arms in awe of the poetry. He was not, at that moment, feeling empathy for the forlorn protagonist. Only admiration for the lines on the page.

He read more verses.

"The man begins to feel *bronca*," which means "anger" in lunfardo.

His voice and expression turned angry. I could see the actor in him. At the end of the reading, we both looked at each other's eyes and said in unison: "Ah ... what a tango!," sharing a good laugh after some tears.

This man was a living history book of the golden age of tango, from 1939 up to the present. It was like he stepped out of the fog from that time and walked into this café to sit with me. I related to him that in one of my courses at the Academy of Tango, the instructor had said Podestá was the one singer who was always impeccable, no matter with which orchestra he performed. I asked him how that could be, and he answered: "Because I never changed my style."

The conversation then turned to Discépolo, one of my favorite tango poets. I asked what type of person Discépolo was, since he wrote the most acid tango lyrics of all time: was he a cynical or angry man? "Discépolo was a rather introverted person," he answered, "quite friendly, who had many loyal friends; one of them accompanied him during his last days before he died."

"Was not Tania with him when he died?" I asked.

Podestá reacted to the name of Tania with a dismissive gesture, as most porteños do, resenting her lack of loyalty to the great poet of Buenos Aires, nicknamed the "Schopenhauer of tango." The singer continued: "When I was a young singer, Discépolo used to tell me, '*Pibe* [kid], each one of your arms is bigger than two of my legs put together.'"

"You were chubby, weren't you? Aníbal Troilo used to call you *Gordurita.*"

He nodded affirmatively, and we laughed. All along, as we were talking, he was stroking my arm and hand in his porteño way. What a faucet of affection this man was!

He suddenly looked at his watch and said, "When will we see each other again, Beatriz?"

"Anytime, anywhere," I said quickly. I was moved by his generosity.

"I have to go now, my love, I have a doctor's appointment."

We departed with a kiss on the cheek, the porteño way. During the rest of the day and the rest of my stay in Buenos Aires, I knew I had come face to face with the beating heart of the tango. I no longer wanted to talk about lyrics with him. I wanted to continue experiencing him!

The View from the Shadows of the Seats

I saw Podestá perform three times during my stay.

The first time was at *Club del Vino*, a café concert where artists and audience share an intimate space. Maestro Lisandro Adrover, former musical director of the world-touring musical *Forever Tango*, began with a virtuoso bandoneón performance, rising and descending with the instrument in mid-air. In the silence of the audience I could hear the reverence porteños have for tango music. Podestá then gave us seven songs with the Adrover orchestra. His voice was virile and tender, rich in textural expression, and rounded even when he sang rage. "Tinta roja" made me shiver as he, the protagonist, returned to visit his place of birth and saw it changed. With his right hand placed on his aching heart, he sang with sadness and *dolor*:

> *¿Dónde estará mi arrabal...?*
> *¿Quién se robó mi niñez...?*
> *En qué rincón, luna mía,*

Part III. The Poetry

Volcás, como entonces
tu clara alegría?

Veredas que yo pisé,
malevos que ya no son,
bajo tu cielo de raso,
trasnocha un pedazo
de mi corazón...

Where is my neighborhood now?
Who stole my childhood?
In what corner, my moon,
do you pour your clear joy
as you did back then?

Sidewalks that I trod,
brawlers that are no more,
under your satin sky,
a piece of my heart
stays up all night.

After each song the audience shouted requests for their favorite tangos. People loved Podestá! We gave him a standing ovation: waves of affection traveled back and forth in a connecting invisible circle between him and us. We wanted more singing, but he was done for the evening and began to step down onto the floor where people were sitting at small tables for two. With an impish look, maestro Adrover began playing the tango "A Media Luz" ("With the Lights Down Low"), assuming that it would seduce Podestá to return for one more song. Podestá was indeed seduced; he looked back at Adrover, smiled, and climbed back to the stage once again for the last performance of the evening.

How could his voice have lasted so long? He was 82, he had sung for over half a century, and I heard no strain in it. His technique, so highly developed, refined and natural, was imperceptible.

The second performance I attended was at *La Cumparsita* in San Telmo, where I arrived at 10 P.M. The doorman told me Podestá was scheduled to sing at about 1 A.M., so I went out for a short stroll. Walking in San Telmo at night felt like living in a postcard of Buenos Aires at the turn of the century: only the carriages of the 1880s were missing. How romantic were the old wet cobblestones, bathed by the soft light of old gas lamps! After walking back in time under the *garúa*, I went back to La Cumparsita. Its ordinary and non-touristy tango ambiance also felt like part of the past. It was congruent with the down-to-earth tango, with the real tango.

192

Behind the humble walls of this old typical building in San Telmo, in the small tango venue La Cumparsita, an international circle of hands embracing the singer Alberto Podestá came together. *Photograph courtesy of Ivan Prado Froes (Kiev, Ukraine).*

San Telmo at night. A walk through this barrio, with its earthy cobblestones, melancholic mist (*garúa*), and romantic gas lamps, can produce a feeling of transport back to the early, bygone days of the tango's beginnings. Today many stage tango shows and tango bars are located in this nostalgic area. *Photograph courtesy of Gregorio Donikian (Buenos Aires).*

Empty tables were still waiting for customers at 10:30. I sat down and fixed my eyes on a picture that decorated the small unpretentious stage: it was the portrait of the handsome, robust, dark-haired singer who invented how tango was to be sung. The man whose pictures I had seen during my formative years in buses, taxis, store windows, shoe shiner's boxes, absolutely everywhere. I smiled at him until he became a living human being in my mind; with a left-hand motion I invited him to sit next to me. He emerged from the frame, stepped down onto the stage, and came to my table with two glasses of champagne. "*Salud*," I said, in unison with his eyes. I was overtaken not only by his looks but also by his continental finesse, which showed no traces of his humble origins. Now I know why women found him irresistible; why I had heard so many stories about his lovers in Paris, Nice, Buenos Aires, Spain, Uruguay…. This was my chance to ask Carlitos, as we porteños call him, questions about his mysterious life. What was it like for you to invent the singing style of our music? You performed the first *tango canción* in 1917; you set the style for how tango was to be sung ever since! I was humbled, I said, by the scope of what you accomplished. How could you, just one person, express the sentiments of all the people of Buenos Aires? He seemed interested in listening to my questions, so I went on. Did it surprise you that you became a sought-after companion of the rich and famous in Argentina and in Europe? That after growing up poor in *barrio Abasto* you wore tuxedos as if you had been born in them? Did your loyalty to your mamá Doña Bertha keep you unattached and unmarried? Carlitos avoided all my questions, but his silence implied that not being attached left room for all women to dream about him. I told him that the mystery of his love life had kept us talking about his sexuality ever since he died. Your friend, the jockey Leguizamo, said that you were good at having women fall in love with you without getting involved. Carlitos gave me one of his inscrutable smiles in lieu of an answer, so I moved on to a different subject. What was it like to die in that airplane accident that killed you at 45? Was it really an accident, or did it happen because you were fighting? Are you sad you missed the golden years of the tango? Do you regret that you never got to see Astor Piazzolla as a full-grown musician? What do you think of your porteño fans, who still go to your burial place and keep your statue with a cigarette always lit between your fingers? What do you think about how we still say, "Carlitos sings better every day"?

Customers were beginning to show up and fill the tables around us. I had more questions to ask, but he would not have answered them. Questions about his dark side, his rumored associations with the mafia as he was growing up, his never wanting to return to Buenos Aires in spite of his emotive rendition of the tango "Volver" ("To Return").... In my mind's eye I watched Carlitos go back to the stage ... step back inside the frame ... and that myth named Carlos Gardel, with whom I shared a moment in the privacy of my fantasy, was his photograph again.

When the show got started, each performer expressed the tango in his very distinct way. Some got so possessed they seemed in a trance with their shut eyes, high concentration, and wet foreheads, shaking in emotional labor. When it was Podestá's turn, at 1 A.M., he ascended the tiny stage and began to kid back and forth with the musicians. I could see this was his way of preparing an informal cocoon for music and song between himself and the musicians and also between the stage in the lights and the audience in the shadows. He suddenly became serious and began the ceremony of singing with total immersion in the ritual. His voice melded stage and audience in high drama. My heart was pierced by each of his utterances.

Later that night, there was an incident that gave the North American me a bit of a shock. When Podestá sat down at my table after performing and we were conversing, a man came by, placed his cheek in front of him, and said: "Alberto, give me a kiss."

Podestá did, naturally. A straight man felt free to ask another straight man for a kiss! I realized how true the poet Horacio Ferrer was when he said tango was a way of life. In a conversation Ferrer and I had a few days before, he mentioned that tango men kiss each other and explained that Aníbal Troilo, the musician and orchestra director, started the trend. Troilo used to say that men should kiss other men with the same naturalness they kiss their fathers, brothers and sisters with. My mind flashed to a poster I had seen during my stroll in San Telmo that night, in which maestro Adrover was planting a kiss on Podestá's forehead. Somehow it seemed totally logical that Podestá was a magnet for kisses.

I attended another Podestá performance with maestro Adrover at *La Trastienda*, another café concert venue in San Telmo. When Podestá got ready to sing "El bazar de los juguetes," he dedicated the song to me because, he said humorously, I had been following him for a month as if he owed me money. After the show, we arranged to meet one-on-one for the last time.

The Boy in the Story

We met a few days later. He came to La Biela in his usual sunny mood at about 10 P.M. As old friends do, we exchanged our latest news. Our conversation kept being interrupted by people who knew him and kept coming out of the woodwork to kiss him on the head.

I told him "El bazar de los juguetes," the lyric he wrote, always makes me cry inside because I can see the protagonist remembering how he used to look at a store window as a kid, longing for the toys he was not going to have. The part that makes me cry the most, I said, is when the child feels compassion for his mother, who is unable to buy holiday presents for her kids. "I watched you sing it with a broken heart; with longing, sorrow, and tragedy in your voice" —

> *Si mi vieja era tan pobre*
> *le faltaba siempre un cobre*
> *para comprarnos el pan*

> My mother was so poor
> she was always a penny short
> to buy the bread for us

"Your voice can put together the frustration, the immense tenderness and gratitude of the boy toward his mother" —

> *Yo sé lo que es sentirse besado tiernamente*

> I know how it feels to be kissed so tenderly

He told me the lyrics were autobiographical. I admired his honesty! When I mentioned that somehow the lyrics were attributed to Reinaldo Yiso, not to him, he did not seem bothered by it. (I later checked the archival sources and found that Podestá is listed as the first author of the music and lyrics, although it's under his real name — Alé Alejandro Washington — and not his stage name. The second author is Roberto Rufino, and the third is Reinaldo Guiso — who appears cited as "Yiso" in various sources.) Then he added: "This poetry touches everybody because we all, in one form or another, at one time or another, have felt like the boy in the story. We wish to have something others have, and we can't have it."

I noticed he never made the conversations all about himself. He was always very attentive to where I was, always interested in what I was experiencing in Buenos Aires, in whether I liked my life in the United States, in knowing how I liked the milongas I was going to. He asked me how I got interested in the tango, why was I writing a book. I told him how much the tango had been part of my roots, and how I was finding my roots and myself again as I was discovering more about it. "Oh," he remarked, "it is good that you did not start from your head. You started from your heart."

Spending this time with him, and sensing the enormous sensitivity register of Alberto's personality, led me to develop a new appreciation for the singer's role. Talented singers like Podestá transform the magnificent written word into electrifying outpours of emotion. He is the one singer that porteños consider of excellent voice and diction no matter with which orchestra he sang. I told him that tango books tend to enshrine composers, musicians, and poets, and to underplay the role of singers; but that without gifted singers like him, who are able to feel and express a whole range of emotions, many lyrics would have remained in obscurity. In addition to great lyrics, it is the singer's delivery that makes people tremble. After tacitly agreeing with the viewpoints I was proposing, Podestá gave me examples of lyrics that went nowhere in the voice of a certain singer, and became a success when recorded by someone else.

Before departing, Podestá said that he liked the United States, where I live; but, pointing at his watch, he added: "It is past midnight; we have been talking for two-and-a-half hours. Unfortunately people do not have this in the United States." We stepped out onto the busy sidewalk and began walking *del bracete* (arm in arm) as he looked at the changed Recoleta neighborhood and told me stories about the various tango places that once punctuated the three blocks we were walking.

It was hard for me to depart from this man. I felt he was a part of me, one of those parts I had lost when I migrated from my native city. I was refusing to let go again. So I insisted on accompanying him to the corner of Las Heras and Uriburu to catch the cab that would take him to La Cumparsita. He did not want me to, but we fought a little, and I won. I was prolonging the time with him. He quietly slipped a present into my hands — a parcel wrapped in brown paper, which hadn't caught my eye, but which he had with him the whole time in the café —

and as I was sadly closing the door of the cab at the curb, he said: "I am going to miss you…. *Hasta mañana*—we will say *hasta mañana*; it is easier."

When I got back to my apartment, I opened his present and found his last CD, *Alma de Bohemio*. It had been recorded around 1996, with a voice exquisitely seasoned by time. Inexplicably, I also found an unpublished original recording of live radio broadcasts from Radio El Mundo and Radio Belgrano. How did Podestá know what shows my father listened to? How did he know he was giving me a bridge to sounds, voices, and emotions that were part of my earliest home? I listened to these recordings, dated 1963: no longer in my memory but now emanating from my speakers was the voice of my ghost friend, the MC. I found his impeccable diction exactly as I remembered it. He recited *glosas*— poetic prose — to introduce songs, singers, and orchestra directors; for Podestá, singing "El vals soñador," the *glosa* went this way:

> *Luminosa ilusión de estrella y luna que cae desde el cielo al corazón. Es romántica visión de una eterna primavera del amor que siempre espera, que nunca sufre ni llora. Este vals les traigo ahora que no es para aquel que quiere sino para aquel que adora.* [Luminous illusion of star and moon that falls from the sky to the heart. It's a romantic vision of an everlasting springtime of the heart that always yearns, that never suffers or cries. I bring you this waltz then, which is not for those who desire but for those who adore.]

The music begins blending in with "que adora." Thunderous applause marks Podestá's entrance on the stage, and a few moments later he sings.

I realized then that Podestá and I had tangoed without dancing for the past four weeks.

Ripples of Connection

Back in the United States, I frequently play *Alma de Bohemio* after turning the car engine on. Many of the lyrics are about goodbyes, like "Adiós" and "Ave de Paso." I pretend that Podestá is singing them to me as he departed in the cab for his gig at La Cumparsita.

I have missed this man's protective quality, his sensitivity, his ageless sensuality, his "kissability," his tango way of life always making time for another cafecito. He stands for what tango poetry means to me: passion, conversation, intimacy, openness, candor. He stands for what Buenos Aires means to me, the warmth, the touching, the readiness to make time for meeting new friends or old strangers, the salt and pepper of a bit of mischief.

After settling in the United States again, I emailed a friend who travels the world for tango, to ask him if Podestá's songs were played at milongas throughout the world. This was the beginning of an unstoppable chain of events. He placed my request for information on an online forum that reaches tango DJs throughout the world: responses began pouring in from the United States, Canada, Europe, and Australia. That's how the circle began to grow around the globe and around Podestá. Most DJs had assumed he was no longer alive; a few DJs emailed me directly, saying they started playing more Podestá songs and listening to them differently. One of the responding DJs from Montreal was particularly emotive in his response. He had seen Podestá in Montreal in the 1990s, before he knew much about tango. He called himself a "poor dumb Canuck" and promised to make up for his ignorance back then by spending a "lot of time cleaning and enhancing" Podestá's vintage recordings. I contacted him to find out how he gave new life to old recordings. He told me he specialized in taking away "the artifacts of time" and restoring "the purity of sound." He was thrilled to find out that this legendary singer was alive and asked if, through me, he could get these audio restorations to Podestá. In the process of our correspondence, I felt that his dream could easily materialize and at the same time give Podestá a moment of nostalgic joy.

Though unknown to us at the time, the international circle of hands would, through him, soon be made complete. Friends of his from Australia were coming to Montreal on their way to Buenos Aires; they would be going to La Cumparsita and would convey a CD to Podestá, along with a greeting from this DJ, which I translated into Spanish. Three months after my own return, these Australians, now in Buenos Aires themselves, sent to Montreal a message that read:

> The night with Podestá was amazing. A smoky little old bar with the best singers and musicians and a big photo of Gardel in the background. It was like a jam session. About two square meters to dance in, but it was great. The owners were in on it, and we surprised him after his bracket. Our friend H. read out your greeting. The other singers (five) all waited around. When we played his music (one of the Caló valses), he choked back the tears. He said he was 16 when he sang that song. Have it all on video and will send it on when we get back.

Epilogue:
The Tango in All of Us

We embarked on a quest to discover why the most iconic dance of the 20th century is much more than a dance, much more than can be seen by the eye.

Watching how tango utterly possesses dancers from all points of the globe compelled me to ask: What is the power in the heart of this dance? What enabled it to rise above cultures and to resonate around the globe as loudly as it does?

Our quest did not take us to the fishnets and fedoras of dancers who perform tango onstage in musicals. It took us instead to the emotions and experiences of ordinary people who dance embraced to one another in one of the purest and most intimate forms of human interaction.

We met the people, visited the places, resonated to the poetry of tango and kept discovering intangibles — a heart, a soul, a way of being, a way of thinking, an ethic, a culture.

In the connecting glue of the city of Buenos Aires we felt part of a grand circle of life. We became enraptured by the desire to connect, the curious gaze, the romanticism, and the playfulness of porteños. These invisibles were as palpable as the lavender flowers of the jacaranda trees. In the city's dance halls we met regular people who live the tango lifestyle, who are enamored of this dance that is an extension of what they feel, of who they are, of the way they live, walk, talk, and think about life. Buenos Aires gave us her essence, energy, and heart in the form of tango, an art full of paradoxes, beset by contradictions. An art that is all of us.

During our visit to La Boca, a strong perfume of tango took us close to the unreplicable recipe of this art with its unique genetic pool from the world, its stubborn autonomy and solidarity. Here we understood why the dance shakes us to the core with the undiluted passion, beauty, and rebellion that were bred into it by working-class people who had a lot to say, and who still cling tenaciously to this district.

A symphony of imagination surprised us in San Telmo. We wound through the crowds and found in the colorful vendors and performers — all of them street artists, many of them satirical or nonsensical — the inventive creativity that finds its way into the dance. We encountered the same creativity in the evocation of an old tenement house, where the people who danced the early tango had to invent how to live day by day.

Almost six thousand miles away from Buenos Aires, in the global tango scene of the Virtual Age, we saw an alternative tango festival in the Midwestern United States. There we heard the stories of six dancers — most of them immigrants, all of them perpetual tango travelers — who reinvented their daily lives to put tango at the center. All of them felt defined by the dance. Their stories are tango's invisible legacy in today's world, as it becomes not only a lifestyle but also an identity.

Traveling through the subjective gamut of nostalgia in the poets' souls, we discovered that the lyrics are as conversational, personal, and intimate as the dance itself. In the poets' hearts we found a mirror for our own. We indulged in that sweet nostalgia that hurts a little when we think about lost places, times, and loves. We traced the evolution of a major character in the lyrics — Milonguita — and saw how tangos are connected not only to the real world, and to the life of the collective psyche, but also to each other. And we learned that lyrics are not words to accompany a melody; they are a cosmo-vision, a passionate ideology. In their ethics of integrity, which focuses on what really matters, we found a set of values that exudes humanity and realness. The poetry, we found, needs the singer as much as the singer needs the poetry. The singer's interpretation and performance endows the written text with its unique pathos. We got up close to one of those legends in person, Alberto Podestá, in whom we found the incarnation of tango. We shared many evenings with him at café concerts, intimate bohemian places where the intimate tango is sung by intimate singers.

Whether through the music, the dance, the people, the poetry or the singing, we arrived at the same invisible essence: intimacy, sentiment, earthiness, humanity.

At the end of our quest, a question remains unanswered: What is the power in the heart of this dance? Why does the tango — born of the angst inherited from the 19th century and the tensions of the 20th — speak so compellingly to people of the 21st century now?

Something in it feeds our hunger for being on a level with others. Something in it understands our rebellion and soothes our longing for "home," giving us a sense of belonging and a shared communication that knows no barriers. Something in it mirrors our nostalgia. We are nostalgic, each of us, historically: we all have emigrated from the warm, the safe, and the personal. Our feelings parallel those of the

A moment at the "Alma Porteña" milonga in Brescia, Italy. The tango is all of us in life's common places, connecting generations. *Photograph courtesy of architect Giuseppe Bianco (Piacenza, Italy).*

inventors of tango, who left their familiar homes to arrive in a city where they saw their dreams for a better future crushed by an unexpected reality. They had to reinvent themselves and adapt to a world of sudden and rapid change. Our world no less than theirs puts us face to face with a grave uncertainty about the future: they did not know if they could survive in the small locality of the Río de La Plata; we do not know if we can survive in a global world that veers us away from our most precious possessions — our subjectivity and our hearts.

The malaise of our times — the philosophy "any gain is good" — demands that we look outside for direction, that we put our status ahead of our hearts, that we treasure possessions over human connections and subjective fulfillment. What we lose in these exchanges are our "homes," our hearts, our values. We are irredeemably nostalgic for that. Historically we have arrived at a nightmare of greed and its consequences: terror, endless competition, infinite careerism, alienation.

We are not only nostalgic. The "any gain is good" attitude is the culprit of another malaise: we are developing the uncanny homesickness that descends upon people who are still at home but feel estranged from the place they have lived all their lives. It has been called "solstalgia": it occurs when ecological changes leave people watching their gardens becoming infertile, their birds disappearing, their crops and animals perishing.

The 19th century-born tango understands our 21st century "algias," our nostalgia and solstalgia, our isolation-algia, our fragility, our immigrant condition, our anger at human-manufactured threats to life. That's how this dance of tenderness and connection eases our return to a safe and warm "home."

Whether as music, dance, poetry, lifestyle, or identity, the tango still fulfills human needs and soothes our 21st century angst. This is its power, but … is this all that propelled it to rise above cultures and to resonate around the globe? As I pondered this question, I flashed back to two experiences. I copy them here from my life notes; this is the first:

> I wanted to participate in the miracle of birth, as an observer. The mother had to be someone I did not know. I was allowed into the delivery room, which was the mother's private hospital room. Decorated in shades of green, everything was impeccably sterile.
>
> When labor began, the "all" of life looked me straight in the eyes. There it was, staring me down. At its rawest. Unedited.
>
> Mother's ecstasy. Mother's agony. Cries of joy. Cries of pain. Hard labor. Sweat. Blood. Strange body materials. Malodorous fluids. A mother's body without will. Nature pouring her insides out. A thunderstorm agitating the ocean.
>
> A mother's suffering became a baby's head, then a baby's body, then a little person who could cry his very own terror out loud with his brand new lungs. This new human being could only calm down when his father's arms held him securely and tightly close to his chest.
>
> The birthing mother could have been an English queen surrounded by an entourage of caretakers, giving birth in the luxury of a palace. Or a woman from the Argentine pampas. Or a slave on an antebellum Southern plantation in the United States. Or a Muslim with a veil. The baby could have been any color. As never before, the basic common experience of all mothers and all babies struck me as being uncannily identical.

In that delivery room, I felt myself made of the "stuff" tango is made of: the beautiful and the ugly, the joy and the pain, the blood and the sweat, the fragrances and the odors. Tango has earth in its soul. It melts down differences by zeroing in on our commonality. Tango is all of us in life's common places. It is who we are at the core, behind our social masks.

How is it that other social dances do not take us there? I believe that the physical tango embrace is a one-second ticket to emotions so old we do not have names for them, to the moment we enter this world as a creature. In the embrace, we are held in the same exact vertical position against someone's chest, feeling safe and connected, engaging in a myriad of bodily duets. This ineffable universal "home," the beginning of our ontology, still matters to us in that zone of the "unconscious," where present and past are one and the same.

> I heard the sound of silence during my visit to the Galápagos Islands, off the coast of Ecuador, in the wildlife that inspired Charles Darwin, in the habitat that remains largely as it was when he studied it. We were not supposed to disturb the animals while touring the islands. When we encountered, on our narrow path, the Blue-footed Boobies with their white and black outfits and blue painted feet, they did not walk away or fly off. We humans stopped in our tracks. Then we detoured so as not to bother them.
>
> They owned the place. The familiar differences between urban animals and humans did not exist in Galápagos. In that semi-pristine landscape, it was crystal clear that they had more rights than we did.... Detouring around them, we reached the ocean; a sea lion had given birth on the beach. I could tell because a solitary placenta was basking in the sun, waiting to become food for another species. Perfect cycles of nature: one's discard becomes food for another.
>
> On that beach, for the first and only time in my life, I listened to a new sound of silence. Not the one that results from absence of noise. A silence that enveloped the earth and the skies and everything in a larger dimension, where human and animals lived in a shared space and had equal rights. This zone transcended both our species.

The delivery room and the Galápagos confronted me with something basically human ... maybe bigger than human ... cosmic perhaps.

In both memories I encountered a point, as it is at the beginning of life and (I imagine) as it is at the end of life. Between these two points, we do the dance of life that pushes them apart.... We grow away from our common stock, from our one same story, believing that our different affiliations to country, religion or ethnicity separate us. We kill for those beliefs. And in many cultures we deny our bodies as inferior to our minds and spirits. Tango bypasses all these camouflages of the self and goes right into the ineffable zone of the cosmic where we were in the first place, to that

205

ineffable story of sameness, those points where our bodily nature screams its existence.

Tango's power also resides in how it works in our psyches from the inside. The carnal embrace destabilizes our polar tendencies, while giving us a visceral sense of being more complete. The dance is a meeting ground of opposites and a synthesis of the extremes that are in our very cores: man and woman, masculinity and femininity, oneness and separation, spirituality and carnality — all of these universally human polarities clash and blend in the embrace. We dance our man and woman to the fullest, in halves that need and complement each other. Yet, in this dance where the polar genders meet, I feel strands of androgyny that we dance, that we hear in the music, that we experience in the poetic text and in the singing. Many compositions insist on the beat; they seem more masculine. Others are melodically slower and gentler; they seem more feminine. Others are balanced in their melodic and rhythmic aspects. Men and women singers switch from grave "masculinity" to tender "femininity" in voice and feeling in a fraction of a second. So do poets, who, in a macho culture, felt free to express their "feminine" emotions.

The opposites of oneness and separation do their own dance as well. The embrace summons us back to a wonderful oceanic experience, where two of us become one — for three minutes — until we recover our boundaries. The distinguished psychoanalyst Otto Fenichel used the expression "oceanic" to refer to the blurring of boundaries between self and world (which is uncannily similar to the experience of "merging" reported by dancers in moments of transport). It is a wonderful metaphor for the connection we feel but that others cannot see. In certain moments of the dance we go back to the ocean. In the rhythmic tides of the music we rise and fall; we are waves with a form that merge with the water, but that soon enough acquire individuality again. As dancers directly or indirectly told us, even in nonspectacular moments, we often feel snatches of a vast zone beyond ourselves and a sense of connection to more than what our senses perceive.

Not only does the dance fulfill needs, but it also confronts us with our ineffable nature, with a mystery our minds cannot understand but our emotions do.

Whether as dance, lifestyle or identity, song lyric or alternative culture, the tango has proven itself able to fulfill universal human needs. Most popular dances celebrate the happy side of life and put the tragic off to the side; the tango speaks to our pain and losses without trivializing or erasing them. Instead by in fact confronting and intensifying what is usually left in the margins, it summons us back to our realness.

Its initial spread and its current resurgence around the world show that, despite the disparities of time and place, language, skin color, religion or social status, we find ourselves, we find each other, we find the tango's strength in strangers' arms.

Bibliography

Historical References

(Based on archival documentation)

Donato, Marisa. 1995. "Aluvión de tangos." In *Documentos e investigaciones sobre historia del tango*, 11–15. Buenos Aires: Instituto del Tango.

Lamas, Hugo and Binda, Enrique. 1998. *El tango en la sociedad porteña 1880-1920*. Stuttgart: Editorial Abrazos

Novati, Jorge and Cuello, Inés. 1980. *Antología del tango Rioplatense. Desde sus comienzos hasta 1920*. Vol.1. Buenos Aires. Instituto Nacional de Musicología "Carlos Vega"

Other Books and Journals Consulted

(The list includes references directly and indirectly related to the tango in its non-historical aspects. Sources related to the early history of tango may not be strictly supported by archival documentation.)

Abadi, Sonia. 2003. *El Bazar de los Abrazos*. Buenos Aires: Ediciones Lumiere.

Akhatar, Salman. 1999. The immigrant, the exile, and the experience of nostalgia. *Journal of Applied Psychoanalytic Studies*, I: 123–130.

Andrews, George R. 1980. *The Afro-Argentines of Buenos Aires 1800–1900*. Madison: University of Wisconsin Press.

Apicella, Mario. 2005. "Noche de 'puro' tango en el Colón." *La Nación*. December 14, 2005.

Assuncão, Fernando. 1984. *El Tango y Sus Circunstancias*. Buenos Aires: Editorial el Ateneo.

Astigueta, Fernando. 2000. "Tango and its meaning for a culture." *American Journal of Psychoanalysis,* 28 (3), 483–500.

Azzi, María Susana. 1991. *Antropología del Tango. Los Protagonistas*. Buenos Aires: Ediciones de Olavarría.

_____ and Simon Collier. (2000). *Le grand tango. Astor Piazzolla*. New York: Oxford University Press.

Barbero, María Inés, and Fernando Devoto. 1983. *Los Nacionalistas (1910-1932)*. Buenos Aires: Centro Editor de América Latina.

Bates, Héctor, and Luis J Bates. 1936. *La Historia del Tango*. Buenos Aires: Taller Gráfico de la Compañía General Fabril Financiera.

Benarós, León. 1999. "El tango y los lugares y casas de baile." In *La Historia del Tango: Primera Época*. Buenos Aires: Corregidor.

Bibliography

Borges, Jorge Luis. 1969. *Fervor de Buenos Aires.* Buenos Aires: Editorial Emecé.

Boym, Svetlana. 2001. *The Future of Nostalgia.* New York: Basic Books

Caamaño, Roberto. 1969. *La Historia del Teatro Colón, 1908–1968.* Buenos Aires: Editorial Cinetea.

Canaro, Francisco. 1957. *Mis bodas de oro con el tango y mis memorias 1906–1956.* Buenos Aires: Corregidor.

Carella, Tulio. 1966. *Tango: Mito y Esencia.* Buenos Aires: Centro Editor de América Latina.

Carretero, Andrés. 1999. *El Compadrito y el Tango.* Buenos Aires: Ediciones Continente.

_____. 1999. *Tango Testigo Social.* Buenos Aires: Ediciones Continente.

_____. 2004. *El Tango, La Otra Historia.* Buenos Aires: Ediciones Margus.

Castellanos, Pintín. 1948. *Entre Cortes y Quebradas, Candombe, Milonga y Tango.* Montevideo: Colombino Hermanos.

Castro, Nelson. 2007. "Arturo Toscanini: tragedia y pasión en Buenos Aires." *La Nación: ADN Cultura.* August 25, 2007.

Cautère, Fernando. 2008. *En el Nombre del Tango.* Buenos Aires: Editorial Santa María.

Cibotti, Ema. 2005. *Sin Espejismos: Versiones, Rumores y Controversias.* Buenos Aires: Editorial Aguilar.

Cibotti, Ema. 2008. "Del desencanto de una elite, en clave de tango." Paper presented at the International Congress Tango Tres Siglos. Buenos Aires: December.

Collier, Simón, Artemis Cooper, María Susana Azzi and Richard Martin. 1995. *Tango! The Dance, the Song, the Story.* London: Thames & Hudson Ltd.

Conde, Oscar. 2004. *Diccionario Etimológico del Lunfardo.* Buenos Aires: Editorial Aguilar.

Cormier, B. 2005. "Dance, Shop, Eat, Sleep." *Bakerfield Californian.* October 9, 2005.

Cutler, Kim-Mai. 2005. "The new tango trades cheek to cheek for hot, fast moves." *The Wall Street Journal.* August 2005.

Del Priore, Oscar, and Irene Amuchástegui. 2008. *Cien Tangos Fundamentales.* Buenos Aires: Editorial Aguilar

Dinzel, Rodolfo and Gloria Dinzel. 2000. *Tango: An Anxious Quest for Freedom* Stuttgart: Editorial Abrazos.

Elizabetta Piqué. 2008. "Roma también vibra con el tango." *La Nación.* September 2008.

Erlán, Diego. 2005. "Ni tan clásicos ni tan modernos. A 70 años de la muerte de Gardel." *Clarín, Revista de Cultura, Edición Especial.* Buenos Aires. 2005.

Escobar, Raúl Tomás. 2004. *Diccionario Lunfardo del Hampa y del Delito.* Buenos Aires: Editorial Distal.

Estévez, Carlos Alberto (Petróleo). 1989, 1990, 1991. "*Tango.*" *Publicación interna del Banco Europeo.* Buenos Aires: Banco Europeo para América Latina SA.

Feder, Stuart. 1982. "The nostalgia of Charles Ives: an essay on affects and music." *The Annals of Psychoanalysis,* X: 301–332.

Fenichel, Otto. 1945. *The psychoanalytic Theory of Neurosis.* New York: Norton.

Ferrer, Horacio. 1960. *El tango, su historia y su evolución.* Buenos Aires: Ediciones Continente.

_____. 1998. *La Epopeya del Tango Cantado.* Vols. I-II, Historia. Buenos Aires: Manrique Zago Editor.

_____. 2000. *Los tangos de Piazzolla y Ferrer. Mi loco bandoneón.* Buenos Aires: Ediciones Continente.

Fumagalli, Mónica. 2004. *Jorge Luis Borges y el Tango.* Argentina: Abrazos Books.

Gálvez, Lucía, and Enrique Espina Rawson. 2002. *Romances de tango.* Buenos Aires: Puntos de Lectura.

Germani, Gino. 1966. "Mass immigration and modernization in Argentina." *Studies in Comparative International Development*, 2 (11).

Gesualdo, Vicente. 1961. *Historia de la música en la Argentina*. Buenos Aires: Editorial Libros de Hispanoamérica.

_____. 1992. "Eloisa D'Herbil de Silva. El Chopin con faldas." *Todo es Historia*, 304: 35–41.

Gobello, José. 1980. *Crónica General del Tango*. Buenos Aires: Editorial Fraterna.

_____. 1999. *Breve Historia Crítica del Tango*. Buenos Aires: Corregidor.

_____, and Irene Amuchastegui. 1998. *Vocabulario Ideológico del Lunfardo*. Buenos Aires: Editorial Corregidor.

Groppa, Carlos G. 2004. *The Tango in the United States*. North Carolina: McFarland & Copany, Inc., Publishers.

Guillermoprieto, Alma. 2003. "Tango, soul of a nation." *National Geographic*. December 2003, pp. 34–53.

Güiraldes, Ricardo. 1968. "Tango." In J. L. Borges and S. Bullrich, eds., *El compadrito, su destino, sus barrios, su música*. Buenos Aires: Compañía General Fabril Editora, pp. 155–156. (First published in 1915.)

Guy, Donna. 1990. *Sex and Danger in Buenos Aires: Prostitution, family, and nation in Argentina*. Lincoln & London: University of Nebraska Press.

Hey, Barbara. 2003. "Denverites turn passionate for the dangerous dance." *Denver Post*. June 24, 2003.

Holland, Bernard. 2004. "Critic's notebook; passion for tango. West Coast and East." *New York Times*. March 3, 2004.

Korn, Francis. 1974. *Los Huéspedes del 20*. Buenos Aires: Editorial Sudamericana.

Konish, Lorie. 2006. "Let your feet follow your heart." *The Kansas City Star*. February 2006.

Krauss, Clifford. 1998. "Buenos Aires journal; doctor, why do I keep dreaming of Argentina?" *The New York Times*. May 20, 1998.

Krystal, Henry. 1966. "Giorgio de Chirico: Ego states and artistic productions." *American Imago*, 23: 210–226.

Kukkonen, Pirjo. 1996. *Tango Nostalgia: The language of love and longing*. Helsinki: Yliopistopaino, Helsinki University Press.

Kuri, Carlos. 1997. *Piazzolla, la música límite*. Buenos Aires: Corregidor.

Lee, Denny. 2008. "Argentine nights." *The New York Times*. March 2008.

López Vicente Fidel. 1968. "Las orillas hacia 1810." In J. L. Borges and S. Bullrich, eds., *El compadrito, su destino, sus barrios, su música*. Buenos Aires: Compañía General Fabril Editora, pp. 113–116. (First published in 1884.)

Lugones, Leopoldo. 1968. "Las orillas hacia 1870." In J. L. Borges and S. Bullrich, eds., *El compadrito, su destino, sus barrios, su música*. Buenos Aires: Compañía General Fabril Editora, pp. 119–120. (First published in 1911.)

Mafud, Julio. 1966. *Sociología del Tango*. Buenos Aires: Editorial Americalee.

Mármol Augusto Fernando. 2007. *Buenos Aires Antiguo. Old Buenos Aires. Cambios Urbanos. Urban Changes. 1880–1940*. Buenos Aires: Ediciones del Viajero.

_____. 2007. *Buenos Aires Antiguo. Old Buenos Aires. Vida Cotidiana. Daily Life 1900–1940*. Buenos Aires: Ediciones del Viajero.

Mássimo Di Marco and Monica Fumagalli. 2007. *Carlos Gavito su Vida, su Tango*. NYN Opera Tango.

Matamoro, Blás. 1996. *El Tango*. Madrid: Editorial Acento.

Milkewitz, Harry. 1964. *Psicología del Tango*. Montevideo: Editorial Alfa.

Miller, Milton L. and M.D. Boston. 1956. *Nostalgia. A Psychoanalytic Study of Marcel Proust*. Boston: Houghton-Mifflin.

Molinari, Alejandro, Roberto Martínez

and Natalio Etchegaray. (1998). *Tango y Sociedad, De Garay a Gardel, la Sociedad, el Hombre Común y el Tango: 1580–1917.* Argentina: Ediciones Biblioteca Nacional.

Moreno, María. 2001. "Women in tango." *Revista Pugliese.*

Natale, Oscar. *1984. Buenos Aires, Negros y Tango.* Buenos Aires: Peña Lillo Editor.

Oliveri, Marcelo Héctor. 2005. *El Tango del Tercer Milenio.* Buenos Aires: Editorial Del Cachafaz.

Páez, Jorge. 1970. *El Conventillo.* Buenos Aires: Centro Editor de América Latina.

Pelinski, Ramón. 2000. *El Tango Nómade. Ensayos Sobre la Diáspora del Tango.* Buenos Aires: Corregidor.

Plazaola, Ricardo. 2008. *Yo Quería Bailar. Carlos Gavito, Vida, Pasión y Tango.* Buenos Aires: Editorial Dunken.

_____. 2010. *I Wanted to Dance. Carlos Gavito: Life, Passion and Tango.* Stuttgart: Editorial Abrazos.

Pujol, Sergio. 1966. *Discépolo, una Biografía Argentina.* Buenos Aires: Editorial Emecé.

_____. 1989. *Las Canciones del Inmigrante. Buenos Aires: Espectáculo Musical y Proceso Inmigratorio. Desde 1914 Hasta Nuestros Días. Buenos Aires:* Almagesto.

_____. 1999. *Historia del baile, de la milonga a la disco.* Buenos Aires: Emecé.

Romano, Eduardo. 1990. *Las Letras de Tango: Antología Cronológica 1900–1980.* Rosario: Editorial Fundación Ross.

Romeo, Alberto F. 1997. *Aproximación al Tango.* Buenos Aires: Ediciones de la Universidad Católica.

_____. 2009. "Enrique Santos Discépolo, una reflexión sobre los exilios." Paper presented at Esquina Osvaldo Pugliesse. Buenos Aires.

Ruti, Mari. 2005. "From melancholia to meaning: How to live the past in the present." *Psychoanalytic Dialogues*, 15 (5): 637–660.

Sábatos, Ernesto. 1965. *Tango.* Buenos Aires, Editorial Losada.

Salas, Horacio. 2004. *El Tango.* Buenos Aires: Emecé Editores.

Santos, Estela dos. 2001. *Damas y Milongueras del Tango.* Buenos Aires: Corregidor.

_____. 1972. *Las Mujeres del Tango.* Buenos Aires: Centro Editor de América Latina.

Savigliano, Marta. 1995. *Tango and the Political Economy of Passion.* Boulder: Westview Press.

Sebrelli, José. 1964. *Buenos Aires, Vida Cotidiana y Alineación.* Buenos Aires: Editorial Sudamericana.

Selles, Roberto. 1976. "Sur, paredón y después…" In Benarós, León, Ernesto Goldar, Roberto Selles, J.C. Martini Real, and Juan Sasturian. *La Historia del Tango. Sus Poetas.* Buenos Aires: Corregidor.

_____. 1998. *El Orígen del Tango.* Buenos Aires: Academia Porteña del Lunfardo.

_____ and León Benarós. 1977. *La Historia del Tango: Primera Época.* Buenos Aires: Ediciones Corregidor.

Shua, A. 2004. "El dolor y el destino humano, pero con humor." *Clarín.* January 3, 2004.

Sierra, Luis. 1997. *Historia de la Orquesta Típica.* Buenos Aires: Editorial Corregidor.

Tallón, José S. 1964. *El Tango en sus Etapas de Música Prohibida.* Buenos Aires: Instituto Amigos del Libro Argentino. (First published in 1959.)

Thompson, Robert Farris. 2005. *Tango: The Art History of Love.* New York: Random House.

Uchitel, Myriam. 1994. "Exilio, nostalgia, melancholia … as origens do tango." *Precurso*, 13, pp. 37–46.

Ulla, Noemí. 1967. *Tango, Rebelión y Nostalgia.* Buenos Aires: Editorial Jorge Álvarez.

[Unsigned] 1912. "En Nueva Pompeya.

Protesta contra la desidia official." *La Prensa*. May 1912.

[Unsigned] 1914. "Tango teacher asks for $4,000. His suit against the Archbishop of Paris to be heard soon." Wireless telegraph from Paris. *The New York Times*. January 1914.

[Unsigned] 1918. "Vatican prohibits tango." *The New York Times*. Special cable from Rome. January 1918.

[Unsigned] 2001. "A sense of where you were." *The Economist*. December 2001.

Vallejos, Soledad. "Ya hay 56,000 psicólogos en la Argentina." *La Nación*. October 2005.

Watson, Ricardo, Lucas Rentero and Gabriel Di Meglio. 2008. *Buenos Aires Tiene Historia*. Buenos Aires: Editorial Aguilar.

Zalko, Nardo. 2001. *Paris/Buenos Aires: Un Siglo de Tango*. Buenos Aires: Ediciones Corregidor.

Ghi, Fernanda and Gullermo Merló. 2006–2007. International tango instructors. Interviews: *One tango or many tangos?* Buenos Aires.

Lazzari, Eduardo. 2006. Argentine historian. Interview: *History of the Recoleta cemetery*. Buenos Aires.

Podestá, Alberto. 2006. Tango singer. Interviews. Buenos Aires.

Pucci, Humberto. 2009. Researcher at Centro Educativo del Tango de Buenos Aires. Interview: *Picture of school children apparently dancing tango in 1901*. Buenos Aires.

Rajschmir, Sylvia. 2009. Electronic communication. *Milongas in Tel-Aviv and Jerusalem*.

Villagrán Alvaro. 2009. Licenciate in History. Presentation: "*Historia y política: los autores nacionalistas de principios de siglo XX*." Buenos Aires: Centro Cultural Ricardo Rojas.

Interviews

(Conducted by the author while doing fieldwork for this book.)

Arquimbau, Eduardo and Gloria. 2006. International tango instructors. Interview: *The tango culture in barrio Pompeya*. Illinois, USA.

Cautère, Fernando. 2009. Researcher at Centro Educativo del Tango de Buenos Aires. Interview: *Evangelism and anticlericalismo: 1880–1920*. Buenos Aires.

Del Curto, Héctor. 2006. Bandoneón player. Interview: The experince of tango music for foreign audiences. Kansas City, Missouori, USA.

Ferrer, Horacio. 2008. Tango poet. Interview: *Sense of time and androgyny in tango lyrics*. Buenos Aires.

García, Nito and Elba. 2007. International tango instructors. Interview: *What foreign audiences like about stage tango shows in Buenos Aires*. Buenos Aires.

Multimedia

12 Tangos—Adios Buenos Aires. 2005. Film. International DVD edition. Direction and script: Arne Birkenstock. Production: Arne Birkenstock, Thomas Springer, Helmut G. Weber. Fruitmarket Filmproduction and Tradewind Pictures. 86 minutes.

Astor Piazzolla in portrait. 2005. DVD. BBC: Opus Arte. Producer: Ferenc van Damme. 106 minutes.

Buenos Aires: Días y noches. Rubén Juarez, Horacio Ferrer y Juanjo Domínguez. 2005. DVD. Dolby Digital.

Cadícamo, Enrique. Tangos clásicos e inéditos. 2003. DVD. Volumen 1. Producer: Melopea. Buenos Aires. 98 minutes.

Cuesta abajo. 1934. Film. Paramount. Filmed in Long Island, New York. Language: Spanish. Director: Louis Gasnier. Script: Alfredo Le Pera. 74 minutes.

El amarillo. 2006. Premiered 2009. Independent film. Production, script and direction: Sergio Mazza. 87 minutes

El café de los maestros. 2008. Film. Producer: Gustavo Santaolalla. Director: Miguel Kohan. Distributor: Alfa Films. 90 minutes.

El café de los maestros. 2008. Live performance. Teatro Grand Rex. Buenos Aires: December.

El último aplauso. 2008. Film. Director and Screenwriter: Germán Kral. Producer: Germán Kral Filmproduktion / Happinet Corporation Una co-producción de Monogatari Films SRL / Indiecito SA / Estudio Massa SA. 90 minutes.

El último bandoneón. 2009. Film. Director: Alejandro Saderman. Una producción ASP and Malkina. 80 minutes.

Homero Manzi, un poeta en la tormenta. 2009. Film. Production: Tronera Screenplay. Direction: Eduardo Spagnuolo.

Los capos del tango. Aníbal Troilo. Celebrities of tango history. 2005. DVD. Producer: Solo Tango. 93 minutes.

Luces de Buenos Aires. 1932. Film. Paramount. Filmed in Joinville, France. Script: Manuel Romero and Luis Bayón Herrera. Music: Gerardo Matos Rodríguez. Orchestra: Julio De Caro. 85 minutos.

Tango! 1933. Film. Dirección: Luis José Moglia Barth. Production: Argentina sono film SACI. 75 minutes.

Tango. 1998. Film. DVD: Sonic Classics. Production: Juan C. Codazzi, José María Calleja, Alejandro Bellaba. Direction: Carlos Saura. 119 minutes.

Tango, the obsession. 1998. Documentary film. Script, production and direction: Adam Boucher. Adam Boucher Films.

Tangos among friends. Daniel Barenboim in Buenos Aires. 1997. DVD. NVC, ARTS, WDR and Telepiu Classica Co-production. Warner Music Group. 54 minutes.

Tango bar. Videocasette release of 1935 film by Éxito Productions. Distributed by International DVD Group S.A. 58 minutes.

Tango: our dance. 1999. Videorecording. Script, production and direction: Jorge Zanada. Chicago, Ill. Facets Video. 66 minutes.

Un Tal Gavito. 2006. DVD. Volume 3. Producer: Solo Tango.

Yo no se que me han hecho tus ojos. 2003. Documentary film about Ada Falcón. Muñoz, Lorena and Sergio Wolf, filmmakers.

Table of Lyrics

As with many genres of popular song, tango lyrics have been republished in numerous sources, often with a bewildering number of minor textual variants. For this book, my primary source was *Epopeya del Tango Cantado. II. Antología*, edited by Horacio Ferrer, which reprints the lyrics in the form of their initial publication (often preserving non–standard punctuation). For lyrics not included in Ferrer's edition, I have followed the text in *Las letras del tango*, edited by Eduaro Romano. Romano's edition also served as my primary source for date of publication; in cases where a song has different dates of copyright registration, first performance, and first recording, Romano selected the earliest date on record. For lyrics not included in either Ferrer or Romano, I have followed the online text provided by TodoTango.com (a website produced by Ricardo García Blaya, member of the National Tango Academy of Buenos Aires). My ultimate source for establishing authorship and publication date, especially for lyrics not included in either Ferrer or Romano's editions, is the SADAIC copyright registry. The translations provided by Jake Spatz follow the texts printed here, although they do not always reproduce the punctuation of the originals.

Lyrics used by permission of SADAIC:

Así se baila el tango. 1942. Music: Elias Rubinstein. Lyrics: Elisardo Martínez Vilas. Ed. Select.

Ave de paso. 1936. Music: Carlos Pérez de la Riestra. Lyrics: Enrique Domingo Cadícamo. Ed. Universal.

Buenos Aires conoce. 1977. Music: Raúl Miguel Garello. Lyrics: Rubén Nestor Garello. Ed. Universal.

Cafetín de Buenos Aires. 1948. Music: Mariano Martínez (Mariano Mores). Lyrics: Enrique Santos Discépolo. Ed. Peermusic.

Caminito. 1924. Music: Juan de Dios Filiberto. Lyrics: Gabino Coria Peñaloza. Ed. Pirovano.

Chorra. 1928. Music and lyrics: Enrique Santos Discépolo. Ed. Warner.

Como dos extraños. 1940. Music: Pedro Laurenz. Lyrics: José María Contursi. Ed. Pirovano.

Decime Dios ... dónde estás? 1965. Music: Bernardo Manuel Sucher. Lyrics: Laura Ana Merello (Tita Merello). Ed. Peermusic.

Table of Lyrics

El bazar de los juguetes. 1954. Music and lyrics: Alé Alejandro Wahington (Alberto Podestá), Roberto Rufino, Reinaldo Ghiso. Ed. Warner.
En esta tarde gris. 1941. Music: Mariano Martínez (Mores). Lyrics: José María Contursi. Ed. Warner.
Garúa. 1943. Music: Aníbal Carmelo Troilo. Lyrics: Enrique Domingo Cadícamo. Ed. Warner.
La morocha. 1905. Music: Enrique Saborido. Lyrics: Ángel Villoldo. Ed. Pirovano.
Malena. 1942. Music: Lucio Demare. Lyrics: Homero Nicolás Mancione (Homero Manzi) . Ed. Pirovano.
Mano a mano. 1920. Music: Carlos Gardel and José Razzano. Lyrics: Celedonio Esteban Flores. Ed. Pirovano.
Martirio. 1940. Music and lyrics: Enrique Santos Discépolo. Ed. Warner.
Milonguita. 1920. Music: Enrique Pedro Delfino. Lyrics: Samuel Linning. Ed. Universal.
Nada. 1944. Music: José Dames, Lyrics: Horacio Basterra (Horacio Sanguinetti). Ed. Select.
Oro muerto. 1926. Music: Julio Navarrine. Lyrics: Juan Raggi. Ed. Tempo.
Percal. 1943. Music: Domingo S. Federico. Lyrics: Homero Aldo Expósito. Ed. Warner.
Sur. 1948. Music: Aníbal Carmelo Troilo. Lyrics: Homero Nicolás Manzione (Homero Manzi) . Ed. Warner.
Talán ... talán. 1924. Music: Enrique Pedro Delfino. Lyrics: Bartolomé Angel Vacarezza. Ed. Universal.
Tinta roja. 1941. Music: Sebastián Piana. Lyrics: Cátulo Ovidio González Castillo. Ed. Comar.
Tita de Buenos Aires. 2003. Music and lyrics: Humberto Vicente Castaña (Cacho Castaña). Ed. Emi.
Tristeza de la calle Corrientes. 1942. Music: Domingo S. Federico. Lyrics: Homero Aldo Expósito. Ed. Warner.

Lyrics used by permission of OMSA:

Nostalgias. 1935. Music: Juan Carlos Cobián. Lyrics: Enrique Domingo Cadícamo

Lyrics in the public domain:

Volver. 1935. Music: Carlos Gardel. Lyrics: Alfredo Le Pera.

Index

Index

Index

219

Index

Index